D1170662

THE INTEREST GROUP SOCIETY

THE INTEREST GROUP SOCIETY

Jeffrey M. Berry
Tufts University

LITTLE, BROWN AND COMPANY
BOSTON · TORONTO

Library of Congress Cataloging in Publication Data

Berry, Jeffrey M., 1948–
    The interest group society.

    Bibliography: p.
    Includes index.
    1. Pressure groups—United States.   I. Title.
JK1118.B395   1984   322.4'3'0973   83–25155
ISBN 0–316–09212–6

COPYRIGHT © 1984 BY JEFFREY M. BERRY

ALL RIGHTS RESERVED. NO PART OF THIS BOOK MAY BE REPRODUCED
IN ANY FORM OR BY ANY ELECTRONIC OR MECHANICAL MEANS
INCLUDING INFORMATION STORAGE AND RETRIEVAL SYSTEMS
WITHOUT PERMISSION IN WRITING FROM THE PUBLISHER, EXCEPT
BY A REVIEWER WHO MAY QUOTE BRIEF PASSAGES IN A REVIEW.

LIBRARY OF CONGRESS CATALOG CARD NO. 83–25155

ISBN 0-316-09212-6

9 8 7 6 5 4 3 2 1

MV

PUBLISHED SIMULTANEOUSLY IN CANADA
BY LITTLE, BROWN & COMPANY (CANADA) LIMITED

PRINTED IN THE UNITED STATES OF AMERICA

For Jessica and Rachel

Preface

As I was writing *The Interest Group Society,* I had three major goals in mind. First, I wanted to provide readers with a solid, comprehensive understanding of how interest groups operate. Extensive coverage is given not only to how groups lobby, but also to such topics as how groups form, how they raise money, and how they govern themselves. Second, I tried to place this analysis and description within the context of democratic theory. How do we justify the role of interest groups in a democracy? Do restrictions on interest groups violate our fundamental freedoms? A final goal was to relate interest group politics to broader developments in the American political system. Emphasis has thus been placed on subjects like the relationship between political parties and interest groups, and changes in campaign finance practices.

I began to work on this book while in residence at the Lincoln Filene Center for Citizenship and Public Affairs at Tufts University. I am indebted to Stuart Langton, Executive Director, and to all the members of the staff of the Filene Center for their support and encouragement.

A special word of thanks must go to the fifty or so lobbyists who took time from their busy schedules to be interviewed. The interviews were conducted by telephone during 1982 and 1983. These individuals came from a diverse set of organizations active in trying to influence government. Many were kind enough to send me packets of information about their organizations.

A number of the interviews were conducted by Jan Meriwether, a graduate student at Tufts. I was also helped in various ways by Anne Doyle, Bill Fisher, Charles Rosenberg, and David Wolin. Rob Horn spent many hours handling the word processing for the manuscript.

I deeply appreciate the capable assistance of all these individuals. During my work, I was provided with material by the *Baltimore Sun,* Boyden Associates, Burson-Marsteller, the Conference Board, Golightly and Company International, and the Institute of Politics at Harvard University.

A draft of the entire manuscript was read by Jack Walker, Burdett Loomis, and Kay Lehman Schlozman, and Jerry Goldman and Kent Portney read sections of it. I profited greatly from their many excellent suggestions. I benefited too from working with Will Ethridge and Don Palm, my editors at Little, Brown. I also owe thanks at Little, Brown to Sally Stickney and Dave Lynch.

J.M.B.
Medford, Mass.

Contents

THE INTEREST GROUP SOCIETY

CHAPTER ONE

Madison's Dilemma

A troubling dilemma lies at the core of the American political system. In an open and free society in which people have the right to express their political views, petition their government, and organize on behalf of causes, some segments of the population are likely to pursue their own selfish interests. Dairy farmers will push Congress to adopt price subsidies even though it means consumers will have to pay more for milk at the grocery store. Auto companies and auto workers will want the government to impose import restrictions against Japanese car manufacturers, despite the great popularity these cars have won with Americans. And environmentalists will fight for increasing the number and area of parks and wilderness preserves though development of those lands might provide jobs for some who are out of work. In short, people will pursue their self-interest even though the policies they advocate may hurt others, and may not be in the best interest of the nation.

The dilemma is this: If the government does not allow people to pursue their self-interest, it takes away their political freedom. When we look at the nations of the world in which people are forbidden to organize and to freely express their political views, we find that there the dilemma has been solved by authoritarianism. Although the alternative — permitting people to advocate whatever they want — is far preferable, it carries dangers. In a system such as ours, interest groups constantly push government to enact policies that benefit small constituencies at the expense of the general public.

This dilemma is as old as the country itself, yet never more relevant than today. As lobbying has grown in recent years, anxiety has mounted over the consequences of interest group politics. Political

1

the pursuit of self-interest = freedom
the denial of " " " = authoritarianism

action committees (PACs) threaten to dominate financing of congressional elections. Liberal citizen groups are blamed for slowing economic development with the regulatory policies they have fought for. Labor unions are held responsible because America fails to compete effectively in many world markets, while recent tax cuts granted to influential business lobbies seem to increase their profits at the expense of huge federal budget deficits.[1] Beyond the sins allegedly committed by segments of the interest group community is a broader worry. Is the sheer number of interest groups and their collective power undermining American democracy?

Many agree that interest groups are an increasingly troublesome part of American politics, yet there is little consensus on what, if anything, ought to be done about it. The dilemma remains: Interest groups are no less a threat than they are an expression of freedom.

int grps undermining dem?

CURING THE MISCHIEFS OF FACTION

Is there no middle ground between these two alternatives? Must a government accept one or the other? Contemporary discussions of this question inevitably turn to *The Federalist,* for James Madison's analysis in essay No. 10 remains the foundation of American political theory on interest groups.[2] With great foresight, Madison recognized the problem that the fragile new nation would face. Although at the time he was writing the country had no political parties or lobbies as we know them, Madison correctly perceived that people would organize in some way to further their common interests. Furthermore, these groupings, or "factions" as he called them, were a potential threat to popular government.

Factions were not anomalies, nor would they be occasional problems. Rather, as Madison saw it, the propensity to pursue self-interest was innate. The "causes of faction" he warned, are "sown in the nature of man." [3] As any society develops, it is inevitable that different social classes will emerge, that competing interests based on differing occupations will arise, and that clashing political philosophies will take hold among the populace. This tendency was strong in Madi-

econ causes

[1] On the consequences of interest group development, see Mancur Olson, *The Rise and Decline of Nations* (New Haven: Yale University Press, 1982).
[2] *The Federalist Papers* (New York: New American Library, 1961), pp. 77–84.
[3] *Federalist Papers*, p. 79.

son's eyes: he warned that free men are more likely to try to oppress each other than they are to "co-operate for their common good." [4]

Madison worried that a powerful faction could eventually come to tyrannize others in society. What, then, was the solution for "curing the mischiefs of faction"? He rejected out of hand any restrictions on the freedoms that permitted people to pursue their own selfish interests, remarking that the remedy would be "worse than the disease." [5] Instead, he reasoned that the effects of faction must be controlled rather than eliminating factions themselves. This control could be accomplished by setting into place the structure of government proposed in the Constitution.

In Madison's mind, a *republican* form of government, as designed by the framers, would provide the necessary checks on the worst impulses of factions. A republican form of government gives responsibility for decisions to a small number of representatives who are elected by the larger citizenry. Furthermore, for a government whose authority extends over a large and dispersed population, the effects of faction would be diluted by the clash of many competing interests across the country. Thus, Madison believed that in a land as large as the United States, so many interests would arise that a representative government with its own checks and balances would not become dominated by any faction. Instead, government could deal with the views of all, producing policies that would be in the common good.

Madison's cure for the mischiefs of faction was something of a leap of faith.[6] The structure of American government has not, by itself, prevented some interests from gaining great advantage at the expense of others. Those with large resources have always been better represented by interest groups, and the least wealthy in society have suffered because of their failure to organize. Still, even though the republican form of government envisioned by Madison has not always been strong enough to prevent abuse by factions, the beliefs underlying *Federalist* No. 10 have endured.

[4] *Federalist Papers*, p. 79.
[5] *Federalist Papers*, p. 78.
[6] There is an extensive literature on *Federalist* No. 10, but probably none more important than Robert Dahl's *A Preface to Democratic Theory* (Chicago: University of Chicago Press, 1956). A new and fresh interpretation of *Federalist* No. 10 is offered by Gary Wills, *Explaining America* (New York: Penguin, 1981).

This view that the natural diversity of interests would prevent particular groups from dominating politics found a later incarnation in American social science of the 1950s and 1960s. *Pluralist* scholars argued that the many (that is, plural) interests in society found representation in the policy-making process through lobbying by organizations. The bargaining that went on between such groups and government led to policies produced by compromise and consensus. Interest groups were seen as more beneficial to the system than Madison's factions, with emphasis placed on the positive contributions made by groups in speaking for their constituents before government. Although the pluralist school was later discredited for a number of reasons (these will be outlined shortly), it furthered the Madisonian ideal: groups freely participating in the policy-making process, none becoming too powerful because of the natural conflict of interests, and government acting as synthesizer of competing interests. This ideal remains contemporary America's hope for making interest group politics compatible with democratic values.

INTEREST GROUPS AND THEIR FUNCTIONS

One purpose in this book is to reexamine the fundamental questions raised by *Federalist* No. 10. Can an acceptable balance be struck between the right of people to pursue their own interests and the need to protect society from being dominated by one or more interests? That is, can we achieve true pluralism, or is a severe imbalance of interest group power a chronic condition in a free and open society?

Our means of answering this question will be to look broadly at behavior among contemporary interest groups. We will often follow research questions that political scientists have asked about the internal and external operations of lobbying organizations. Data for this study come not only from the literature on interest groups, but also from recently completed interviews with Washington lobbyists.[7] Although the topics I will address are varied, one argument runs

---

[7] In doing the interviews for this study I decided to focus on topics in which the literature is relatively weak. The interviews themselves are drawn upon most heavily in discussing the internal operations of interest groups, but in many other areas as well. Unless otherwise cited, quotations in the text are taken from these interviews.

throughout: Some important changes have been made in interest group politics in recent years, because of which renewed thought must be given to controlling the effects of faction.

Before proceeding, let us define some essential terms and outline the basic functions of interest groups. To begin with, *an interest group is an organized body of individuals who share some goals and who try to influence public policy.* What falls within and outside the boundaries of this definition? "Farmers" do not constitute an interest group, yet the National Association of Wheat Growers, the American Farm Bureau Federation, and the National Milk Producers Federation are all bona fide interest groups. The critical distinction between "farmers" and any one of these groups is *organization.* Farmers are people in a similar occupation and may share some views on what the government's farm policy should be. But farmers do not all belong to an organization that acts on their behalf in attempting to influence public policy. The larger distinction here may be between *interests* and *interest groups*. People may share an interest, a common concern, without belonging to the same interest group.[8]

The distinction may seem like an exercise in semantics; it is common to hear of congressmen worried about how "farmers" (rather than any particular organization) will react to legislative proposals. Part of the reality of politics is that most interest groups represent only a part — possibly a very small part — of their potential membership. Government officials rightly care about what the larger constituency feels on policy issues as well as being attentive to specific interest group organizations. Just why it is that not all people who share an interest join an organization representing that interest is an

---

[8] It is difficult to precisely and succinctly define the universe of organizations that should fall within the coverage of a book on interest groups. At least a few qualifications ought to be mentioned here. There are some lobbies that are not groups in the sense of having any kind of membership. There are public interest law firms and poor people's lobbies, for example, that are really staff organizations. Corporations are not described best as groups either, because their employees or stockholders are hardly equivalent to the members of other kinds of lobbies. On this point, see Robert H. Salisbury, "Interest Representation: The Dominance of Institutions," *American Political Science Review*, forthcoming. Both types of organizations are acknowledged as distinct cases under the definition here and are included in this study. See also Robert H. Salisbury, "Interest Groups," in Fred I. Greenstein and Nelson W. Polsby, *Nongovernmental Politics*, Handbook of Political Science, Vol. 4 (Reading, Mass: Addison-Wesley, 1975), pp. 171–228.

important question, which we will address at length in Chapter 4. Interest groups are thus important not only because of their actual
memberships, but because they may represent the views of even
larger constituencies.

When an interest group attempts to influence policy makers, it can
be said to be engaging in *lobbying.* (The word comes from the practice of interest group representatives standing in the lobbies of legis-
latures so that they could stop members on their way to a session and
plead their case. In earlier times, when many legislators had no office
of their own, the lobbies or anterooms adjoining their chambers were
a convenient place for a quick discussion on the merits of a bill.)
Although "lobbying" conjures up the image of an interest group representative trying to persuade a legislator to vote in the group's favor,
we should see it in a broader context. Lobbying can be directed at any
institution of government — legislative, judicial, and executive. Interest groups can even try to influence those institutions indirectly by
attempting to sway public opinion, which they hope in turn will influence government. Lobbying also encompasses many tactics. Initiating
a lawsuit, starting a letter-writing campaign, filing a formal comment on a proposed regulation, talking face to face with a congressman or bureaucrat; just about any legal means used to try to influence
government can be called lobbying.

Roles

In their efforts to influence government, interest groups come to play
diverse roles in American politics. First and foremost, interest groups
act to *represent* their constituents before government. They are a
primary link between citizens and their government, forming a channel of access through which members voice their opinions to those
who govern them. The democratic process can be described in the
most eloquent language, and be based on the noblest intentions, but
in the real world of politics it must provide some means by which
manufacturers, environmentalists, construction workers, or whoever,
can speak to government about their specific policy preferences and
have the government listen. For many people, interest groups are the
most important mechanism by which their views are represented before the three branches of government.

Interest groups also afford people the opportunity to *participate* in
the political process. American political culture leads us to believe

that participation is a virtue, apathy a vice. A person who wants to influence public policy making may not find voting or other campaign-related activity to be enough. Elections come only at intervals and do not render decisive judgments on most issues. If one wants a larger role in the governmental process, other ways of participating must be found. A major reason for the popularity of antiabortion and pro-choice groups, for example, is that they offer members a chance to do something about an issue they feel strongly on. If you care deeply about abortion, voting by itself is not likely to make you feel that you've done much to resolve the question. By contributing money to a lobbying organization, and possibly participating through it to do other things such as writing letters or taking part in protests, members come to feel they have a more significant role in the political process. Interest groups give them that opportunity.

Another function performed by interest groups is helping to *educate* the American public about political issues. With their advocacy efforts, publications, and publicity campaigns, interest groups can make people better aware of both policy problems and proposed solutions. An inherent trait in interest groups is that they present only their side of an issue to the public, offering facts and interpretations most favorable to their position. Despite the obvious bias in educational efforts by any group, lobbying organizations still make a valuable contribution to people's understanding of political issues. Antinuclear citizen groups like the Clamshell Alliance and the Abalone Alliance have added to public knowledge about the risks associated with nuclear power plants. The utilities that run such plants have tried to convince people otherwise with their own educational activities. Americans have profited from this exchange: public discussion and knowledge about nuclear power would be much poorer without the spirited fight over the "facts" by the opposing interest groups.

A related activity is *agenda building*. Beyond simply educating people about the sides of an issue, interest groups are frequently responsible for bringing the issue to light in the first place. The world has many problems, but not all are political issues being actively considered by government. Agenda building turns problems into issues, which become part of the body of policy questions that government feels it must deal with. The work of labor unions has helped to put specific problems of occupational health and safety on the political agenda. Their advocacy has contributed significantly to awareness among congressmen and administrators of how coal miners can *oversight*

be debilitated by black lung disease and how textile workers get brown lung by exposure to cotton dust.

E.   Finally, interest groups are involved in *program monitoring*. Lobbies closely follow programs affecting their constituents, and will often try to draw attention to shortcomings they observe through such tactics as issuing evaluative reports and contacting people in the media. They may also directly lobby agency personnel to make changes in program implementation or even go to court in an effort to exact compliance with a law. The American Iron and Steel Institute and individual steel companies carefully monitor prices of foreign imports of steel to watch for any illegal "dumping" (selling below producer costs) by their overseas competitors. The American steel industry, of course, has the greatest incentive to follow such complex transactions.

Understanding Interest Groups

Important as these roles are, interest groups remain misunderstood and maligned organizations. Americans distrust interest groups in general, but value the organizations that represent them. People join an interest group not simply because they agree with its views, but because they equate those views with the "public interest." Groups that stand on the opposite side of the same issues are regarded with disdain. Intellectually we accept the legitimacy of all interest groups; emotionally we separate them into those we support and those we must view with suspicion.

The basis of any reasoned judgment about interest groups is a factual understanding of how they operate. This is no easy task, for though interest groups all have the same goal — to influence government — organizationally and politically they seem endlessly diverse. Yet patterns are recognizable, and we have tried throughout to use such factors as size, type of membership, and resources to distinguish basic forms of interest group behavior.

But to place this analysis in perspective, we must step back to see how perceptions and attitudes of political scientists toward interest groups have changed in the latter part of the twentieth century. This is more than an interesting piece of intellectual history: a critical change in the thinking of political scientists helped broaden acceptance of the role of interest groups in public policy making. That change, in turn, helped spur the growth of interest groups.

Theory

Ｄαʰⁱ

THE RISE AND FALL OF PLURALISM

The early forerunner of pluralism in political science was known as "group theory," most widely associated with David Truman's *The Governmental Process*, published in 1951.[9] Truman makes a simple assertion: Politics can be understood only by looking at the inter- action of groups. He casts his lot with Madison, agreeing that "ten- dencies toward such groupings are 'sown in the nature of man.' "[10] He also draws on cultural anthropology and social psychology to prove his case that political man is a product of group influences. "In all societies of any degree of complexity the individual is less affected directly by the society as a whole than differentially through various of its subdivisions, or groups."[11]

The pluralist influence in political science reached its zenith a decade later when Robert Dahl published *Who Governs?*, a study of local politics in New Haven, Connecticut.[12] Dahl examined three areas of local politics to see just who influenced policy outcomes. His crucial finding was that in the three areas — political party nomina- tions, urban redevelopment, and public education — different groups of people were active and influential. New Haven did not have a small, closed circle of important people who together decided all the important issues in town politics.

Dahl found policy making in New Haven to be a process by which loose coalitions of groups and politicians would become active on issues they cared about. Although most citizens might be apathetic about most issues, many do get interested in the issues that directly affect them. Businessmen were highly active on urban redevelopment, and teachers, school administrators, and the Parent-Teacher Associa- tion (PTA) were involved in school politics. Politicians, always on the lookout for supporters, would court groups, hoping to build their own resources. Consequently, groups representing different interests were not only active, but their support was sought and their views carried weight.

---

[9] David B. Truman, *The Governmental Process* (New York: Knopf, 1951). Truman traces the roots of a group theory of politics back to Arthur F. Bent- ley's *The Process of Government* (Chicago: University of Chicago Press, 1908).
[10] Truman, *The Governmental Process*, p. 17.
[11] Truman, *The Governmental Process*, p. 15.
[12] Robert A. Dahl, *Who Governs?* (New Haven: Yale University Press, 1961).

Dahl argued that a realistic definition of democracy was not 50 percent plus one getting their way on each and every issue. Elections indicate little about actual majority preferences on each issue. Rather, as he wrote in an earlier work, the "normal" American political process is "one in which there is a high probability that an active and legitimate group in the population can make itself heard effectively at some crucial stage in the process of decision." [13] Through bargaining and compromise between affected groups and political elites, democratic decisions are reached, with no one group consistently dominating.

The influence of pluralist thought, and Dahl's writings in particular, was enormous.[14] He had gone a step further than Truman by putting his findings in such an approving light. That is, he not only seemed to be saying this is the way things are, but this is the way things should be. Policy making through group interaction is a positive virtue, not a threat to democracy.[15] Placing interest groups at the center of policy making revived democratic theory by offering an explicit defense of the American political process.

Elegantly and systematically, pluralism made sense of the bargaining between interest groups and government officials. There was a reason to it beyond the selfishness of individual groups. To most social scientists who stood in the ideological mainstream of their disciplines, pluralism was an attractive counterpoint to radical critiques of American society. Books like C. Wright Mills's *The Power Elite* (1956) had gained a good deal of attention with the claim that America was ruled by a small stratum of wealthy and powerful individuals.[16] This power elite of corporate executives, fabulously rich

[13] Dahl, *A Preface to Democratic Theory*, p. 145. He later reflects on this sentence in his *Dilemmas of Pluralist Democracy* (New Haven: Yale University Press, 1982), pp. 207–209.

[14] The rise of pluralist thought in American political science is detailed in G. David Garson, *Group Theories of Politics* (Beverly Hills, Calif.: Sage Publications, 1978).

[15] Responding to a critique by Jack Walker, Dahl denied that pluralism was intended to be read in such a normative vein. Whatever Dahl's intentions, *Who Governs?* was widely interpreted as praise and defense of the system as well as a description of reality. See Jack L. Walker, "A Critique of the Elitist Theory of Democracy," *American Political Science Review* 60 (June 1966), pp. 285–295; Robert A. Dahl, "Further Reflections on 'The Elitist Theory of Democracy,'" *American Political Science Review* 60 (June 1966), pp. 296–305; and Garson, *Group Theories of Politics*, pp. 119–152.

[16] C. Wright Mills, *The Power Elite* (New York: Oxford University Press, 1956). See also Floyd Hunter, *Community Power Structure* (Chapel Hill: University of North Carolina Press, 1953).

 Hunter.

families, military leaders, and politicians were said to be the true decision makers in society, "democracy" being an effective illusion per-
petrated on the masses. But if the power elite thesis was false, as
most social scientists believed it was, what was the countertheory?

Pluralism thus became the refutation of this damning interpretation of American politics. *Who Governs?* acknowledged that political elites had disproportionate amounts of resources, but said that
the use of these resources in ways inimical to the system was pretty
well countered by the natural working of interest group politics.
Elected officials responded to different groups on different issues,
seeking those groups out to enhance their own power. Group politics
forced elites to be responsive to a broad range of constituencies rather
than to a small group of powerful individuals.

Dahl's considerable reputation as a scholar and the book's brilliant
documentation of New Haven politics raised the pluralist case to
preeminence in political science. At the same time, the unquestioned
importance of the book marked the beginning of pluralism's decline.
It is the natural progression of scientific inquiry for an accepted
model of some social, biological or physical system to come under
close scrutiny, to have its faults exposed, and eventually to be replaced with a new model. The attention paid to *Who Governs?*
quickened this process as social scientists began to examine the underlying assumptions that guided the pluralists. Two main lines of
scholarly criticism soon came to the fore, one *methodological* and the
other *normative*.

The methodological criticism of pluralism was that studies like
Who Governs? focused on far too narrow a set of questions.[17] Wanting to know who actually made policy decisions, social scientists using
a pluralist framework would do research on selected issues being debated by the relevant government authorities. On those issues, there
may well have been participation by a number of affected interest
groups, but critics argued that this did not mean that the governmental process was truly democratic. What of the larger issues, such
as relative distribution of wealth among different segments of society,
which really are never directly addressed by governmental bodies?
The issues Dahl analyzed did not threaten to change the basic structure of New Haven society or its economy, no matter how they were

---

[17] The methodology of pluralism is best defended by Nelson W. Polsby, *Community Power and Political Theory*, 2nd ed. (New Haven: Yale University
Press, 1980).

resolved. In this view, only issues that do not fundamentally alter the position of elites enter the political agenda and become subject to interest group politics. In sum, critics of the methodology said that pluralists asked biased questions and therefore got misleading answers.[18]

A second strain of criticism stressed the consequences of pluralist theory rather than the research questions that guided it. Critics like Jack Walker[19] and Theodore Lowi[20] attacked pluralism because it justified the status quo. In *The End of Liberalism* Lowi concludes that government through interest groups is conservative because it creates resistance to change.[21] He points out that lobbying groups arise to protect the interests of some segment of society. Once government begins to make policies by bargaining with those groups, they then act to favor them at the expense of others. This privileged access of groups even favors them against newly organizing interests from the same strata of society, such as business competitors trying to enter a tightly regulated market.

These critics were not making the more radical argument of those who, like Mills, said America was governed by a small ruling class. Rather, they were saying that there was disproportionate privilege, and that privilege was rationalized by pluralism. Not all relevant interests were adequately represented by interest groups, and pluralism falsely suggested that all those significantly affected by an impending decision were taken into the policy-making process.

The validity of pluralism was thrown open to question not only by scholars, but by real-world events as well. The civil rights movement that began in the early 1960s made it all too clear that blacks were wholly outside the normal workings of the political system. As the marches and occasional violence continued during the decade, the inadequacy of pluralist theory to explain the positions of blacks in society became increasingly evident. On top of the civil rights movement came the anti-Vietnam War movement. Spreading disillusionment with the war increased alienation toward the federal govern-

[18] A forceful statement of this position is in Peter Bachrach and Morton S. Baratz, "Two Faces of Power," *American Political Science Review* 56 (December 1962), pp. 947–952. A further elaboration is provided by John Gaventa, *Power and Powerlessness* (Urbana: University of Illinois Press, 1980).
[19] Walker, "A Critique of the Elitist Theory of Democracy."
[20] Theodore J. Lowi, *The End of Liberalism*, 2nd ed. (New York: Norton, 1979).
[21] Lowi, *The End of Liberalism*, p. 60.

ment. Questions arose in people's minds not only about the wisdom of the war, but about the way the government was run. By the end of the 1960s, neither intellectuals nor ordinary citizens were likely to believe contemporary interest group politics was the basis for democratic policy making.

PLURALISM AS A GOAL

Although pluralism was no longer considered accurate, it nonetheless remained desirable. Dahl's vision of what American politics should look like was still appealing. Pluralism could not simply be discarded like a rejected hypothesis in a small research project; to admit that it could never be an accurate theory of American politics would call into question the legitimacy of interest groups in a democracy. Either a new theory had to rationalize the role of interest groups in a democracy, or the system had to be changed to make pluralism come true.

It is difficult and inherently imprecise to try to trace the force of an idea. How did Keynesian economics come to be so dominant for so many years? The exact force of pluralist thinking is impossible to measure directly. Yet in examining the modern behavioral period (roughly since World War II) in political science, there seems little doubt that pluralism has been the most widely debated theory of American politics. At a time when the discipline was so preoccupied with the methodology of political inquiry, pluralism combined an empirical "scientific" approach to the study of power with a broad theory of democracy.

Why has this theory, no longer considered to be true, had such an important legacy? First, no new theories of comparable scope that give broadly accepted explanations of American politics have come forward. This may seem a damning critique of the social sciences and political science in particular. In the past twenty years, why has no new theory replaced pluralism? The reason, in short, is that the task of formulating one is extremely difficult. The new theory would need to provide an all-encompassing explanation and an integrated framework for understanding American government. The American political system is extremely complex, with highly differentiated actors and institutions. To create a theory that would explain American government and the relationships among its parts, and would combine empirical verification and normative assumptions, is a truly herculean task. It is almost pretentious for a social scientist to try. Most political scientists find it more fruitful to work on narrower, and in their minds more realistic research problems.

A second reason for the pluralist legacy's continued significance is that the Madisonian dilemma remains unresolved. Pluralists adapted Madison's leap of faith to modern American politics by stressing the natural opposition of competing interest groups within the policy-making process. With pluralism declining as an accepted interpretation of American politics, the problem of how to rationalize interest group participation in a democracy again had to be addressed. If interest groups are not part of some type of balance in society, they begin to present dangers. Failing a new resolution to the Madisonian dilemma, the solution has been to try to make pluralism a reality. As we will discuss, scholars, political activists, and policy makers have tried to justify interest group politics by proposing means to make it more balanced.

The residual force of the pluralist vision surely results in part from the leading role of pluralism in political science teaching during the 1960s and early 1970s. Any student enrolled in an American government course (required at many schools) was exposed to the pluralist debate. Indeed, the differences between the pluralist and the power elitist schools of thought was the theme of many courses on American national government and urban politics. The conflicting arguments between those who believed that this country was a democracy and those who thought that a ruling class governed, offered a challenging way to study the American political process. It was a broad question that forced students to think about the democracy in a lively, debatable context. The methodological questions about pluralist and elitist research also facilitated discussion about political inquiry.

The force of pluralist thinking was not, however, restricted to the classroom or the pages of academic journals. More popular works were aimed at larger audiences. The writing of American intellectuals at this time conveyed a similar message in many contexts. A principal theme of this era was that a cause of the malady in American politics was the lack of participation by broad segments of the population. This view was common among those who analyzed the "urban crises." As the cities deteriorated, those trying to stem the tide cited the need for a greater sense of community among remaining city dwellers. Translated into specific policies, this plan meant involving people more in the decisions that affected their lives. The philosophy was incorporated in legislation like the Economic Opportunity Act (1964) and Model Cities (1966), which required citizen participation in the programs' development.

Through a troubled and turbulent time, the solution to the ills of our democracy was more democracy. More people needed to participate in politics so that policies would more closely approximate the true wishes of the citizenry. *More participation inevitably meant more interest groups.*

CONCLUSION

During the 1960s, Americans became increasingly dissatisfied with the way their democratic system was operating.[22] For their part, American political scientists were more and more disillusioned with the dominant theory in their discipline that purported to explain how that democracy worked. Both alienation from American government and scholarly rejection of pluralism contributed to a powerful new idea: Increased participation was needed to balance a system of interest groups that skewed policy making toward organizations unrepresentative of the American people.[23]

Although no new theory as such came along to replace pluralism, the idea of expanded interest group participation by the chronically underrepresented was at least a first step toward finding a new solution to the dilemma of *Federalist* No. 10. The real-world events and the philosophical musings of scholars that contributed to the movement toward increased participation by interest groups could not be selective in their influence. The new interest group politics went far beyond citizen participation programs and public interest groups for those traditionally unrepresented in the governmental process. Rather, extraordinary growth in all types of lobbying organizations raised anew questions about curing the mischiefs of faction.

[22] Arthur Miller, "Political Issues and Trust in Government: 1964–70," *American Political Science Review* 68 (September 1974), pp. 951–972.

[23] See Andrew S. McFarland, *Public Interest Lobbies* (Washington, D.C.: American Enterprise Institute, 1976).

CHAPTER TWO

The Advocacy Explosion

This is not the first period of American history in which an apparent increase in the numbers and influence of interest groups has heightened anxiety.[1] Uneasiness over the power and influence of interest group politics is part of the American political tradition. Yet the widespread concern today does contrast with attitudes in recent American history. The New Deal, for example, was known for its positive acceptance of interest groups because of the greater role trade associations came to have in the policy making of newly established regulatory agencies.[2] As recently as the 1960s, scholars were arguing that interest group politics contributed to democratic politics.[3]

Currently, a pervasive, popular perception is that there has been an unprecedented and dangerous growth in the numbers of interest groups, and that this growth continues unabated. This view is echoed constantly in the press. *Newsweek* says that "Every conceivable issue seems to have competing pressure groups." [4] David Broder, the widely respected syndicated columnist, states that until strong political parties return, "single-interest groups will ride rampant through the system."[5] *The New York Times* calls K Street in Washington, where

---

[1] Some arguments here were first published in Jeffrey M. Berry, "Public Interest Vs. Party System," *Society* 17 (May/June 1980), pp. 42–48.

[2] Theodore J. Lowi calls this "interest group liberalism." See *The End of Liberalism*, 2nd ed. (New York: Norton, 1979).

[3] See Robert A. Dahl, *Who Governs?* (New Haven: Yale University Press, 1961).

[4] "Single-Issue Politics," *Newsweek*, November 6, 1978, p. 48.

[5] David S. Broder, "One-Issue Groups: The New Force in Politics," *Boston Globe*, September 13, 1978.

16

many interest groups have their headquarters, "the equivalent of a new branch of government." [6]

Politicians, too, see a rising tide of special interest groups, altering the governmental process for the worse and making their job more difficult. Senator Gary Hart of Colorado says, "I hate to get on the plane for Denver. For three hours, the lobbyists just line up in the aisle to get a word with me." [7] Former Minnesota Senator Wendell Anderson also paints a dreary picture of interest group politics. "The single-interest constituencies have just about destroyed politics as I knew it. They've made it miserable to be in office." [8] And President Jimmy Carter, in his farewell address to the nation, blamed interest groups for many shortcomings of his administration:

> . . . We are increasingly drawn to single-issue groups and special interest organizations to insure that whatever else happens our own personal views and our own private interests are protected. This is a disturbing factor in American political life. It tends to distort our purpose because the national interest is not always the sum of all our single or special interests.[9]

Scholars too find interest groups to be at the heart of this country's problems. Economist Lester Thurow states unequivocally that, "Our economic problems are solvable," but adds that "political paralysis" stands in the way. The source of that paralysis in Thurow's eyes is an expanding system of effective interest groups that makes it impossible for government to allocate the pain that comes with realistic economic solutions.[10] Political scientist Everett Ladd blames special interest politics for our economic woes as well. "The cumulative effect of this pressure has been the relentless and extraordinary rise of government spending and inflationary deficits." [11]

In short, the popular perception is that interest groups are a

---

[6] Lynn Rosellini, "Lobbyists' Row All Alert for Chance at the Budget," *The New York Times*, February 26, 1981.

[7] Single-Issue Politics, p. 48.

[8] Broder, "One-Issue Groups."

[9] "Prepared Text of Carter's Farewell Address on Major Issues Facing the Nation," *The New York Times*, January 15, 1981.

[10] Lester C. Thurow, *The Zero-Sum Society* (New York: Penguin Books, 1981), pp. 11–15.

[11] Everett C. Ladd, "How to Tame the Special Interest Groups," *Fortune*, October 20, 1980, p. 66ff.

cancer, spreading unchecked throughout the body politic, making it gradually weaker, eventually killing it.

THE INTEREST GROUP SPIRAL

Political rhetoric aside, has there really been a significant expansion of interest group politics? Or are interest groups simply playing their familiar role as whipping boy for the ills of society?

The answer to both questions is "yes." Surely nothing is new about interest groups being seen as the bane of our political system. The muckrakers at the turn of the century voiced many of the same fears that show up today in *Newsweek* or David Broder's columns. Scholars like Thurow and Ladd are almost polite in criticizing interest groups compared to the wholesale indictments of privilege in earlier works like Charles Beard's *An Economic Interpretation of the Constitution* or C. Wright Mills's *The Power Elite*.[12] Politicians, too, have always been plagued by the demands of lobbyists.[13]

Yet even if the problem is familiar, it is no less troubling. The growth of interest group politics in recent years should not simply be dismissed as part of a chronic condition in American politics. As we will articulate at length in Chapter 3, this growth took place during a period of party decline. The United States is not just a country with an increasing number of active interest groups, but a country whose citizens look more and more to interest groups to speak for them in the political process. The implications are disquieting.

Before addressing some of the larger problems that arise from this trend, we must document the increasing number of interest groups. The statistics we have show an unmistakable increase in interest group activity in Washington. The best available data are in Jack Walker's recent survey of 564 lobbying organizations in Washington[14] (see Figure 2.1). The historical evidence shows a clear pattern of growth, with appropximately 30 percent of the groups originating

---

12 Charles A. Beard, *An Economic Interpretation of the Constitution of the United States* (New York: Macmillan, 1913), and C. Wright Mills, *The Power Elite* (New York: Oxford University Press, 1956).

13 See Kay Lehman Schlozman and John T. Tierney, "More of the Same: Washington Pressure Group Activity in a Decade of Change," *Journal of Politics* 45 (May 1983), pp. 351–377.

14 Jack L. Walker, "The Origins and Maintenance of Interest Groups in America," *American Political Science Review* 77 (June 1983), pp. 390–406.

Figure 2.1
Interest Groups and Their Year of Origin

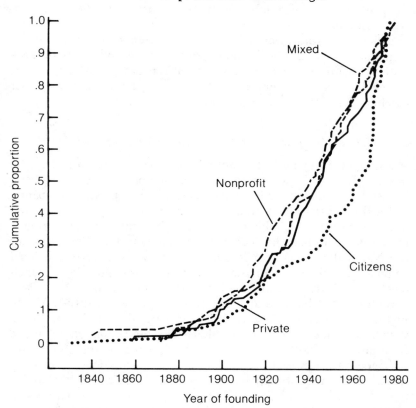

Source: Survey of voluntary associations by Jack L. Walker, "The Origins and Maintenance of Interest Groups in America," *American Political Science Review* 77 (June 1983), p. 395. The "mixed" category represents groups which have members from both the public and private sectors.

between 1960 and 1980.[15] The figures do not, however, precisely indicate how many new groups have been started in different eras because we cannot calculate how many were started in earlier periods but have

[15] See an earlier version of the Walker article, similarly titled, presented at the annual meeting of the American Political Science Association, New York, September 1981, p. 14.

since ceased to exist. Still, Walker's results show such large differences that it can be confidently concluded that there has been a sharp upturn in the number of groups even though the precise increase cannot be determined.

When we break down the growth of interest groups into smaller components, specifically the number of corporate offices, trade associations, political action committees, citizen groups, and law firms, the evidence is even more compelling; some of these give us firmer baselines for measuring the increases.

Trade Associations and Government Relations Offices

Washington lobbying in the world of business has taken a dramatic upsurge. Business representation in Washington is done in two basic forms. First are the trade associations, which represent companies engaged in a particular economic activity. Some are quite broad, such as the National Association of Manufacturers, but most have a much narrower scope, like the National Funeral Directors Association or the National Independent Retail Jewelers. Second, large individual corporations are commonly represented in Washington by a branch office for "Governmental Relations" or "Public Affairs."

Both types of business lobbying have visibly increased their Washington-based activity. Between 1977 and 1980, the number of professional and trade associations headquartered in Washington jumped from around 1,700 to about 2,000. The Greater Washington Board of Trade estimates that one or two national associations arrive every week. "The main attraction," says a Board official, "is the lobbying." [16] Between 1970 and 1980, the proportion of national associations that made Washington their headquarters went from 21 percent to 28 percent.[17] Similar trends can be found among individual businesses. Between 1968 and 1978, the number of corporations with public affairs offices in Washington increased from 100 to more than 500.[18] A Boston University School of Management study of over

[16] Robert D. Hershey, Jr., "The Magnet for Lobbyists," *The New York Times*, August 18, 1980.

[17] David Vogel, "How Business Responds to Opposition: Corporate Political Strategies During the 1970s," paper delivered at the annual meeting of the American Political Science Association, Washington, D.C., September 1979, p. 15; and Hershey, "The Magnet for Lobbyists."

[18] Vogel, "How Business Responds," p. 15. See also Phyllis S. McGrath, *Redefining Corporate-Federal Relations* (New York: Conference Board, 1979).

Figure 2.2
Corporate Offices in Washington, D.C., by Year of Origin

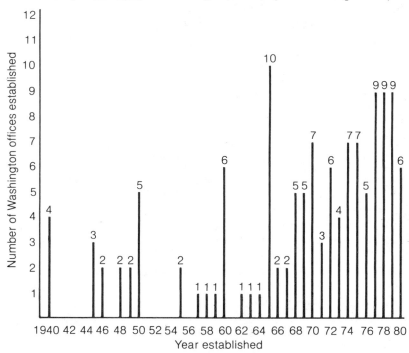

Year established

Source: Survey of Corporations by Boston University School of Management, reported in *Public Affairs Offices and Their Functions*, (Boston: Boston University School of Management, 1981), p.8.

400 firms revealed that of those with Washington offices, roughly half started that office in the last decade[19] (see Figure 2.2).

Equally important is that corporations are upgrading their Washington offices. The *Wall Street Journal* reports, "Faced with wrestling a Hydra-headed bureaucracy, many corporations have been adding or expanding government-relations activities, and upgrading the post that used to go to a public-relations functionary into that of a top corporate officer." [20] The Boston University study shows that 63 per-

[19] *Public Affairs Offices and Their Functions* (Boston: Boston University School of Management, 1981), p. 8.
[20] Vasil Pappas, "More Firms Upgraded Government-Relations Jobs Because of Sharp Growth in Federal Regulations," *Wall Street Journal*, January 11, 1980.

cent of the corporate public affairs departments surveyed had increased their professional staffs in the past five years.[21] General Motors went from a three-person office in 1968 to a staff of twenty-eight in 1978.[22] In the past few years, such large companies as Anheuser-Busch, Allied Chemical, and INA Corp., a large insurer, all created posts of vice-president for government relations.[23]

Citizen Groups

Before the recent rise in the number of citizen groups, they were not generally considered to be important actors in national politics.[24] As Figure 2.1 indicates, citizen groups show more likelihood of being formed in recent years than other types of lobbying organizations. In the early 1970s I surveyed 83 "public interest groups" active in Washington. Almost half the sample (47 percent) were started in the five years between 1968 and 1972.[25] Again, as with the Walker study, the amount of increase is probably overstated because the number of groups that ceased to exist before the survey could not be measured.[26]

The growth of citizen group politics is surely even greater at the local level than in Washington. By the end of the 1970s, the National Commission on Neighborhoods had identified 8,000 grassroots neighborhood groups across the country. The Department of Housing and Urban Development compiled its own list of 15,000 citizen groups.[27] Many of these are quite small and depend heavily on vol-

---

[21] *Public Affairs Offices and Their Functions*, p. 4.

[22] Vogel, "How Business Responds," p. 15.

[23] Pappas, "More Firms Upgraded Government-Relations Jobs."

[24] See, for example, the leading interest group texts of the 1950s by V. O. Key and David Truman. Their books include only negligible references to citizen groups. V. O. Key, Jr., *Politics, Parties, and Pressure Groups* (New York: T. Y. Crowell, 1942; 5th ed., 1964); and David B. Truman, *The Governmental Process* (New York: Knopf, 1951).

[25] Jeffrey M. Berry, *Lobbying for the People* (Princeton: Princeton University Press, 1977), p. 34.

[26] Data collected by Kay Lehman Schlozman shows that these organizations have a higher mortality rate than other types of interest groups. She suggests that this adds to the bias in favor of business in the interest group system. "What Accent the Heavenly Chorus?: Political Equality and the American Pressure System," working paper, Boston College, 1983.

[27] Stuart Langton, "Citizen Participation in America: Current Reflections on the State of the Art," in Stuart Langton, ed., *Citizen Participation in America* (Lexington, Mass.: D. C. Heath, 1978), p. 2.

unteer labor. Collectively, however, they have helped to change the political environment of this country. No one has a firm count of citizen groups that today have lobbying offices in Washington, but it continues to grow. Many new conservative groups have started up in the past few years, in contrast to the wave of liberal groups that began in the late 1960s and early 1970s. Most important, though, is that citizen group leaders and followers of both the left and the right have come to share the belief that they can influence government, that citizen groups stand a real chance against opposing groups, and that the interest group model of political activism makes sense compared with the alternative of political party work.

Political Action Committees

The proliferation of political action committees (PACs) is clearly the most worrisome aspect of the increase in interest groups. These are fund-raising units organized to collect and disburse campaign contributions. They are formed by corporations (such as Republic Steel); labor unions (International Ladies' Garment Workers' Union); professional associations (American Medical Association); farm groups (Associated Milk Producers); ideological groups (Fund for a Conservative Majority); and other types of organizations. The PACs themselves do not usually lobby beyond their donations, but are often adjuncts to a lobbying office of a parent organization.

Widespread PAC activity is a relatively recent phenomenon: Close to 3,400 PACs were registered in 1982, compared with about 600 in 1974 [28] (see Table 2.1). The amount of money contributed by PACs grew apace, going from roughly $12.5 million for congressional candidates in 1974 to an estimated $83 million in 1982.[29] More than 40 percent of the PACs registered in 1982 were sponsored by corporations and they donated roughly a third of PAC money to congressional candidates. Trade association PACs were an additional source of business money.

Unlike the other manifestations of increased interest group activity, the upsurge in PACs is rooted in federal law. Throughout this

[28] "PACs Increase in Number," Federal Election Commission, January 14, 1983.
[29] "1981–82 PAC Giving up 51%," Federal Election Commission, April 29, 1983; and Herbert E. Alexander, *Financing Politics*, 2nd ed. (Washington, D.C.: Congressional Quarterly, 1980), p. 85.

Table 2.1
Growth of PACs

Year	Number of PACs
1974	608
1975[a]	722
1976	1,146
1977	1,360
1978	1,653
1979	2,000
1980	2,551
1981	2,901
1982	3,371

[a] Through November.
Source: Federal Election Commission.

century, corporations had been forbidden to contribute funds to candidates for federal office. Although restrictions were relaxed somewhat for PACs in 1971, it was not until the passage of the Federal Election Campaign Act Amendments of 1974 and its subsequent interpretation by the Federal Election Commission, that corporations were fully free to set up committees that could solicit voluntary contributions. After these changes in the law, the number of corporate PACs began to skyrocket. (The reforms are described more fully in Chapter 8.)

The formation of so many PACs in recent years is not, however, wholly attributable to modifications in the law. Noncorporate PACs too have significantly increased in numbers and in funds contributed since 1974. Interest groups are aware that their work is competitive, and as other groups escalate their efforts, they try to respond in kind.

Law Firms

The expansion in Washington lobbying activities is also manifested in the sharp jump in the number of lawyers practicing in Washington: Between 1972 and 1983, the Washington bar went from around 11,000 to 38,000.[30] Washington has more lawyers than Los Angeles, a city three times its size.[31]

[30] Source: Washington, D.C. Bar Association.
[31] Donald F. Pike, "Rise of the Power Brokers," *U.S. News and World Report,* March 10, 1980, pp. 52–56; and Bryce Nelson, "A Gold Rush for Lawyers in Legal Hills of Washington," *Boston Globe,* December 8, 1980.

Washington law is lobbying law. Firms are hired by individual corporations, trade associations, foreign governments, and others to work with the government to try to solve specific problems. They are most in demand to help clients with the complexities in the regulatory process. If a manufacturer in Duluth is having trouble meeting pollution standards set by the Environmental Protection Agency (EPA), it may find that hiring a Washington law firm is a first step toward finding a solution. A Washington firm like Beveridge, Fairbanks & Diamond, whose partners have experience working in the EPA, may seem better suited than a Minnesota firm to advise the company on its options, to press EPA for a change, or, if necessary, even to protect its client in court.[32]

Because so much of Washington law is related to the regulatory process, the rapid growth of regulations and new regulatory agencies during the 1970s dictated an increase in the supply of lawyers to meet the demand. Not only did firms expand, and new ones start up, but large out-of-town firms opened branch offices. To serve their corporate clients well and to protect their business, many out-of-town firms found they needed a Washington branch office. Well-known firms like Dewey, Ballantine, Bushby, Palmer & Wood (New York), O'Melveny & Myers (Los Angeles), and Vinson & Elkins (Houston) started branch offices in Washington during this time. Felix Laughlin of Dewey, Ballantine explains:

> The old school said that you could sit in New York and do everything, or maybe get on a plane and come down here for a day. But if you're here full time you're in almost daily contact with the regulatory agencies, and you get things done a lot faster.[33]

A major area of growth has also been in new, specialty firms that emphasize one policy area or agency. This is an effective way for a new firm to compete with the large, established firms.[34] A new firm that has expertise in a specialized field, will naturally attract particular clients, as do recently formed firms like Epstein & Becker

32 James W. Singer, "Practicing Law in Washington — An American Growth Industry," *National Journal*, February 4, 1978, p. 177.
33 Steven V. Roberts, "Federal Magnetism Draws Law Firms," *The New York Times*, January 11, 1978.
34 Singer, "Practicing Law in Washington," pp. 172–179.

(health), or Brownstein, Zeidman, Schomer & Chase (housing).[35] For every lobbying problem, Washington lawyers abound.[36]

The increase in interest group advocacy seems incontrovertible. The statistics reflect a tremendous increase in interest groups and in resources devoted by groups to lobbying activities. But documenting the rise of interest groups does not explain it. Why is it that so many new interest groups have developed over the past fifteen years?

THE RISE OF CITIZEN GROUPS

The growth of interest group advocacy in different sectors of society comes from many of the same roots. At the same time, the sharp growth in numbers of interest groups also reflects different sectors of society responding to each other. As one segment of the interest community grew and appeared to prosper, it spurred growth in other segments eager to equalize the increasing strength of their adversaries. This spiral of interest group activity began in large part in the civil rights and antiwar movements of the 1960s.

Movement Politics

A legacy of the civil rights and anti-Vietnam War movements was that they succeeded in influencing the course of public policy.[37] This effect is most evident for the civil rights movement, which began to gather steam with the 1954 Supreme Court decision banning school segregation and the 1955 Montgomery, Alabama bus boycott. In Montgomery, blacks refused to ride the segregated system (whites in front, blacks in the back), quickly depleting the financial resources of the city's transit system. Although it took a Supreme Court order to force integration of the system a year later, many

---

[35] Some evidence says that unprecedented growth in the last decade along with the deregulation and recession of the Reagan years has finally brought down the spiraling rate of increase. See Stephen Wermiel, "Washington Lawyers Seeing Signs That the Boom Times Have Passed, *Wall Street Journal*, March 18, 1982; and Robert D. Hershey, Jr., "Deregulation Cuts Lawyer Need," *The New York Times*, June 1, 1981.

[36] And if a lawyer is not needed, there are many public relations specialists who can be hired instead. The public relations industry in Washington has also expanded as the demand has grown for lobbying experts. See Chapter 6.

[37] On the influence of the civil rights and antiwar efforts, see David Vogel, *Lobbying the Corporation* (New York: Basic Books, 1978), pp 23–68.

other boycotts and sit-ins followed, increasing national awareness of discrimination. Public opinion was not fully galvanized, however, until the early 1960s, when blacks began marches and demonstrations, many of which ended in confrontation with white authorities. Some ended in violence, with marchers being attacked by policemen. The demonstrations, shown on network news telecasts, helped to turn the public decidedly in favor of civil rights legislation.[38] The immediate outcome was the Civil Rights Act of 1964, outlawing many basic forms of discrimination, and the Voting Rights Act of 1965, which ended exclusion of blacks from voting in many areas in the South.

The anti-Vietnam War movement took form in the mid-1960s as American involvement in the war increased. Its success is not as clear-cut as that of the civil rights movement because so many American soldiers continued to fight and die during years of protest. Many Americans also became hostile toward the antiwar movement because they felt it was disloyal for people not to support American soldiers once they were committed to a military action. Most would agree, however, that the antiwar movement hastened the end of American participation in the war in Vietnam. The unpopular war helped push President Johnson out of office and brought pressure upon President Nixon to end American participation in the fighting. The antiwar groups spearheaded opposition to the war and their periodic demonstrations were visible evidence of growing public anger over the fighting.

The lessons of the civil rights and antiwar movements were clear to other would-be reformers. Citizens' interest groups, such as the Southern Christian Leadership Conference of the civil rights movement, or the Student Mobilization Committee of the antiwar movement, could have an effect. These groups worked completely outside the party system, stood independently on their own resources, and did not compromise principle to achieve political accommodation.

The model of citizen group advocacy was soon copied by those suffering from discrimination who saw parallels between blacks and themselves. Hispanic farmworkers in California were organized for the first time by Cesar Chavez and his United Farm Workers union. Gays would later organize into groups like the Lambda Legal Defense and Education Fund, which works for civil rights for homo-

[38] David J. Garrow, *Protest at Selma* (New Haven: Yale University Press, 1978).

sexuals. Most conspicuous is the rise of the women's movement, deeply influenced by the citizen advocacy of the 1960s. Women saw the tools of these earlier groups as directly applicable to their own plight. Sara Evans writes of how the National Organization for Women (NOW) was formed:

> The lessons of the NAACP and its legal defense arm were not lost on the women who founded NOW: to adult professional women in the early 1960s the growth of civil rights insurgency provided a model of legal activism and imaginative minority group lobbying.[39]

Evans points out that many of those who became pioneers in the women's movement first gained experience working in those earlier causes.

Minorities and women were not the only ones influenced to organize by the civil rights and antiwar movements. Political activists began to look at the range of policy areas that interested them, such as consumer rights, environmental affairs, hunger and malnutrition, corporate responsibility, access to media, and so on.[40] Although the success of civil rights and antiwar groups inspired formation of new groups in these areas, the protest orientation of these earlier organizations seemed inappropriate. Leaders of these new groups wanted to transcend "movement politics" with organizations that could survive beyond periods of intense emotion. The organizations that were needed could put the idealism of young, liberal activists in harness with the financial support and policy interests of the middle class.

Public Interest Groups

Many of the new organizations in the late 1960s and 1970s became popularly known as "public interest groups." [41] These were lobbying

---

[39] Sara Evans, *Personal Politics* (New York: Knopf, 1979), p. 25.

[40] The thinking of this new generation of activists is captured well in David S. Broder's *Changing of the Guard* (New York: Penguin, 1981), especially pp. 225–253.

[41] When pressed, lobbyists from these groups will reject the untenable philosophical position that their organization embodies the public good or "public interest." William Butler of the Environmental Defense Fund says, for example, that his organization does not claim to speak on behalf of the public interest, but that they represent the "unrepresented and under-represented" segments of society. Timothy E. Clark, "After a Decade of Doing Battle, Public Interest Groups Show Their Age," *National Journal*, July 12, 1980, p. 1138.

groups without economic self-interest, or more precisely, "a public interest group is one that seeks a collective good, the achievement of which will not selectively and materially benefit the membership or activists of the organization." [42] The most prominent of the new groups were Common Cause and the Ralph Nader organizations. Common Cause, which focuses on opening up and reforming the governmental process, was founded in 1970 by John Gardner, a liberal Republican and former Cabinet secretary in the Johnson administration. Declaring that "Everyone is represented but the people," Gardner used full-page newspaper ads and direct mail solicitations to build a membership of 230,000 in little more than a year, an astonishing feat for a voluntary organization. [43]

Ralph Nader came into the public eye in 1965 when *Unsafe at Any Speed*, attacking the automobile industry, was published. Nader quickly became known as a champion for consumers and in his first decade in Washington put together more than a dozen lobbying organizations. Many of his groups, including the Public Citizen Litigation Group, the Health Research Group, and the Center for the Study of Responsive Law, have been major actors in Washington politics. [44]

Many other groups, such as the Environmental Defense Fund, Zero Population Growth, and the Children's Foundation, started up as well. Older groups such as Consumers Union, the League of Women Voters, and the Sierra Club, prospered too and devoted new resources to Washington lobbying. Indeed, public interest groups have existed for years; and the most recent wave of groups is in the tradition of reform movements in America. Public interest groups are distinguished from earlier reform movements, though, by the breadth and durability of the lobbying organizations.

Public interest groups of this era directly benefited from the growing force of the pluralist ideal. The lack of an acceptable alternative theory of democracy and the reality of interest group politics made pluralism a compelling idea, a goal toward which America should strive. As it became accepted that pluralist democracy did not in fact exist, how was its absence to be remedied? The solution was

---

[42] Berry, *Lobbying for the People*, p. 7.
[43] Berry, *Lobbying for the People*, pp. 29–30.
[44] On Nader's rise, see Charles McCarry, *Citizen Nader* (New York: Saturday Review Press, 1972).

1960's + 1970's:
Ideological Legitimacy

quite simple: The influence of existing groups had to be *balanced*.[45]
Madison's words were echoed: Democracy could be achieved not by
limiting the freedom of private interests to lobby, but rather by "controlling" the "effects" of the one-sidedness. The Ford Foundation
articulated this simple premise in defending their sponsorship of
public interest law firms during the early 1970s:

> A central assumption of our democratic society is that the
> general interest or the common good will emerge out of the
> conflict of special interests. The public interest law firm seeks
> to improve this process by giving better representation to cer-
> tain interests.[46]

The liberal public interest movement was thus built on a vision
of how democracy could work. The leaders of these groups came to
a common conclusion as to how reform could be achieved. Broad,
sweeping reform through legislation that would limit the role business could play was given little attention. Nor was working through
the political parties, or initiating a third party given much credence
as an alternative way of achieving their goals. The philosophy of
the public interest movement of this period was that no matter how
much government was reformed, government by itself was inherently
incapable of protecting the common good. Left to its own devices,
the government would always be overly influenced by private sector
groups. The only solution was continuing involvement by citizen
groups in policy making to balance the influence of other organizations. Making pluralism come true was the answer.[47]

Citizen Participation

It was not only citizen activists who adopted pluralism as a goal.
The federal government, too, acknowledged that the interest group
system was not balanced and that action had to be taken to ensure
that affected interests became represented interests. This attitude was
manifested in the citizen participation programs that were adopted
for administrative policy making. By embracing citizen participation,

[45] Andrew S. McFarland, *Public Interest Lobbies* (Washington, D.C.: American
Enterprise Institute, 1976.
[46] *The Public Interest Law Firm* (New York: Ford Foundation, 1973), p. 8.
See also, "Ford Ends Public Interest Law Program," *Citizen Participation* 1
(January/February 1980), p. 9.
[47] Berry, "Public Interest Vs. Party System."

the government tacitly admitted that their agencies and regulatory bodies, created to protect the public, could not properly do so without more public input. It reflected the belief, fostered by social scientists, that administrators are most responsive to the private interests they regulate rather than remaining independent in their decision making.[48]

The first of the new citizen participation programs was mandated by the Economic Opportunity Act of 1964, the heart of President Johnson's War on Poverty. The law, with a phrase now familiar, called for "maximum feasible participation" by the poor in the community action programs funded by the government. The law and the legislative record said little more about what "maximum feasible participation" meant, leading to a great deal of local conflict between citizen groups and city agencies.[49] Nevertheless, as new domestic programs were initiated, or old ones amended, requirements for citizen participation were written in. In laws such as the Airport and Airways Development Act, the Federal Water Pollution Control Act, the Coastal Zone Management Act, and the Energy Reorganization Act, Congress said that some provision must be made for citizens to participate in policy making.[50]

Generally, Congress remained vague about what exactly it wanted, leaving the specifics of citizen participation up to the administering agencies. Typically, agencies would fulfill their mandate by holding open hearings to which any interested citizens could come and speak their mind. Yet these programs were really vehicles for citizen *groups*, because people believe that there is power in numbers. Thus, citizen participation programs encouraged formation of citizen groups across the country.

Liberals hoped that government-sponsored pluralism would nourish a failing system. Citizen participation would be one means of empowering people, part of a broader citizens' movement that would make America a true democracy. Looking back on the growth of this philosophy, activist Harry Boyte writes, "Such a democratic vision

[48] See Marver H. Bernstein, *Regulating Business by Independent Commission* (Princeton: Princeton University Press, 1955); and Paul H. Weaver, "Regulation, Social Policy, and Class Conflict," *Public Interest* 50 (Winter 1978), pp. 45–63.
[49] Daniel P. Moynihan, *Maximum Feasible Misunderstanding* (New York: Free Press, 1969).
[50] Langton, "Citizen Participation in America," p. 3.

represented a rekindled faith in the citizenry itself, a conviction that, given the means and the information, people can make decisions about the course of their lives...." [51] This vision proved popular. By 1977 there were approximately 225 separate citizen participation programs under federal law and countless more state and local programs.[52] Walter Rosenbaum points out, however, that their growth was a "counterfeit prosperity," for many of the programs turned out to be disappointing.[53] Such programs were built on a naive assumption that bureaucracies would willingly share their authority with citizen groups. Instead it became easy for administrators to implement their citizen participation programs without ever having to go beyond symbolic gestures. In the Community Development Block Grant program, public hearings are frequently the only form of participation. Commenting on research on the program, one analyst concluded that "Generally, the impact of hearings on final decisions appeared minimal, producing minor concessions by officials in some cases and no recognizable responses in others." [54]

Although liberals have been disappointed that citizen participation has not had more direct influence in swaying policy making toward their preferences, it has achieved one major goal: increased participation. The participation ethos that these programs contributed to led to an explosion in the number of citizen groups in the United States. Not everyone found these thousands of new groups or "grassrooting of the system" to be a desirable turn of events.[55] Some neoconservatives, like Harvard political scientist Samuel Huntington, began to wonder if the governmental process was being "overloaded" with so many competing demands.[56] Others argued that citizen groups and citizen participation programs had worked in favor of the middle-class elite who, for example, frequently prevailed upon

[51] Harry C. Boyte, *The Backyard Revolution* (Philadelphia: Temple University Press, 1980), p. 7.

[52] Walter A. Rosenbaum, "Public Involvement as Reform and Ritual," in Langton, *Citizen Participation in America*, p. 84.

[53] Rosenbaum, "Public Involvement as Reform and Ritual," p. 81.

[54] Barry Checkoway, "Public Hearings Are Not Enough," *Citizen Participation* 1 (May/June 1980), p. 7.

[55] The phrase is Janice Perlman's, "Grassrooting the System," *Social Policy* 7 (September/October 1976), pp. 4–20.

[56] Samuel P. Huntington, "The Democratic Distemper," *Public Interest* 41 (Fall 1975), 9–38.

But, new ethos? → new groups,

local authorities to restrict development projects in the name of environmental preservation.[57] Ironically then, the legacy of citizen participation has been both liberal and conservative disenchantment.

The New Right

The surge in citizen groups was not limited to the liberal side of the political spectrum. The rise in conservative public interest groups did come later, however, and indeed, seemed stimulated in part by the growing success of liberal public interest groups. By 1980, though, the "new right" had an impressive array of groups dedicated to changing the direction of domestic and foreign policy. One reason the new right came to be called "new" is that many of the recently formed organizations focus exclusively on single issues like abortion or school prayer, whereas older conservative organizations like the American Conservative Union and the Young Americans for Freedom have a broader outlook. Yet nothing is new about single-issue groups in American politics; nor are all the new conservative citizen groups so narrow in their coverage of issues. All that was really new about the new right was the large number and notoriety of these groups.

As with the liberals, rising conservative dissatisfaction with government has its roots in the controversies over civil rights and the Vietnam War. The civil rights acts and the Great Society programs that were aimed mainly at minorities made large numbers of people feel that their own interests were being ignored. Civil rights was part of a larger range of "social" issues that they found disturbing. School busing, "crime in the streets," growing welfare programs, and an expanding federal government that seemed ever more intrusive contributed to a belief that the government was out of touch with Main Street. Conservatives also became angry that the United States failed to pursue an all-out military effort against North Vietnam. In their eyes, Washington did not seem to have the will to win. In the 1968 campaign, third-party candidate George Wallace appealed to many working-class whites because of his hostility toward blacks while he was governor of Alabama and because of his attacks on the federal government. He struck a responsive chord when he belittled Lyndon Johnson's "sissy attitude" on law and order, and ridiculed

[57] Bernard J. Frieden, *The Environmental Protection Hustle* (Cambridge: MIT Press, 1979).

Particular interests feed within conservative (liberal) ideology

the "pointy-headed" bureaucrats for their attempts at social engineering.[58]

With so much conservative dissatisfaction about government, it may seem surprising that right-oriented citizen groups did not form in great numbers as their liberal counterparts in the late 1960s and early 1970s had. One reason may be that the Wallace vote offered an outlet for some frustrated conservatives. His voters may have felt satisfied that their voices had been heard. Other conservatives may have thought the election of Republican Richard Nixon in 1968 heralded a return to responsible government. Nixon campaigned for an honorable end to the Vietnam War and for a conservative course on domestic policy. Finally, the growth of conservative citizen groups may have been delayed by the disdain conservatives felt for the liberal groups that became active in the 1960s. The protest orientation of the civil rights and antiwar groups gave citizen advocacy an unappealing image in conservative eyes. To those on the right they surely appeared to be organizations of radical blacks and young, countercultural whites, and thus presented an organizing model that seemed inappropriate. The public interest lobbies that soon came to Washington to represent other liberal interests, however, created a new model that slowly took hold with conservatives.

The wellsprings of the new right movement that developed in the late 1970s was a belief that the American way of life is threatened. The threat comes not only from our enemies abroad, but from the moral decay that is eating away at the country from within. In particular, new right groups like the Moral Majority and the Eagle Forum worry about the decline of the American family. Policies seen as threatening to traditional family life, such as abortion on demand, the Equal Rights Amendment, prohibition of school prayer, and gay rights, are associated with liberal groups that stand behind them. A historian of the new right, Alan Crawford, says this movement embodies "the politics of resentment." [59] Much of this resentment is directed toward a government that is thought to be overly influenced by the lobbies of the left.

The most prominent new right organizations are probably the Moral Majority and the National Conservative Political Action Com-

---

[58] Theodore H. White, *The Making of the President 1968* (New York: Atheneum, 1969), pp. 402–403.
[59] Alan Crawford, *Thunder on the Right* (New York: Pantheon, 1980).

mittee (NCPAC). The Reverend Jerry Falwell, an evangelical Baptist minister from Lynchburg, Virginia, founded the avowedly political Moral Majority in 1979. Its purpose is to bring a Christian presence into policy making by forcing those in government to recognize fundamentalist religious values. The organization has proved to be quite controversial because many feel that advocacy aimed at promoting Christian policies runs against the grain of separation of church and state in America.[60]

The NCPAC first came to national prominence with its work against liberal, Democratic Senators in the 1980 elections. The group acted independently of the Republican challengers and spent money on its own to discredit the incumbents. Voters of South Dakota were told in advertisements that "While the energy crisis was brewing, George McGovern was touring Cuba with Fidel Castro." [61] McGovern and three other targeted incumbents lost, giving NCPAC the aura of great power. In the 1982 congressional elections, though, they were generally unsuccessful in their campaigns, making many realize that the group was not quite the giant killer it had been held out to be. Like the Moral Majority, NCPAC has built a strong financial base with direct mail operations that tap the anger and pocketbooks of hundreds of thousands of small donors around the country.

Together with the election of Ronald Reagan in 1980, conservative citizen groups have helped to change the agenda of American politics. They have focused public attention on issues dealing primarily with traditional concepts of morality and the nuclear family. They have yet to succeed in getting most of their major proposals enacted into law, but their presence is sure to be felt for some time to come.

BUSINESS FIGHTS BACK

The rapid rise of liberal and conservative citizen groups in recent years can easily obscure the equally dramatic growth in business lobbying. As the figures cited earlier show, the number of business-related groups active in trying to influence government has shot up. Still, business has always been well represented in Washington, and

---

[60] Frances FitzGerald, "A Disciplined, Charging Army," *New Yorker*, May 18, 1981, pp. 53–141.
[61] Bernard Weinraub, "Million-Dollar Drive Aims to Oust Five Liberal Senators," *The New York Times*, March 23, 1980.

enjoyed what Charles Lindblom calls a "privileged position" in American politics.[62]

The Plague of Regulation

When business executives are asked why they've opened up a Washington office or expanded one already there, the inevitable response is increased government regulation. Business people feel their corporations or trade associations have little choice but to try to counter the encroachments of federal regulatory bodies. Patrick Rowland of the Borg-Warner Corporation comments: "Without someone in Washington, all we know is what's published in the *Federal Register* — and by then it's too late." [63] Likewise, Jerry Breiter of the U.S. Hide, Skin, and Leather Association says, "This is where the action is, if you've got problems with the government." [64] Bernard Falk of the National Electrical Manufacturers' Association emphasizes the government's changing role: "In the past, going back ten or fifteen years, you didn't have a consumer movement. The manufacturer controlled the makeup of his own product, and Washington could be ignored. Now we all have a new partner, the federal government." [65]

Surveys of business executives point unmistakably to the influence of regulation. A Conference Board study revealed that of those executives citing a change in their government-relations work, 71 percent cited increased government activity as the reason.[66] This corporate perception of increasing regulation is no mirage. In the 1960s and the 1970s many new regulatory laws were passed and new regulatory agencies were begun. The Environmental Protection Agency (EPA), the Occupational Safety and Health Administration (OSHA), and the Department of Energy were all created during this time.

The regulatory process is particularly conducive to interest group advocacy because it deals with the most complex and esoteric aspects of public policy. As technology has complicated policy in such areas as air and water pollution, nuclear power, communications, and occu-

[62] Charles E. Lindblom, *Politics and Markets* (New York: Basic Books, 1977).
[63] Pappas, "More Firms Upgraded Government-Relations Jobs."
[64] Rosellini, "Lobbyists' Row All Alert."
[65] Steven V. Roberts, "Trade Associations Flocking to Capital as U.S. Role Rises," *The New York Times*, March 4, 1978.
[66] McGrath, *Redefining Corporate-Federal Relations*, p. 1. See also, "New Laws/ New Jobs," Golightly & Co. International, New York, N.Y., n.d., p. 1.

pational health, the opportunity for regulatory advocacy has increased too. Regulatory decisions in areas like these must be made after considering relevant technical data — data often difficult to obtain and open to competing interpretations. No one has more incentive to collect industry data than the industries themselves. At its heart, regulatory lobbying is a process of interest groups bringing their data to policy makers and trying to make these data the information base from which decisions flow.

Far from being the unfinished details of legislation, regulatory decisions frequently are critical policy determinations. Often these are needed because new regulatory legislation passed by Congress is vague, leaving key decisions to administrators. The ninety-nine pages of the Energy Policy and Conservation Act of 1975 are described by one expert as:

> a potpourri of mandatory provisions, optional and discretionary authorizations, invocations to planning, and reporting requirements, ranging far and wide over the entire range of energy issues. But what has been gained in breadth has been lost in clarity. Indeed, if obfuscation had been the intention, the manner in which the statute is drafted could not have more successfully accomplished the purpose.[67]

Sometimes Congress gives agencies great regulatory latitude because no political consensus can be found in the House and Senate on which policies need to be adopted. Sometimes Congress does not know the answer to particular problems, and so it gives agencies the flexibility to try different solutions. Sometimes it must be vague to accommodate competing goals embodied in a piece of legislation. Regulation of natural gas is an example. The Federal Power Commission (later reorganized as the Federal Energy Regulatory Commission) was given the responsibility of protecting consumers from price gouging as well as ensuring that gas producers made enough profit to pursue further gas exploration. Its mandate was to set "just and reasonable" wellhead prices for gas, but there has never been agreement on how to measure the production costs of gas. Because of the imprecision in the regulatory mandate, "Defenders and critics of FPC regulation assaulted each other with conflicting data, interpretations of data, and extrapolations from data that left certain only the con-

---

[67] John M. Blair, *The Control of Oil* (New York: Pantheon, 1976), p. 355.

tinuing employment of economists to fuel the controversy with further analysis." [68]

The agencies created in recent years have greatly expanded the reach of governmental regulation, because many of them have jurisdiction over broad problem areas, such as pollution or occupational health, rather than specific industries like broadcasting or banking. The breadth of regulatory authority for agencies like EPA or OSHA is immense, and large numbers of industries find themselves subject to their regulation. Businesses have found the new "social" regulation especially disturbing, "with its more detailed, multi-industry intrusions into areas of long-standing managerial discretion and its cost- and liability-enlarging potential." [69]

In time, businesses and trade associations without Washington representation find themselves at a disadvantage. Administrative agencies issue regulations continuously and must be monitored constantly. For most large companies, having the vice-president for public affairs fly into Washington from the corporate headquarters in New York or Chicago is simply not an adequate way to deal with the government. Broad-scale regulation demands that business equip itself with effective Washington-based representation. Ironically, even in periods of deregulation (as during the Reagan administration), the incentives are equally great to be fully represented, because the manner in which deregulation is carried out can hurt the bottom line (by increasing competition, for example) as well as help it.

Seizing the Initiative

But the sum of increased lobbying is more than the parts of individual industries responding to specific regulatory problems. The business community as a whole reacted to an increasingly hostile public attitude toward business. Business entered the 1970s on the defensive, beset by a vigorous and popular public interest movement, a skeptical public distrusting business ethics, angry young people blaming it for the war in Vietnam, and a government that did not seem to care about its problems.

[68] Walter A. Rosenbaum, *Energy, Politics and Public Policy* (Washington, D.C.: Congressional Quarterly Press, 1981), p. 154.
[69] Edward S. Herman, *Corporate Control, Corporate Power* (New York: Cambridge University Press, 1981), p. 185.

All lobbies want to believe they have a special relationship with government, where legislators and administrators place primary importance on their interests. They want to believe that policies are made only after detailed consultation with them. They want to believe that their views carry more weight than those of other relevant interests. Finally, they want to believe that they have some control over the agenda in their policy area, where the issues they want heard are brought to the surface, and those they find distasteful can be killed or moderated by sympathetic officials. It is in this sense that businesses felt they had lost their special relationship with government between the late 1960s and the mid-1970s. David Vogel describes this attitude:

> For nearly a decade, most of the issues placed on the political agenda affecting business were initiated not by business, but by those who represented constituents hostile to business. Environmental protection, occupational health and safety, consumer protection, price controls on energy, affirmative action, product liability, expansion of the welfare state, prohibitions on corporate overseas payments, corporate governance, campaign reform, restrictions on corporate compliance with the Arab boycott of Israel — not a single one of those issues originated with business. To be sure, business was successful in ... influencing many of these areas, making them less threatening than their proponents preferred. But what is critical is that for most of the decade, business was fighting its political battles on terrain set by its opponents.[70]

The resurgence of business as a force in national politics is symbolized by creation of the Business Roundtable, a lobbying group composed of 200 or so chief executive officers (CEOs) from the nation's largest firms. Started in 1972, the Roundtable draws extensively on the resources of its member corporations and involves the CEOs themselves in lobbying. It has been highly successful in fighting a number of prolabor initiatives, and quickly established itself as a leader in presenting the business point of view to government. What is especially significant about the Roundtable is that it fights on behalf of *general* business issues (such as labor law reform) rather than on the narrower issues that might activate only one industry. Although other business "peak" associations have long existed, includ-

[70] Vogel, "How Business Responds to Opposition," p. 6.

ing the Chamber of Commerce and the National Association of Manufacturers, none has so effectively utilized the resources of its membership as the Roundtable. The Roundtable's success, however, is a major reason both the Chamber and the NAM have expanded their staffs and become much more aggressive in their lobbying efforts.[71]

This expanded advocacy by business reflects an effort to seize the initiative in the political process rather than having to respond to the hostile agenda of others. Among matters bothering business was the burgeoning public interest movement in Washington. Its proregulation and seeming antigrowth philosophy was affecting public policy. The somber business magazine *Fortune* went so far as to ascribe the founding of the Business Roundtable to corporate fear of citizen advocacy: "Nader was winning victory after victory . . ." and so business had to respond in kind.[72] Nader's push for an Agency for Consumer Protection deeply troubled the business community, which saw in it the specter of even more federal regulation. It prompted a new cooperative spirit among business lobbyists in Washington who worked together to defeat the proposal and continued working together on initiatives of their own.[73]

Big business also recognized that part of the problem they were having with government was weakening public support. They undertook attempts to educate the American people about the value of the free enterprise system. To inspire in the public a more probusiness attitude, a number of corporations purchased newspaper and magazine advertising to extol the virtues of the free market system. Businesses also became more aggressive in donating money to think tanks and university research centers for studies on problems of business.

Increasing its influence also meant a heavy involvement in electoral politics once corporate PACs became fully legal. Few in the business community doubt the efficacy that business PACs have had in making Congress more sympathetic toward their interests. Business has also taken the initiative by expanding its advocacy to the states,

---

[71] Mark Green and Andrew Buchsbaum, *The Corporate Lobbies* (Washington, D.C.: Public Citizen, 1980); Kim McQuaid, "The Roundtable: Getting Results in Washington," *Harvard Business Review* (May/June 1981), pp. 114–123.

[72] Walter Guzzardi, Jr., "How to Win in Washington," *Fortune*, March 27, 1978, p. 53.

[73] William J. Lanouette, "Business Lobbyists Hope Their Unity on the Tax Bill Wasn't Just a Fluke," *National Journal*, October 24, 1981, pp. 1896–1898.

where regulatory agencies can be just as troubling as on the federal level. Corporations and trade associations are developing statewide PACs in attempting to influence policy making at that level.[74]

Business advocacy has also been buoyed because its traditional adversary, organized labor, has failed to improve its position. Indeed, labor is probably the only segment in the interest group community that has not prospered recently. This has much to do with change in the American work force, as it moves toward white-collar jobs and away from the declining smokestack industries. Beyond a shrinking labor force in areas most fertile for union organizing, labor has been hurt by the weakening American economy and the apparent need to devise policies beneficial to business so that the economy may expand.

By the 1980s, business had met the challenge to its authority. Expanded advocacy was the tool it used to regain its primacy in Washington.

DEMYSTIFYING INTEREST GROUP ADVOCACY

Clearly, the rise of interest groups has many sources. Different kinds of groups responded to particular events, the growth of adversary groups, changes in the law, and evolutionary changes in the political environment. These stimuli that contributed to expanding advocacy by lobbying organizations were enhanced too by a cumulative learning process.

During the 1960s and 1970s, interest group politics was "demystified." A broader segment of the population came to believe that interest group advocacy had great potential. More and more people came to understand that interest groups were vital to protecting and furthering their own interests. And more and more people came to understand how interest groups operate in practice, and how new groups could be formed.

At the heart of this demystification was, of course, the development of pluralist ideology. Political scientists and public policy makers had justified interest group activity, placing it at the center of democratic policy making. Lobbying was now a virtue, its image as an inherently nefarious activity dimmed. Political science also justified

---

[74] Daniel W. Gottlieb, "Business Mobilizes as States Begin to Move into the Regulatory Vacuum," *National Journal*, July 31, 1982, pp. 1340–1343; and Timothy D. Schellhardt, "Corporate PACs Turning Attention to the States as Deregulation Gains," *Wall Street Journal*, October 28, 1982.

pluralism as a goal when it became evident that a pluralist democracy did not in fact exist. As the impediments to organization became clearer, and the advantage of elites in interest group politics was accepted as the "natural" state of things, ways to promote pluralism were devised. Citizen participation, in particular, became a way of *teaching* people to lobby.

Interest group leaders (and prospective organizers) learned by watching other interest groups; lobbying organizations are inveterate copiers. The rapidity with which citizen groups copied the successful civil rights and antiwar organizations reflects the breadth of this movement. Not only did other minorities copy the black civil rights organizations, but new liberal citizen groups were started to appeal to middle-class interests as well.

Conservative citizen groups that arose in the 1970s directly responded to the success of the liberal citizen groups. There was a sense that everyone was represented but the conservatives. The liberal citizen groups appeared to be enormously successful, with major victories such as establishing regulatory agencies like the Consumer Product Safety Commission and the EPA, the constant media attention given to Ralph Nader and Common Cause, and a stream of successful environmental lawsuits. Most important, liberal groups seemed to have the ear of government and thus were influencing its agenda.

Business too was influenced by the liberal citizen groups' growing advocacy. Even though the most direct stimulus was increased regulation, the public interest movement was seen as primary instigator of "excessive" government regulation. Business has made great use of all major strategies of effective lobbying. The success of business and conservative citizen groups with political action committees has caused many liberal groups to create PACs of their own.[75]

There is no automatic mechanism in politics whereby new groups cause opposing groups to form as a countervailing power; the reality is much more complicated. In recent years, though, proliferation of groups has been facilitated by rapidly increasing knowledge about interest groups. From academic works to the omnipresent eye of the mass media, both laymen and elites have learned how these groups

---

[75] See Phil Gailey, "A Political Action Unit of the Left," *The New York Times*, February 10, 1982; Warren Weaver, "Political Action Group Focuses on the Elderly," *The New York Times*, January 1, 1982; and Maxwell Glen, "Liberal Political Action Committees Borrow a Page from the Conservatives," *National Journal*, July 4, 1981, pp. 1197–1200.

operate. The development of public policy, and the interest groups' role in that process, have been reported and analyzed in excruciating detail. Thus the costs of acquiring information about interest groups became cheaper. People found it easier to find out what they needed to know to form groups, and once they were formed, what they needed to know to operate them effectively. More specifically, the growth of interest groups was furthered by increasing knowledge about three subjects.

ORGANIZATIONAL MAINTENANCE. Interest group leaders have become more effective at raising money and broadening their base of support. Their growing utilization of direct mail is the most obvious example; leaders of newly forming or existing groups can buy lists of likely prospects. Foundations and government became primary sources of money for interest groups during this time when groups were forming so rapidly. Businesses moved quickly to use the newly acquired right to form PACs to collect money from corporate executives. For interest group leaders who feel they need help in maintaining their organization, many consultants in Washington have expertise in direct mail and how to secure government grants.

LOBBYING SKILLS. Through the years, lobbying has had an unsavory behind-the-scenes image of unctuous group representatives using their contacts in government to do the groups' bidding. Yet today, typical lobbyists will often find themselves actually trying to gain recognition and publicity for what they are doing rather than trying to hide it (see Chapter 6). Lobbying has quickly become an anyone-can-do-it activity and little mystery is left on what successful lobbyists do. One does not have to have close friends in high places (though it certainly doesn't hurt), but other attributes are commonly accepted as vital to effective lobbying. Chief among these is policy expertise. The ability to "network" (form coalitions), to utilize the media, and to develop lasting professional relationships with staffers and policy makers are other well-known fundamentals of lobbying. It is much harder to raise the resources for lobbying than it is to figure out what to do with those resources.

COMMUNICATIONS. Lobbying has been furthered by a growing recognition that information is power and that the best lobbyists are the people back home. Interest group leaders emphasize the communications networks between themselves and the members of their organizations, and between themselves and other interest groups.[76] The Washington newsletter is now a staple of Washington politics. Constituents back home receive frequent mailings on the issues that are being decided by government, and what they need to do to influence them. Computerized lists of constituents facilitate mailings to members in key congressional districts when a critical vote is coming. Some groups have special networks of activists, who can be instructed to contact those in government when the need arises.

The growth of interest group politics thus comes in part from learning: successful groups set the example for others. Washington is really a town of few secrets, and what works for one group is quickly copied by others. Consultants, lawyers, and public relations specialists who work for different clients, the huge Washington media establishment, and the lobbyists who interact constantly with one another, make learning about what interest groups do ever easier.

CONCLUSION

Writing about foreign trade legislation between 1953 and 1962, the authors of the highly acclaimed *American Business and Public Policy* concluded, "We note ... how few were the congressmen who had heard anything from the major pressure groups and how many there were who were genuinely puzzled as to how they should vote and who would have appreciated clear indications of where their constituencies stood and what the issues were." [77] Two decades later it is inconceivable that anyone doing research on any important public policy issue would find many congressmen who had heard nothing from interest group lobbyists or the constituents they represent back home. By any standard, the amount of lobbying in Washington has expanded significantly. Many previously unrepresented interests are now represented before the government by recently formed organizations. Interests that were already represented in Washington tend to be even better represented today.

Although the reasons for lobbying's rise in different sectors of society vary, some common threads appear in the broad movement toward

[76] Jo Freeman, *The Politics of Women's Liberation* (New York: David McKay, 1975).

[77] Raymond A. Bauer, Ithiel de Sola Pool, and Lewis Anthony Dexter, *American Business and Public Policy* (New York: Atherton, 1963), p. 351.

interest group politics. Pluralist theory contributed to the idea that interest group pluralism was a desirable goal for society. Expanding governmental activity in the 1960s and 1970s (usually at the behest of interest groups) directly affected more and more constituencies and helped catalyze increased advocacy. Finally, as new interest groups form, they stimulate other constituencies to organize because new groups increase awareness about what various interests are doing and, further, their formation threatens their natural adversaries. New groups do not always form to directly counter others, but the learning has been cumulative as incipient groups come to copy successful organizing models and tactics of friend and foe alike.

Beyond these causes of proliferation, one more is the recent period of party decline.

CHAPTER THREE

Parties and Interest Groups

The relationship between political parties and interest groups has always been uneasy. When it suits their needs, interest groups push congressmen to take issue stands that are contrary to those of their party leaders. In this era of political action committees, parties and interest groups compete for the financial resources of the politically active. Yet the relationship is not one that is always at odds, because there are good reasons for parties and interest groups to seek support from each other. Parties want the backing of interest groups at election time and will work hard to bring potentially supportive groups into their electoral coalitions. Likewise, interest groups recognize the value of cooperating with party leaders to help them change or protect preferred policies.

The rise in numbers of interest groups did not cause the recent decline of political parties. As we will show, the origins of this trend seem independent of the growing movement toward interest group politics. Rather, what is being argued here is that interest groups benefited from party decline and, further, that the relationship between parties and interest groups has been altered by these recent political trends.

We begin by briefly reviewing the evidence on party decline. Next, a question: Why has disenchantment with the party system not extended to interest groups? Then we turn to the evolving relationship between parties and interest groups, focusing on both coalition building and campaign finance.

PARTY DECLINE

It has become a truism of American politics that our parties have somehow declined.[1] Exactly what party "decline" means, however, is not always clear. Although many quantitative measures bear this change out, it is easy to overstate. Parties have not fallen from some recent period of omnipotence. The United States, unlike many other western democracies, has never had a "responsible party" system wherein legislative candidates must pledge themselves to vote with their party on vital issues. Separation of powers has made the president the leader of his party while making him highly independent of it.[2] A prevailing image of American parties, says Austin Ranney, is that "They have never been more than short-lived, ad hoc coalitions of state and local party leaders and followers, labor and business leaders, and issue and candidate enthusiasts."[3]

Measuring the Trend

Acknowledging that party decline cannot be measured against an era of strong, centralized parties still does not resolve the problem of measuring the changes that have taken place. No one time is recognized as the start from which to measure partisan decline. The most common reference point for political scientists, though, is probably the 1950s. It was a time of relative tranquility, postdating the Great Depression and World War II and predating turbulence in the 1960s. Indeed, the very stability of the 1950s distinguishes it as an unusual period, making it far from a perfect baseline from which to judge deviations from the norm.

The 1950s are significant in political science less because of political events than because sophisticated survey research had developed

---

[1] The more recent trends in this regard are succinctly captured in William J. Crotty and Gary C. Jacobson, *American Parties in Decline* (Boston: Little, Brown, 1980). The larger historical roots are detailed in Walter Dean Burnham, *Critical Elections and the Mainsprings of American Politics* (New York: Norton, 1970).

[2] See James W. Ceaser, *Presidential Selection* (Princeton: Princeton University Press, 1979).

[3] Austin Ranney, "The Political Parties: Reform and Decline," in Anthony King, ed., *The New American Political System* (Washington, D.C.: American Enterprise Institute, 1978), p. 245.

by then. This tool has allowed scholars to rigorously analyze the hows and whys of voting behavior and party identification. Early statistical research produced *The American Voter,* a seminal book in American politics.[4] *The American Voter* used sample surveys of the electorate during the 1952 and 1956 presidential elections and drew from those data a systematic and detailed explanation for voting behavior. The core of the book was an analysis of the major components in the voting decision. Partisan identification was found to be the most important factor explaining why people vote the way they do.

Drawing upon the impressive body of data generated by survey research since the 1950s, political scientists now rely on a number of indicators to calculate party decline, including partisan identification, issue or candidate voting versus party voting, voting turnout, and levels of confidence in the parties.

PARTISAN IDENTIFICATION. "Perhaps the most dramatic political change in the American public over the past two decades has been the decline of partisanship" concluded the authors of *The Changing American Voter,* a study comparing voters of the 1950s with those of the 1970s.[5] The statistics on partisan identification are revealing. Biennial surveys conducted by the University of Michigan show that in 1952, 75 percent of the sample professed allegiance to a political party. In 1980, that figure stood at 63 percent. Those who claimed to be "strong" Democrats or Republicans fell from 36 to 26 percent during the same time.[6]

The drop in partisanship is extremely significant because identification with a party is so influential in voting decisions.[7] As party ties diminish, voters become less predictable in their voting habits. Everett

[4] Angus Campbell, Philip E. Converse, Warren E. Miller, and Donald E. Stokes, *The American Voter* (New York: John Wiley, 1964).

[5] Norman H. Nie, Sidney Verba, and John R. Petrocik, *The Changing American Voter* (Cambridge: Harvard University Press, 1976), p. 47.

[6] Warren E. Miller, Arthur H. Miller, and Edward J. Schneider, *American National Election Studies Data Sourcebook, 1952–1978* (Cambridge: Harvard University Press, 1980), p. 81; and Dick Kirschten, "The 1982 Elections Could Offer Clues to 1984's Main Event," *National Journal,* January 9, 1982, p. 56.

[7] The decline of partisanship is analyzed in Paul R. Abramson, "Generational Change and the Decline of Party Identification in America," *American Political Science Review* 70 (June 1976), pp. 469–478; Philip E. Converse, *The Dynamics of Party Support* (Beverly Hills, Calif.: Sage Publications, 1976); and Paul R. Abramson and John H. Aldrich, "The Decline of Electoral Participation in America," *American Political Science Review* 76 (September 1982), pp. 502–521.

Ladd writes that in such a period of decline, "voters move away from parties altogether; loyalties to the parties, and to the parties' candidates and programs weaken, and more and more of the electorate become 'up for grabs' each election." [8] When voters drift away from the parties, government policy making is increasingly interpreted as independent of Democratic and Republican alternatives.[9]

ISSUE VOTING. Individuals are not only less likely to profess identification with a party, but polls also reveal that they are less likely to rely on partisan attitudes in making their voting decision. While partisanship has declined, issues seem increasingly important in voting. In the same University of Michigan surveys, respondents asked to evaluate the candidates mentioned their issue positions 49 percent of the time in 1952, but 67 percent of the time in 1972. By comparison, those mentioning party ties in evaluating the presidential candidates dropped from 46 percent to 24 percent.[10]

The reasons for this rise in issue voting are more difficult to document. One likely explanation is the highly ideological tone in some of our recent presidential elections. The Johnson versus Goldwater (1964) and Nixon versus McGovern (1972) races were particularly ideological, and differences on issues were heavily stressed. The mass media too have broadened the exposure of citizens to issues. Citizens simply have much more access to campaign-related information in the exhaustive coverage by the media of ever-lengthening presidential campaigns.

Finally, taking the 1950s as a baseline may exaggerate this trend because Dwight Eisenhower, who won two landslide elections over Democrat Adlai Stevenson, was perceived by many to be above politics. His personal popularity transcended normal party politics at a time when ideology was more muted than usual.[11]

VOTING TURNOUT. The reasons for not voting are varied and the underlying causes and consequences are much debated.[12] The de-

[8] Everett Carll Ladd, *Where Have All the Voters Gone?* 2nd ed. (New York: Norton, 1982), pp. 76–77.
[9] Ladd, *Where Have All the Voters Gone?*, pp. 78–79.
[10] Nie et al., *The Changing American Voter*, p. 167. The frequency of references to the personal characteristics of the candidates was high and generally stable during this time.
[11] Nie et al., *The Changing American Voter*, pp. 174–193.
[12] See Raymond E. Wolfinger and Steven J. Rosenstone, *Who Votes?* (New Haven: Yale University Press, 1980).

cline in voting, however, is popularly accepted as indicating a failing party system. The downturn in voting is serious, going from 61.6 percent in 1952 to 53.9 percent in 1980.[13] Another disturbing trend is that more people believe that it makes little difference who is elected. The University of Michigan surveys show that in response to the question, "Generally speaking, would you say that you personally care/cared a good deal which party wins/ won the presidential election this fall, or don't you care very much which party wins/won?" 67 percent of the 1952 sample cared a good deal and 57 percent replied the same in 1976.[14] Voting is the foundation of any true democracy, and it is distressing that fewer people are attracted to the polls or profess interest in election outcomes.

CONFIDENCE IN PARTIES. A direct way of measuring people's attitudes toward the party system is to ask them about their confidence in it. The answer to such survey questions reveal additional evidence of alienation with the party system. When asked "How much do you feel that political parties help to make the government pay attention to what the people think?" those responding "a good deal" declined from 41 percent to 21 percent between 1964 and 1978. Likewise, the number of people who agree with the statement "Parties are only interested in people's votes but not in their opinions" went up sharply from 46 percent in 1968 to 62 percent in 1978.[15]

This lack of confidence in parties mirrors the decline in trust in the political system generally.[16] Fairly or unfairly, the belief is widespread that parties do not do their job well and are unresponsive to the will of the people. As people see a weakening link between the ballot box and outcomes of public policy, they may see less reason to become actively involved in party politics.

By all these indexes, then, the evidence of party decay is unmistakable. Beyond the factors that caused parties to decline in the first place, however, is the difficulty parties have had in revitalizing themselves.

[13] Crotty and Jacobson, *American Parties in Decline*, p. 7; and *Elections '82* (Washington, D.C.: Congressional Quarterly, 1982), p. 23.
[14] Miller et al., *American National Election Studies*, p. 308.
[15] Miller et al., *American National Election Studies*, pp. 261–262.
[16] Arthur Miller, "Political Issues and Trust in Government: 1964–1970," *American Political Science Review* 68 (September 1974), pp. 951–972. See also Arthur Miller, "Is Confidence Rebounding?", *Public Opinion* 6 (June/July 1983), pp. 16–20.

Party Reform, Party Dealignment

Party decline is not inevitable or irreversible. Popular dissatisfaction with the party system creates opportunities for party reform or even for realignment of parties. A concerted effort at reforming the parties has, in fact, taken place. The impetus for such efforts can be traced to the 1968 Democratic convention. The mainstream Democratic contender, Vice-President Hubert Humphrey, was inactive in the primaries because of President Lyndon Johnson's late withdrawal and likely because of his own fear of being defeated by rival candidates. He relied instead on the votes of delegates elected in party caucuses, many of whom were responsive to the wishes of party leaders. For antiwar Democrats who saw one of their candidates, Robert Kennedy, assassinated, and the other, Eugene McCarthy, denied the nomination after being instrumental in pushing Johnson out of the race, Humphrey's nomination seemed a miscarriage of justice. Rightly or wrongly, they saw him as the candidate of the party "bosses" and of a nominating system unresponsive to "the people." Youthful antiwar activists who came to the Chicago convention to protest against Humphrey's nomination confronted a hostile Chicago police force, and the convention was marred by violence in the streets.

The trauma of the 1968 convention led the Democrats to reappraise the nomination process.[17] In an effort to become more attractive to those who had been most critical of it, the party adopted quotas for women, young people, and minorities for each state delegation. Other reforms were intended to reduce the influence of party leaders, such as banning the unit rule (which some states had used to require that all delegates vote with the majority in the delegation); requiring selection of delegates to take place in the calendar year of the convention; and mandating that in primary states where delegates' names are listed on the ballot, those delegates must list the presidential candidate they are supporting.[18]

Events surrounding the 1968 election were a major impetus for another change. More states adopted primaries as their means of selecting convention delegates, thereby opening up the nominating process to rank-and-file voters. Between 1968 and 1972, the proportion of delegates to the Democratic convention selected through

[17] Austin Ranney, *Curing the Mischiefs of Faction* (Berkeley: University of California Press, 1975).
[18] William Crotty, *Party Reform* (New York: Longman, 1983), pp. 44–62.

primaries went from 42 percent to 65 percent.[19] This movement toward primaries clearly worked to the advantage of Senator George McGovern, whose antiwar stance made him unpopular with many moderate and conservative Democratic party leaders. McGovern, however, did well in the primaries, where his strong, activist organization and highly motivated voters prevailed.

The Republicans also made some modest changes, but the major "reform" effect on the GOP was the increasing number of primaries. As with the Democrats, more control over party nominations was placed in the hands of voters and taken from party leaders and elected politicians. By 1976 more than 70 percent of convention delegates for both parties were chosen through primaries.[20] Many wonder if this opening up of the nominating process has gone too far. Primaries are low in voter turnout and those who do vote tend not to be representative of their party as a whole. Thus, a primary-based nominating system makes it easier for someone like a George McGovern, who may be out of step with mainstream voters, to be nominated. Even if the eventual nominee is more centrist, the primaries can make it easier for someone having poor relationships with the party hierarchy to win. And so it was with self-proclaimed Washington outsider, Jimmy Carter. Carter's shortcomings as president are blamed in part on his inexperience in national politics.[21] In short, the efforts at reform by the Democrats and by the states have not revitalized the party system. Indeed, they may have weakened it further.

The chances for party renewal are not, however, limited to deliberate efforts at reform. Periodically the country has gone through a "realigning" election, in which an enduring change in party coalitions is forged. The last realigning election was that of 1932, when the New Deal Democratic coalition of Franklin Roosevelt was formed. Blacks, Jews, Catholics, southerners, and urban workers joined to become the majority coalition, replacing dominance by the Republican party.[22]

[19] Ceasar, *Presidential Selection*, p. 237.
[20] Ceasar, *Presidential Selection*, p. 237.
[21] This argument is made forcefully in Nelson W. Polsby, *Consequences of Party Reform* (New York: Oxford University Press, 1983).
[22] An alternative scenario for realignment has a new party eventually replacing one of the old. Although the change is conceivable, the electoral system makes it very difficult for third parties to enter and become competitive. See Daniel A. Mazmanian, *Third Parties in Presidential Elections* (Washington, D.C.: Brookings Institution, 1974).

The decline of the party system has led many journalists and social scientists to believe the country is on the verge of another realigning era. Both the Nixon and Reagan victories brought speculation that a conservative Republican majority had been formed. The Nixon victory brought no long-term success to the Republican party, and indications from polls and the 1982 congressional elections are that the Reagan victory as well represents no new majority. Political scientists speak more of party "dealignment" and "disaggregation." Instead of a decaying party system renewing itself by realignment, it may well continue to decay with no assurance of revival.[23]

Although party revival has not been brought about by reform or realignment, at least some signs hint that the condition of the party system is improving. Statistics from the 1982 congressional elections show voting up over 1978. The Republican party has developed a strong organizational capability, with impressive fundraising, candidate recruitment, and campaign resources. Both parties, as we will explain, are drawing more on the support of sympathetic interest groups. Possibly a stronger party system will result in years to come. Nevertheless, the period of party decline has strongly affected the American political system. One consequence is furthering the opportunity for interest groups to attract and maintain members.

ADVANTAGES OF INTEREST GROUPS

Interest groups have inherent advantages over American type parties that make them highly appealing to the politically active. The improving ability of interest groups to market themselves in an era of party decline has made these advantages all the more evident. Still, this rising popularity presents a paradox. Why is it that decreasing confidence in the American political system and in the political parties has not affected interest groups?

Interest Group Decline?

In an era of rising alienation from the governmental process, interest groups would seem a logical target of public discontent. They have

[23] See Burnham, *Critical Elections and the Mainsprings of American Politics;* Everett Carll Ladd, Jr., with Charles D. Hadley, *Transformations of the American Party System,* 2nd ed. (New York: Norton, 1978); and Ladd, *Where Have All the Voters Gone?*

always been an object of suspicion and mistrust. It is not only that they pursue their self-interest at the expense of the public good; scandals involving illegal use of money by these groups to achieve their goals have been frequent.

Unfortunately, unethical and illegal activity by interest groups is not a footnote from our distant past. Prior to the 1972 election, a group of dairy cooperatives secretly pledged large campaign contributions to the Republican party contingent upon a favorable decision by the Nixon administration on dairy price supports. After the administration acted, more than $200,000 was contributed to the GOP by milk PACs before the scandal was revealed in the press.[24] Around the same time, the International Telephone and Telegraph (ITT) Corporation was accused of trying to influence a Justice Department antitrust decision by promising to provide substantial financial support for staging the Republican party's national convention. Before the campaign finance laws were changed to fully allow corporate PACs, large companies like American Airlines, Gulf Oil, and Goodyear Tire were convicted of making illegal campaign contributions.[25]

Today, it is the entirely legal activities of political action committees that have brought most controversy over interest group participation in the political process. Contributions from PACs are commonly seen as an unsavory part of the electoral system, because groups appear to be using their wealth to improve their standing with elected officials. People easily assume that policies they dislike are enacted by a Congress unduly influenced by PACs. This popular perception is built not so much on evidence of specific links between money and votes, but from the simple belief that the millions of dollars PACs contribute must be accomplishing something.

We have no way of tracking disillusionment with interest groups like that by which the decline of parties can be measured. Moreover, cynicism toward interest groups has always been such (beginning with *Federalist* No. 10), that even more cynicism may seem hardly noteworthy. Yet, as we saw at the beginning of Chapter 2, unease does seem to be growing about the dangers of interest group politics. Worry about the role of single-issue groups pressing for

---

[24] A summary of this episode is in Carol S. Greenwald, *Group Power* (New York: Praeger, 1977), pp. 3–9.

[25] Herbert E. Alexander, *Financing Politics*, 2nd ed. (Washington, D.C.: Congressional Quarterly, 1980), pp. 74–76.

social change, the impact of preferential policies granted to business and labor on economic growth, and, of course, the rising numbers of political action committees, have all prompted criticism of interest group politics. A symptom of this attitude was the attack on the early Democratic frontrunner for nomination in 1984, Walter Mondale, who was criticized in the press and by his opponents as too much of a broker for special interest groups. Although a president is supposed to be a coalition builder, he must also in this view have the strength to control interest groups and keep them from damaging the nation.

In spite of inherent mistrust of interest groups and growing anxiety over their numbers and power, they are thriving as never before. The increasing alienation and distrust of the political system that characterized the 1960s and 1970s and contributed to the decline of political parties did little to stop the growth of interest group politics.

Policy Maximizers

The reason interest groups can profit when they are generally viewed with suspicion is relatively straightforward: People distinguish between the groups they back and the interest group population as a whole. In an individual's mind, it is easy to believe that one's own group is pursuing policies that are truly in the public interest, and to see other organizations as selfish lobbies. It is only natural for people to believe that their own group is seeking policies that are fair and beneficial to the nation as a whole.

This attitude also somewhat describes the views of people about the party system. To many loyal Republicans, the Democratic party is the devil incarnate, and vice versa. Yet, even for those who have not weakened in their support for one of the two major parties, there is still good reason to see an interest group as essential for achieving their policy goals.

The fundamental advantage of interest groups over political parties is clear. Assume that you are politically active and willing to spend $100 to pursue your political goals during a single year. What is the best way to spend that money so that your chances of achieving those goals will be maximized? If you care about a particular policy — protecting wilderness, fighting regulation of the used-car business, increasing the price support for tobacco, or whatever — you may easily conclude that an interest group is the better "investment" for that $100 than a political party or one of its congressional campaign committees. Even though one cannot confidently predict the real chances that either a party or an interest group will succeed in pushing for that one specific goal, it is clear to you as donor of the money that the interest group will work more intensively and single-mindedly toward that goal. A political party, on the other hand, has a constituency so broad that it will be pushed to move on hundreds of issues. But in any year, relatively few issues will be assigned priority by party leaders, and if an issue is highly controversial, the best political course for the congressional party or the president may be to act in a superficial, symbolic manner or to abstain altogether from acting on the issue.

The advantages of interest groups are accentuated by the character of our two-party system. With plurality elections in single-member districts (and thus no proportional representation), the likelihood is that there will be two very broad parties covering a great deal of ideological ground.[26] To win an election, the parties must build a coalition of some breadth, attracting large numbers of those in the center ("moderates") to go along with those who form the ideological core of the party. By their very nature, then, American political parties are "vote maximizers." To win elections they must dilute many policy stands, take purposely ambiguous stands on others, and generally ignore some, so as not to offend segments of the population that they need in their coalition.[27]

Interest groups are just the opposite. They are "policy maximizers," meaning that they will do better in attracting members if their outlook is narrowly focused.[28] Although a few interest groups like the Chamber of Commerce and Common Cause work on a broad range of issues, the typical group cares only about a few closely related issues. The appeal of the American Soybean Association, the Veterans of Foreign Wars, and the Independent Truckers Association is that each works only on the problems of soybean farmers, veterans, and independent truckers, respectively. A dollar donated to these groups is a dollar spent on their narrow set of issues.

[26] Maurice Duverger, *Political Parties* (New York: John Wiley, 1963); and Anthony Downs, *An Economic Theory of Democracy* (New York: Harper and Row, 1957).

[27] Benjamin I. Page, *Choices and Echoes in Presidential Elections* (Chicago: University of Chicago Press, 1978).

[28] Jeffrey M. Berry, "Public Interest Vs. Party System," *Society* 17 (May/June 1980), p. 47.

Market Forces

Economists often speak of "economies of scale," referring to an organization's ability to do things more efficiently as it grows. A corporation manufacturing widgets can make them more cheaply as it grows, getting a better price on its raw materials because of larger purchases, performing more tasks in-house rather than contracting them out, having more specialization within the organization, and so on. For interest groups, though, the economies of scale are not the same. Large growth may not be beneficial if it means deliberately taking on a broader array of issues. By trying to grow very large, they may lose their distinctive appeal as people come to associate them with a general outlook, not a narrow one. There is enough overlap among interest groups that individuals may decide to move their money from the large, general group to a more narrowly focused one that works intensively on the one issue that most interests them.

Interest groups appeal to their consumers in much the same way as cable television networks appeal to theirs. Unlike the networks on "free" television, cable networks do not try to find the programs with the greatest possible appeal. They seek out a narrow segment of the market and offer those people what they most want to see. Interest groups exist for the same reason, offering a narrow market what it cannot get from other interest groups or parties. The environmentalist who cares about wilderness and national parks will find that the Sierra Club and the Wilderness Society most clearly emphasize those issues. Other environmentalists who see solar energy as a path to the future have the Solar Lobby to join. For those who wish to protect animals, the Fund for Animals and the Society for Animal Protective Legislation speak for that interest. Other environmental issues are covered by the Natural Resources Defense Council, the National Audubon Society, the National Wildlife Federation, the Izaak Walton League, Friends of the Earth, the Environmental Policy Center, the Environmental Defense Fund, Environmental Action, and many more, each of which has areas of specialization that give it some distinctiveness.

The segmentation in these groups' audiences does not mean that they do not want to grow larger in resources. Rather, it means that for a group to try to achieve growth by greater capture of its market makes more sense than trying to enter new ones. Thus the National

Segmentation

Association of Wheat Growers might do worse if it tried to be an all-purpose farm lobby instead of just a wheat lobby. There are already lobbies identified with other major commodities and broad-based farm groups like the American Farm Bureau Federation as well. Many wheat farmers may not want the money they pay for the group's services and lobbying diluted by an expanded focus on sugar and cotton.

Whatever the issue, the market forces of interest group politics push lobbying organizations to create a distinctiveness associated with their coverage of issues. This effect, in turn, brings the politically active individual who cares about that issue to value the purity of their efforts, especially when compared to the vote maximization reality of party politics. Furthermore, as I will show in detail in Chapter 4, interest groups have improved their marketing effectiveness by direct mail and other means. Never have interest groups more aggressively sold what they have to offer.

WORKING TOGETHER

The prosperity of interest groups during a time of party decline has not changed their inescapable need to seek cooperation by political parties. Except for the few groups who focus exclusively on the courts, nearly all lobbies must direct their efforts at the partisan Democrats and Republicans who fill Congress and the appointed positions of any administration. Interest groups are not going to replace the parties, and so they must try to find ways to exert influence within them.

Most lobbying groups will take pains to avoid any official partisan stance, and they usually try to play both sides of the street. They work hard to establish good relations with members of both parties on a key committee in Congress. When they have little access to those in power, they often turn to an intermediary such as a law firm or public relations firm that does.

Yet for a number of groups, it is not enough to try to maintain good relations with both parties. Major policy changes frequently depend on a significant change in the makeup of Congress, election of a Democratic or Republican president, or a policy commitment by a party that goes beyond support of a few committee chairmen. Some groups, therefore, commit themselves to try to change a party's electoral fortunes or outlook on policy. In forging electoral alliances with the parties, groups expect that the cooperation will extend past election day.

People at the top of interest groups are not alone in deciding that the organization must become involved; members at the grassroots can become active on their own. Many interest group members recognize that it is shortsighted not to try to influence the parties because neither is as committed to their policy goals as their own interest group is, and they work for candidates or donate money to party campaign committees. Even though their lobby may work single-mindedly toward a favored policy goal, it still may not be able to get anywhere without some electoral change. Other interest group members become involved with party work because their policy interests are broader than those of the typical interest group. If so, they may want to donate to one of the ideological PACs that solicit them by direct mail.

Coalition Building

The relationship between interest groups and political parties is clearest at election time as each party attempts to put together a coalition of its natural constituents and fence sitters to give it a winning margin. Because most lobbies prefer not to become identified as partisan, those which want to become active will usually limit their efforts to PAC donations to members of both parties. (This type of giving is discussed below.) For a group to become more extensively involved in party politics, it must feel it has little to lose by overt partisanship. Sometimes an organization's views are highly compatible with one party but incompatible with the other, as with most unions and their close relationship with the Democratic party.

Interest groups may direct their efforts toward influencing the party or its presidential candidate in a number of ways. Sometimes the party platforms become a target. Platform fights can take on great symbolic importance even when policy lines already are clearly drawn. In 1980, feminist groups pushed for strong language favoring continued support for the Equal Rights Amendment (ERA) in the Democratic platform, while antifeminist groups fought successfully to keep it out of the Republican platform even though candidate-to-be Reagan already was adamantly opposed to the amendment. A lobby may care less about the language in the platform than about getting presidential support for a specific legislative proposal. When the National Education Association gave its first presidential endorsement to Jimmy Carter in 1976, "association officials made it clear to Mr. Carter that they wanted [a Department of Education] created to give education more visibility in the Cabinet." [29] With Carter's strong backing once he was in office, the NEA got what it wanted. Still other groups may be more interested in ensuring that they will have access and influence on a range of issues than on one proposal. The AFL-CIO's relationship with the Democratic party transcends any one issue. It wants to have access on any important new issues that may arise affecting the economy and domestic policy, as well as on the immediate, high-priority issues that it and its member unions have identified.[30]

A group may have greatest leverage when it enters party politics for the first time (as with the NEA endorsement in 1976) or when it moves in an unusual direction. When the Teamsters Union endorsed Republican Richard Nixon in 1972, they may have been motivated more by a desire for respectability for the scandal-plagued union than by any labor issues. A warm presidential embrace is no small benefit to any lobby's leadership. Yet an endorsement by an interest group guarantees little. Although the air traffic controllers endorsed candidate Ronald Reagan (who made a vague promise to help improve their working conditions) in 1980, Reagan's "support" turned to hostility when the air controllers illegally struck in 1981. With Reagan's concurrence, the striking controllers were fired by the federal government and the union was crushed. A group that was larger and more important to the Republican party electoral coalition probably would have been treated less harshly. Still, what a party or a president is willing to do for an interest group is subject to the constraints of public opinion and other political considerations.

In return for what they offer interest groups, the parties and their candidates expect to receive support at the ballot box and a commitment of organizational resources during the campaign. Campaign contributions are the most obvious resource that an interest group has to offer, but volunteer labor is another precious asset. The work of labor union officials has long been a backbone of Democratic

---

[29] Gene I. Maeroff, "Teachers' Unions Are Courted and Castigated," *The New York Times*, June 26, 1983.

[30] See, generally, J. David Greenstone, *Labor in American Politics* (New York: Vintage Books, 1969).

party campaigns. Another potential benefit comes later, after the election, when a president or a member of Congress will frequently turn to groups who have been strong supporters to ask for their help in getting a bill passed, even though it may not be the group's highest priority.

In trying to build his electoral coalition, a presidential candidate is not restricted to reaching out to the groups who may endorse him. Rank-and-file members of a group may be much more sympathetic to a candidate than their organization's leadership is. Both Richard Nixon and Ronald Reagan made concerted efforts to appeal to union members even though they were unpopular with most union presidents. An interest group's endorsement does not mean that members will necessarily follow it. Moreover, beyond every organization is a larger constituency of people who are not members of that lobby. An incumbent president courts these broad constituencies continually, often by appearing at the annual conventions of related interest groups. The accompanying publicity allows presidents to speak directly to the group's constituency, bypassing the organization's leadership. When education began to appear as a major issue in the 1984 presidential campaign, President Reagan booked an appearance at the convention of the American Federation of Teachers to try to convince public school teachers that he was more sympathetic to the needs of educators than his budget cuts for education might suggest. The group's leadership was anti-Reagan, but Reagan thought he might be able to appeal to the rank and file with his stress on back-to-basics education and his condemnation of the group's rival union, the National Education Association.[31]

There are signs that some interest groups are beginning to believe they should become more active in party politics and elections. To increase its clout within the Democratic party, the AFL-CIO decided that it would make a preprimary endorsement before 1984. By committing its might to one candidate, the group would put the candidate deeper in debt to itself, could be perceived as kingmaker at the convention, and could increase the chances that the candidate most sympathetic to labor would win the nomination. If their candidate lost the nomination, the winner's need for labor support would still give the union access to any Democratic administration. At its

[31] Rich Jaroslovsky, "Reagan Gets Tepid Reception as He Tries to Win Points with Teachers' Federation," *Wall Street Journal*, July 6, 1983.

October, 1983 convention, the AFL-CIO gave its endorsement to former Vice-President Mondale. At about the same time, the National Organization for Women announced that it would make its first presidential endorsement for the 1984 race.

Feeling the Reagan administration's antagonism toward their policy views, black groups also undertook efforts to make themselves a more potent force in electoral politics. A number of civil rights groups like the National Association for the Advancement of Colored People (NAACP) and Operation PUSH (People United to Serve Humanity) instituted voter registration drives, both to help specific black candidates and to give presidential candidates more reason to seek their support. Jesse Jackson's candidacy for the 1984 Democratic nomination was another step in this direction. Already a significant force within Democratic party politics, black groups see an opportunity to become stronger. Similarly, some Hispanic groups such the Southwest Voter Registration Education Project view voter registration as a means of gaining power within the Democratic party and making issues that interest Hispanics more important in elections.

PAC ⟨handwritten⟩

PACs: Party Politics Through Interest Groups

The greatest change in the role of interest groups in party politics and elections comes from the sharply increasing amounts of money PACs donate to congressional campaigns. Labor union donations have long been a major source of revenue for Democratic party candidates, but most corporate giving was restricted until the Federal Election Campaign Act was changed in 1974. Ideological citizen groups have used direct mail to become major fundraisers of PAC money as well.

The great appeal of PACs is that they allow individuals who recognize that electoral change is instrumental in achieving their policy goals to funnel their giving through a recognized interest group. The money comes "labeled" from an identifiable interest rather than from individuals who choose to contribute but don't have a way of clearly expressing their policy concerns. Whether the contributors are executives of Litton Industries, factory machinists, or physicians, they have their own PAC to pool their money and to give their interests heightened visibility in the political process.

Even individuals who wish to promote general liberal or conservative values rather than their occupational interests have good reason

$ = visibility for labeled interests. ⟨handwritten⟩

to give through a PAC rather than through a party campaign committee. A liberal donating money to the Democratic Congressional Campaign Committee does not know if the contribution will ultimately be in the hands of a liberal or a conservative candidate. The same liberal giving money to a PAC such as the National Committee for an Effective Congress knows that the money will be channeled to a liberal.

Political parties remain important sources of funds, contributing directly to candidates as well as making coordinated expenditures on their behalf (such as paying for polls for a group of candidates). The PACs, however, donate more and their contributions are a growing percentage of the funds raised by congressional candidates. At first glance, this change may not seem of great consequence. Labor PACs give all but a small percentage of their funds to Democrats. Many corporations and trade associations draw upon information provided to them by the Republican party or groups such as the Chamber of Commerce and BIPAC (Business-Industry Political Action Committee), to direct money not already designated for incumbents to races in which it will be most helpful to Republican candidates. And many of the nonconnected ideological groups are wholly partisan, giving only to Republicans or Democrats. It could be argued, therefore, that PACs are working closely with the parties and are no great threat to them.

Yet even though a good deal of PAC giving is done on a partisan basis or given in coordination with the parties, the parties have good reason to worry about the growing popularity of PACs. To begin with, PAC giving favors incumbents. If the parties could direct all PAC giving, they would surely distribute more money to challengers and less to incumbents who are highly favored to win. A trade association, however, is going to care more about access to key committee members than about building up one of the parties. The ideological groups are a separate problem. Groups like the Republican-oriented Citizens for the Republic or the Fund for a Democratic Majority compete directly with the parties for funds, but relatively little of the money they collect actually gets to candidates.[32] High operating costs, due largely to direct mail expenses, make these ideological PACs very inefficient fundraisers. If fundraising were cen-

[32] Adam Clymer, "PAC Gifts to Candidates Rose 45% in Latest Cycle," *The New York Times*, April 29, 1983.

tralized through the parties and this duplication and overlap ended, candidates might end up with more money.

Most important, PACs push candidates to be responsive to interest group pressures and those interests frequently conflict with broader party aims. It is surely more difficult to build disciplined, coherent congressional parties when legislators depend heavily on PAC money for their campaigns. As New Right leader Paul Weyrich says of PAC politics, "both political parties would have an all-night celebration if we were to go out of business." [33] Because no reforms on the horizon would eliminate PACs, parties have accepted them as part of the process and are trying to work more closely with them. Or, as Larry Sabato puts it, "Like Willie Sutton who robbed banks 'because that's where they keep the money,' parties have begun to direct their attentions to the overflowing PAC treasuries and have hired consultants to insure that they get their fair share of PAC money." [34]

The efforts of parties to do more to cultivate the PACs seem sensible from their point of view, but it raises some serious questions as well. One is suggested by the Democratic Congressional Campaign Committee's effort to increase business donations to the party's candidates. Under the direction of Representative Tony Coelho of California, the committee has aggressively sought out leaders of business PACs, encouraging them to give to the party. In return, Coelho has not hesitated to contact Democratic members of the House and ask them to meet with these lobbyists and to help them with their problems if they can. Nothing is new in one legislator asking another to meet with a lobbyist, but what is of note here is the tie between a congressional party campaign committee, its eager solicitation of money, and these requests for assistance. It has made some Democrats feel as though their party is on the auction block. [35]

The party is not always the aggressor in this relationship. Some of the larger PACs have used questionnaires and other not-so-subtle forms of pressure to push candidates into committing themselves to

[33] Larry J. Sabato, *The Rise of Political Consultants* (New York: Basic Books, 1981), p. 274.

[34] Sabato, *The Rise of Political Consultants*, p. 273.

[35] Dennis Farney, "Rep. Coelho Makes Money, and Waves, For the Democrats," *Wall Street Journal*, June 14, 1983; Elizabeth Drew, "Politics and Money — I," *New Yorker*, December 6, 1982, pp. 54–149; and Rob Gurwitt, "Democratic Campaign Panel: New Strategy and New Friends," *Congressional Quarterly Weekly Report*, July 2, 1983, pp. 1346–1348.

the group's position. Build-PAC, the political action committee of the National Association of Home Builders, adopted a "get-tough" policy in the 1982 election to get candidates to move closer to the prohousing policies the group wants enacted by Congress. The group used a seven-page questionnaire to calculate each candidate's support for the group's positions, announced it would not support candidates whose stances on housing were only "lukewarm," and then delayed its decisions on donations to add further pressure on incumbents with relevant legislation before them. This tactic prompted the GOP leadership in Congress to circulate a letter encouraging members to work for housing measures to help the industry. A bipartisan housing caucus was also formed.[36]

Again, nothing is new in an interest group's using its campaign funds to reward its friends and punish its enemies. The actions of Build-PAC, though, are more blatant, more aggressive, and a step closer to a quid pro quo between candidate and donor than is normal. They also call into question the desirability of the parties' "if you can't beat 'em, join 'em" philosophy toward PACs. Large PACs, like the Home Builders, which gave approximately $1 million to candidates in the 1982 election, will not hesitate to throw their weight around in their dealings with the parties. More and closer relationships between PACs and parties will help the parties financially, but they would be better served if their fundraising remained largely independent of PACs.[37]

CONCLUSION

The relationship between interest groups and political parties is characterized by continuity and change. Parties still play their traditional role of coalition building around election time, and thus seek out the support of interest groups in much the same manner as they always have. In recent years, though, parties have weakened, beset by declining public support and reforms that have diminished the role of party leaders. In contrast, interest groups have increased in number and their role in campaigns has been enhanced by the Federal Election Campaign Act Amendments of 1974. With the

---

[36] Timothy D. Schellhardt, "Builders Try to Wield Political Cash to Get Housing Aid From Congress," *Wall Street Journal*, March 25, 1982.
[37] PACs and campaign finance are explored in more detail in Chapter 8.

widespread availability of PACs, the politically active can easily work to influence elections through their interest groups.

It would be a mistake to assume that the expansion of interest groups is an adequate substitute for a strong party system. Despite the thousands of interest groups, many Americans are still unrepresented or underrepresented by lobbying organizations. Even with the increase in citizen groups, the universe of lobbying organizations favors business, labor, and the professions at the expense of the poor, minorities, and diffuse, hard-to-organize constituencies like consumers.

For many Americans, voting may well be the only type of political activity they engage in. If they remove themselves from that process because they find the choices meaningless, or not worth the effort, they lose what leverage they have and increase the influence of those who remain in the system. Walter Dean Burnham writes:

> To state the matter with utmost simplicity: political parties, with all their well-known human and structural shortcomings, are the only devices thus far invented by the wit of Western man which with some effectiveness can generate countervailing collective power on behalf of the many individually powerless against the relatively few who are individually — or organizationally — powerful.[38]

Thus, both decline of parties and proliferation of interest groups have worked to the advantage of those already well represented in the political process. Parties can counter the efforts interest groups make to achieve their self-interested goals by articulating broader, national interests. Party renewal is vital to improving representation for the broad constituencies poorly represented through interest group politics. A strong party system is not incompatible with large numbers of interest groups and, hopefully, a growing awareness of the value of parties will lead to an era of party renewal.

[38] Burnham, *Critical Elections and the Mainsprings of American Politics*, p. 133.

CHAPTER FOUR

Origins, Maintenance, and Marketing

The recent impressive growth of interest groups may obscure a simple fact. Even in a bull market for interest groups, not all new ones succeed. Some may be stillborn, not attracting enough money to go beyond initial fundraising efforts. Others may enjoy some initial success, but then find themselves in gradual decline, slowly losing members and income. And some groups around for a long time will even fold. All this points to a significant question about interest groups: Why is it that people join such organizations?

Political scientists approach this question by asking what people expect to receive in return for dues or contributions, and what leaders can do to make their organizations more attractive to potential members. It is not merely a matter of determining which marketing approaches work best for which constituencies. Rather, the problem of who joins and why is, at heart, a matter of _representation_. The better an organization is at finding and retaining members, the better it will be able to represent its constituents' interests.

COMPETING THEORIES

Ideally, political scientists would like to be able to predict when and under what circumstances new interest groups will form. A theory of interest group formation should specify the factors important in this formation, and should further specify which of these factors are crucial to a new group's success or failure.[1] By examining successful

[1] See William Gamson, _The Strategy of Social Protest_ (Homewood, Ill.: Dorsey Press, 1975); and Jeffrey R. Henig, _Neighborhood Mobilization_ (New Brunswick, N.J.: Rutgers University Press, 1982).

groups and groups that died, scholars have tried to isolate the critical determinants in their formation. Each major theory to be examined presents compelling evidence on which factors are most important, but each, as we shall see, also has significant shortcomings.

Disturbances

A starting point for serious discussion of interest group origins is David Truman's classic work, *The Governmental Process*, in which he presents a pluralist vision of how interest groups come to form.[2] For Truman, interest groups are the product of two related forces. The first is society's growing complexity. As the economy and society change, new interests are formed while others lose importance. The Brotherhood of Sleeping Car Porters was formed after the railroads developed. Although railroads transformed the American economy, they eventually declined and the porters' union shrank along with them. Contemporary technology, however, has given America cable television and, as we might expect, a new lobby, the National Cable Television Association. The Washington-based association represents more than 1,600 operators of local cable television systems.

Evolving industry and society give rise to many new interests. Not all new interest groups, however, are directly linked to a new technology or profession. The second part of Truman's explanation, dealing with changing political and economic conditions, has proven to be controversial. Truman states that people in society who share an interest, but are as yet unorganized, are brought together when they are adversely affected by a "disturbance," which is some identifiable event or series of events that alter the "equilibrium" in some sector of society. The economic downturn in the 1870s disturbed the equilibrium of farmers, and that instability spurred development of the Grange. Truman writes, "Between 1873 and late 1874 the number of local Granges increased in number from about three thousand to over twenty thousand, paralleling an increase in mortgage foreclosures."[3]

The disturbance theory has an appealing logic: a cause-and-effect relationship between events and organizing. If people find that their political or economic interests are being adversely affected, they will organize to rectify the situation. This is the essence of pluralism:

[2] David B. Truman, *The Governmental Process* (New York: Knopf, 1951).
[3] Truman, *The Governmental Process*, p. 88.

People organize when they have a stake in the outcome of controversies over issues.

Like pluralist theory itself, Truman's disturbance explanation of interest group origins is deeply flawed. It is based on optimistic and unjustified assumptions about all people's ability to organize. Those who are poor are repeatedly "disturbed" by adverse events, such as the Reagan administration's budget cuts in 1981, but remain persistently unorganized. Equally damning to Truman's theory is that many groups have formed without a distinct, identifiable disturbance. Throughout the twentieth century migrant farm workers in California have been poorly treated by farmers. Low wages, discrimination, and terrible working conditions gave farm workers more than enough reason to join unions during periodic organizing efforts. But even the mighty AFL-CIO failed to organize them. In the late 1960s, though, a poor farm worker named Cesar Chavez succeeded in unionizing much of the California grape industry. The objective condition of the grape pickers was no worse than it had always been. The critical difference in the success of the United Farm Workers was unquestionably not some outside event, but the inspired leadership of Chavez.[4]

Entrepreneurs

It may be that disturbance theory could be refined to take greater account of leadership's influence in starting new groups. Political scientist Robert Salisbury argues convincingly, however, that Truman is fundamentally wrong, and that leadership is the main reason any group succeeds or dies.[5] Salisbury looked at farm groups during the same hard times in the nineteenth century that Truman did, but came up with a different conclusion. He points out that farm organizations began to decline before they had achieved their goals of high, stable commodity prices. If people join groups to overcome some disadvantage, why do they sometimes quit before equilibrium is restored? Salisbury reasons that individuals do not join interest groups strictly because of a disturbance, but because they see that benefits will accrue to them from membership. If, after joining, they feel they are getting their money's worth, they will continue to pay dues. If not, they quit.

[4] Peter Matthiessen, *Sal Si Puedes* (New York: Random House, 1969).
[5] Robert H. Salisbury, "An Exchange Theory of Interest Groups," *Midwest Journal of Political Science* 13 (February 1969), pp. 1–32.

In analyzing membership surge and decline, Salisbury emphasizes the role played by each interest group's organizer or "entrepreneur." He uses this name for the organizer because he likens the founder of a new interest group to the business investor who is willing to risk capital to start a new firm. In the interest group "marketplace" entrepreneurs will succeed if they provide attractive benefits or incentives to potential members. These benefits may be of three kinds.[6]

Purposive benefits are associated with pursuit of ideological or issue-oriented goals that offer no tangible rewards to members. Those who join the Defenders of Wildlife do so because they have deep ideological convictions about the environment, not because they have anything to gain or lose by changes in the laws affecting preservation of wild animals. A second type of reward is *material*. Over the years many farmers have joined the American Farm Bureau Federation because it offers its members financial and marketing services. The incentive for companies joining the Coalition for Employment Through Exports is also material. The group's goal is to protect and expand the lending authority of the Export-Import Bank, which translates into increased sales abroad for these companies.[7] Finally, individuals may join a group because of the *solidary* or social rewards. Those who belong to the League of Women Voters may join it rather than other good-government groups because it has a network of local chapters where members can work together to directly participate in politics. The benefit comes from being part of the group's struggle to achieve policy goals.[8]

There is much to Salisbury's theory, for the quality of leadership and the type of benefits offered unquestionably matter in a group's development.[9] The drawback in his theory, though, is its imprecision. Little has been done to develop the theory into more explicit propositions that indicate which benefits and which leadership traits are most useful under which circumstances. Yet Salisbury makes a con-

---

[6] Salisbury uses the typology from Peter B. Clark and James Q. Wilson's "Incentive Systems: A Theory of Organizations," *Administrative Science Quarterly* 6 (September 1961), pp. 129–166, in describing interest group incentive systems. We will also use the Clark and Wilson typology.

[7] Clyde H. Farnsworth, "A Super Lobby in Action," *The New York Times* (June 5, 1982).

[8] A further elaboration of this typology is offered in James Q. Wilson, *Political Organizations* (New York: Basic Books, 1973), pp. 30–55.

[9] Jeffrey M. Berry, "On the Origins of Public Interest Groups: A Test of Two Theories," *Polity* 10 (Spring 1978), pp. 379–397.

vincing point: Interest groups operate in a competitive marketplace and those which do a poor job of providing satisfactory benefits to members will lose to more skillful "entrepreneurs."

Selective Incentives

Another attack on the pluralist idea that people join interest groups because they are being adversely affected by public policy is in economist Mancur Olson's *The Logic of Collective Action*.[10] Like Salisbury, Olson says that people contribute money to interest groups because they receive some benefit in return. He goes further, though, claiming that it generally makes sense for individuals to contribute to a group only if they get a selective benefit in return. This benefit goes only to group members, unlike a collective good, which can be shared by members and nonmembers alike.

Does it make sense for someone in business to contribute to the Chamber of Commerce to support its lobbying? If the Chamber succeeds in getting a tax bill favorable to business through Congress, people in business will profit whether they are members of the organization or not. A general change in the tax law is thus a collective rather than a selective good. Olson feels, then, that it is irrational for people in business to support the Chamber solely for its political advocacy, because they can be "free riders" and still enjoy benefits from its lobbying. He says a major reason people join is that the local Chambers of Commerce "are good places for businessmen to make 'contacts' and exchange information." [11] Only Chamber members can take advantage of the selective benefit of going to meetings, making contacts, and gaining valuable business information.

Olson makes some allowances in this general theory for cases where selective incentives do not form the basis for a group's success. Individuals in labor unions are exempted because they commonly work in closed shops, wherein membership is mandatory. Groups with small constituencies, such as an industry with only a handful of companies, do not need a selective incentive because they are able to exert peer pressure on nonmembers. Visibly absent nonmembers can be singled out for not doing their part.

[10] Mancur Olson, Jr., *The Logic of Collective Action* (New York: Schocken, 1968).
[11] Olson, *The Logic of Collective Action*, p. 146.

Olson's important contribution is in drawing attention to the importance of selective incentives. They can be powerful inducements for membership in large economic interest groups. For other types of organizations, the theory is considerably weaker. Few national citizen groups offer their members any real benefits other than ideological satisfaction. No selective benefit leads people to contribute to the Natural Resources Defense Council or Citizens for the Republic. Olson acknowledges that his theory works poorly for these "philanthropic" lobbies.[12] Yet there are simply too many citizen groups, attracting too many members and millions of dollars, to be dismissed as anomalous or products of "irrational" behavior.

The pervasiveness of ideological lobbying also throws some doubt on the theory's adequacy when applied to business, farm and professional organizations. Membership surveys show that an economic group's lobbying can be a significant incentive for those who join.[13] Even Olson's own example of the Chamber of Commerce is not wholly persuasive. In recent years the Chamber has become more active and visible in its political work and has seen its membership skyrocket. Its political vigor is surely one reason for that rise.[14] Do business people who join the Chamber of Commerce care less about the free-enterprise system than members of the Sierra Club about the environment? It is difficult to answer with certainty, but business associations do offer members the opportunity to *mix* politics with business.

Olson claims that the lobbying activity of large economic interest groups is a by-product of other organizational activities that draw and hold members. Groups "obtain their strength and support" by offering selective incentives.[15] Viewing lobbying as a by-product may, however, underestimate how important political activities are in attracting and maintaining members. The directors of Washington lobbies make a concerted effort to keep members informed of the political issues facing their organizations and of the lobbying work being car-

[12] Olson, *The Logic of Collective Action*, pp. 159–165.
[13] See Terry M. Moe, *The Organization of Interests* (Chicago: University of Chicago Press, 1980); and David Marsh, "On Joining Interest Groups," *British Journal of Political Science* 6 (July 1976), pp. 257–272.
[14] Ann Crittenden, "A Stubborn Chamber of Commerce," *The New York Times,* June 27, 1982; and William J. Lanouette, "Chamber's Ponderous Decision Making Leaves It Sitting on the Sidelines," *National Journal,* July 24, 1982, pp. 1298–1301.
[15] Olson, *The Logic of Collective Action*, p. 132.

ried out. Although surely many members of economic organizations would not join but for the selective benefits, those who run these groups clearly regard lobbying as an essential part of the organizations' appeal to members.

What can we say in summary about these three theories of interest group formation? In looking at all three together, and assessing their strengths and weaknesses, what is it that social scientists know and don't know about the origins of interest groups?

1. New interest groups do evolve naturally out of changes in technology and the ever-increasing complexity of society. This evolution does not, however, explain why all groups form. Nor does it explain why one organization successfully comes to represent a new interest and other organizations started to represent the same constituency fail.

2. Disturbances (wars, turns in the business cycle, and so on) can help new interest groups form by making potential members aware of the need for political action. Disturbances are not necessary for interest group formation, though, because many groups originate without one.

3. Interest group constituencies vary widely, and some are much more difficult to organize than others. Business executives may respond readily to an organization that allows them to mix their free market politics and social interaction with other businessmen. On the other hand, people who are desperately poor will be hard to organize under any circumstances. The disadvantaged cannot afford to contribute to interest groups and often lack the sense of efficacy to make them believe they have the capacity to influence public policy.

4. Because interest groups operate in a competitive environment, leaders must make their organizations as appealing as possible to current and potential members. Organizations that provide their constituencies with valued benefits increase their chances of survival. Selective incentives add to the attractiveness of membership.

SUPPLY OF BENEFITS

The work of Salisbury and Olson suggests that an organizer's chance of successfully forming an interest group is determined by the benefits offered to potential members. We will now go beyond the abstract marketplace analogies of "collective goods," "selective benefits," and "entrepreneurs" to more concretely discuss the benefits leaders actually offer to their members.[16]

Material Benefits

Any individuals who give their money or that of their company to an interest group do so because they feel something worthwhile will result from the organization's activities. Consciously or subconsciously, potential contributors ask themselves one or both of these questions: (1) "If I donate this money, what will I get in return?" and (2) "If I donate this money, what will society get in return?" Material benefits are the tangible rewards that individuals or companies get in return for their donation.

The most common material reward one can get for contributing to an interest group is information. Nearly every group sends the members some type of publication with articles directed at their interests. Interest group publications are of three basic types. The larger, well-endowed groups will often publish magazines. The purpose is to give individuals an attractive, polished publication with articles covering the readers' broad interests rather than focusing exclusively on political issues. A recent issue of the American Bankers Association's *Banking Journal* was devoted mostly to using advanced technology to train bank personnel. Only as a secondary focus does *Banking Journal* cover Washington politics. Instead, it has another publication, the *Bankers News Weekly*, in an inexpensive newspaper format, which focuses on regulatory activity in Washington.

A newspaper or newsletter is used by most interest groups, whether alone or in conjunction with other publications. All are densely packed with news of government activity in the group's policy field. *Bankers News Weekly* covers Congress, the Farm Credit Administration, the Treasury Department, the Federal Deposit Insurance Corporation, the Federal Home Loan Bank Board, and many other governmental agencies. The primary purpose of a newspaper or newsletter is to serve as a monitoring device for members, keeping them in touch with what's going on in Washington. Ninety-nine percent of the material in an interest group newsletter would never appear in a general-audience newspaper, even particularly good ones like the

---

[16] On lobbying and the political "marketplace," see Michael T. Hayes, *Lobbyists and Legislators* (New Brunswick, N.J.: Rutgers University Press, 1981).

Washington Post or *The New York Times*. To serve their monitoring function effectively, newsletters must be published frequently, and many come out as often as once a week or every other week. Numerous organizations will supplement the newsletter with occasional alerts. These are very brief (usually one page) memos, often written in an emotional style, asking activitists or all members to take action. Typically, an alert tells members they must write or phone their congressmen to express their views on an upcoming vote cataclysmically important to the organization's interest.

When the Senate was considering a number of large cuts in Medicare, Social Security, and other programs affecting the elderly in its budget resolution for fiscal year 1983, the National Retired Teachers Association/American Association of Retired Persons (NRTA/AARP) sprang into action. Their legislative alert warned that without a "massive outpouring" of protest by the elderly, millions of older Americans might not be able to afford "life-sustaining necessities." A few organizations, like the National Association of Manufacturers, have an 800 (toll-free) number that members can call to get a daily recorded update of political developments.

The information published in interest group publications can be very useful to members, educating them on developments in their industry or profession and advising them of government actions that may affect their lives. Yet it is difficult to generalize on just how important publications are to members. No studies in political science provide evidence on how thoroughly they are read.[17] But in reading through samples of different organizations' publications, one is led to the inescapable conclusion that most interest groups provide their rank-and-file members with far more information than they can ever want to read. A lobbyist for a food-industry trade association said, "We bore them with information."

Yet the information overkill by interest groups is not a bad membership strategy — far from it. Washington staff members heavily emphasize publications because these reinforce members' appreciation of what the national organization is doing. Publications are periodic proof that members' money is well spent. For the circle of activists in any organization, they provide useful information to help

---

[17] Moe's study of Minnesota-based interest groups attests to the general importance of information provided to members. *The Organization of Interests*, pp. 201–218.

in their political work. For the larger segment of rank-and-file members of the group, they provide reassurance that someone is speaking on their behalf in Washington.

Another material reward groups can offer their memberships is some form of direct service. The U.S. Conference of Mayors assists individual mayors when they are in Washington to lobby the government on some matter. Its staff is also at the mayors' disposal to work themselves on projects that individual mayors want pushed. Says one lobbyist, "There is constant contact . . . I'd say that I personally speak to five or six mayors each day." Some organizations like the National Federation of Independent Business have "caseworkers" on their staff to handle individual problems brought to them by member businesses.

Although individualized service could be a very attractive inducement for membership, few lobbies actively market it. One reason is that casework could easily overwhelm most organizations' office capacity. For a group like the National Federation of Independent Business, with more than 400,000 members, casework could occupy the time of all twenty professionals instead of the two staffers who have responsibility for it. The organization already "gets more mail than they do in a congressional office," says one Federation lobbyist.

A second reason casework is not heavily marketed is that the professional staffs of lobbies are not especially interested in it. Taking care of members' small problems is not nearly as compelling or rewarding as working on a broader issue that requires a new law or new regulation. Troubleshooting at agencies for members lacks the excitement and the high political stakes of larger policy battles. Frequently, then, individual members of trade associations will find that the Washington lobbying office cannot provide the extensive help they need. They may turn to a freelance lobbyist, usually a lawyer or public relations expert, whom they hire at an hourly fee.

The most important material reward is, of course, a change in public policy that directly benefits members. All groups make vague promises to "deliver," but it is risky to promise specific policy rewards on any immediate schedule. If a group offers its members quick results rather than steady representation in Washington, the lack of success can easily disillusion members.[18] The American Agriculture

---

[18] Even with some immediate success, the lack of continued benefits can be disillusioning. See Lawrence Neil Bailis, *Bread or Justice* (Lexington, Mass.: Lexington Books, 1974).

Movement, a protest-oriented group born late in the 1970s, worked for quick relief from inadequate market prices. After some initial government help no other visible successes followed, and lacking other attractive material benefits, the group began to lose some of its membership.[19]

Although lobbying may be born out of specific policy conflicts ("disturbances"), it is usually best for a group to convince its members that the material policy benefits will accrue gradually. In an organization's early years, the professional staff may find themselves trying to broaden the scope of the lobbying beyond the initial issue that brought members in so that their success will not be seen as tied to that one issue.

Purposive Benefits

When people join organizations pursuing policy objectives that are of no direct, material benefit to them, they are said to be attracted by purposive incentives. Purposive incentives are most commonly associated with citizen groups, though not all of these lobbies pursue rewards that are entirely philanthropic. Civil rights groups seek an end to discrimination that keeps minorities from landing good jobs, obviously a material goal.

Aside from groups that may mix material and ideological rewards, thousands of organizations across the country offer members only one thing: satisfaction that they have done their part to make the world a better place. Whether the group's goal is ending the arms race, putting prayer back in public schools, protecting endangered species, keeping the United States out of another country's civil war, fighting economic development of wilderness areas, ending (or facilitating) abortion on demand, or strengthening consumer protection laws, people join to further a cause, not their own material self-interest.

Why is it that people voluntarily join a group that relies on purposive incentives? Research on political socialization reveals that parents strongly influence their children's political views — not only their partisan identification but also their general ideological atti-

[19] Allan J. Cigler and John Mark Hansen, "Group Formation Through Protest," in Allan J. Cigler and Burdett A. Loomis, eds., *Interest Group Politics* (Washington, D.C.: Congressional Quarterly, 1983), pp. 102–103.

tudes. Political participation is also related to socioeconomic status: more highly educated and wealthier individuals are more likely to participate in all forms of political activity. Schools too socialize children toward believing that participation in politics is vital, and that all citizens must take some responsibility for the well-being of their community. Joining civic organizations is part of the "American way," and adults who belong to any type of political organization believe they are fulfilling part of their civic responsibilities as well as advancing their own political views. Finally, the propensity for becoming involved with political organizations can be influenced by critical events in one's life. The Vietnam War propelled many young people of that era into political activism.

The correlations between variables such as education and political participation reflect tendencies rather than deterministic laws of behavior. We cannot accurately predict why any person will care enough about politics to donate money or time to an ideological organization. But for whatever reasons — family, opportunities, experiences, and individual personality — those who join share the feeling that they must do something beyond just voting.

The benefit you get in return for committing resources to a citizens' lobby is that you have made at least a small contribution to the betterment of society. Although this reward is vague and abstract, the ideological groups pursue visible, substantive issues. Nothing could be clearer to antiabortionists who contribute to a right-to-life group than that their donations will be used to try to save the lives of the unborn. It is a very *direct* way to link one's concern for the unborn with political advocacy on their behalf. The degree to which an individual's contribution works to accomplish such a goal as stopping abortions is obviously rather negligible. Donors adopt the attitude, however, that even though their own contributions cannot possibly be critical to the organization's continuing existence, the organization could not exist if everyone took that view.

Although the changes in policy advocated by ideological groups gratify their members, such changes are not absolutely necessary to retain those members. In recent years there has been little progress in moving Congress toward passing meaningful gun control legislation, yet Handgun Control, an anti-gun group, has slowly built up during this time. Most citizen groups, though, can point to some progress in their field and make convincing claims that members' contributions are having an effect. But in the last analysis, a person's decision to join an ideological group is based not simply on its record, but on whether a donation is seen as the right thing to do.

Solidary Benefits

One advantage of ideological groups is that they are a "cheap" way to participate in politics. For the busy individual who worries about the problem of campaign finance, but has neither the time nor true commitment to work personally on the issue, mailing a $20 check to Common Cause can fulfill a need to do something. For many Americans, though, mailing a check off to Washington is not enough — they want to be involved.

When people volunteer their time to a political organization, they are powerfully motivated by their ideology. Yet they are also motivated by the desire to work and associate with others. Stuffing a check into an envelope is a political act, but it lacks the drama and excitement and enjoyment of politics. The solidary incentive is the inducement to be part of a collective struggle with like-minded colleagues.

One organization that depends heavily on solidary rewards as a membership inducement is the Vietnam Veterans of America. Although the leaders of the organization lobby for many important material benefits, the 8,000-member group is decidedly held together by the fifty-five chapters across the country. Meetings at these chapters offer Vietnam Vets an opportunity to come together with others and discuss the special problems they have — problems that only those who fought there seem able to understand. The real benefit for joining is to be able to talk to combat veterans who shared the horror of the war.

Social incentives are not usually so significant as they are with the Vietnam Vets, but it is common for them to have at least some influence in an interest group. In the National Association of Broadcasters (NAB), the busy corporate executives who run the member television and radio stations can gain social benefits from NAB activities. Like so many other national associations, it has a circle of activists in each state whose responsibility is being grassroots lobbyists. These broadcasters will work to influence their own legislators in Washington. They will do such work at the request of NAB staffers, and derive the satisfaction of taking part in a coordinated advocacy effort to help the industry. Some status too can be gained by dealing with congressmen and their staffs, who are receptive to talking with such important constituents. The NAB's annual convention offers further social (as well as material) inducements that give members a chance to socialize, do business, meet with Federal Communications Commission officials and congressmen who appear there, and enjoy camaraderie in the collective fight for sensible government policy toward broadcasting.

The role of solidary incentives varies among interest groups. These may be at the core of the decision to join the Vietnam Vets, but have nothing to do with the decision to donate money to the National Committee for an Effective Congress. When social incentives do play a role, they must still be combined with other incentives. Solidary benefits can only complement the avowed purposive or material goals of a lobbying organization.

The Mix of Benefits

Each organization has its own benefit structure, which Salisbury and Olson see as critical to its ultimate success. If entrepreneurs cannot offer the proper benefits to their constituency, the group will cease to exist. Can it be said that organizers' *choice* of benefits they are going to offer is an overriding factor in organizational development? It is significant, but it is difficult to explain the rise or fall of many interest groups in terms of specific benefit choices made by leaders. The reasons can be summarized briefly.

THE CHOICES ARE FAIRLY LIMITED. The variety of benefits to choose from is not endless, and the ones that can be used may already be widely available. Nothing is novel about a new interest group publishing a topnotch newsletter, giving members a chance to work at the grassroots, or offering members the satisfaction of belonging and doing their part. Services not readily available elsewhere can sometimes be developed, of course, but cost and administrative feasibility are serious constraints on what may ultimately be offered, especially for modest-sized organizations.

COMPETITION BREEDS IMITATION. Many new interest groups face competition from groups that already appeal to the same constituency. When former Vice-President Walter Mondale solicited support in 1982 for his new PAC, the Committee for the Future of America, it had little to offer donors that distinguished it from other liberal PACs. Money donated to it would go for the same purpose as money given to the Fund for a Democratic Majority or Independent Action. Other than to help Mondale establish himself for a presidential bid in 1984, the donor would get no more ideological satisfaction than with any of the other PACs with a broad, liberal orientation. Although market forces push most groups toward some issue distinctiveness, leaders are also prone to model new groups after successful ones, especially in terms of structure, tactics, and utilization of incentives. In making some benefit choices, entrepreneurs may move more toward imitation than innovation.

SOME GROUPS HAVE LITTLE COMPETITION. Though benefit packages may lose some effectiveness when competing organizations offer most of the same things, the opposite can be true as well. Some organizations, notably some trade associations, have little competition and therefore any standard benefit package they offer will do. The quality of that package may affect membership figures somewhat, but a trade association may be able to depend on a core membership simply by being first off the mark in its field. Many businesspeople will strongly identify with their industry and feel obliged to join their primary trade association. Thus, for manufacturers of computer components, the mere existence of the Semiconductor Industry Association may be sufficient inducement to join.

BENEFITS BLEND. It is often hard for organizers (or political scientists) to know exactly which benefits or combination of benefits bring people into different organizations. In many groups, members receive a "package," and it is not easy to distinguish which part of the package is most essential to their participation. The U.S. Chamber of Commerce is a good example, for it offers social, material, and ideological incentives to join. All appear to be good reasons for businesspeople to belong. Asking members their most important reason for joining could provide some clues, but it may be that the Chamber's overall package is what makes it so attractive. In time, the information an individual receives may turn out to be the most valued part of the membership, but he or she might never have joined if there had not been the promise of aggressive lobbying in Washington. In the real world, the benefits blend in a member's mind, and entrepreneurs can never be sure which parts of their package are critical to making the sum so attractive.

Although every individual joins an interest group because they expect to get something in return, it is difficult to specify what combination of benefits gives rise to successful organizations. This general approach does help us to understand the development of interest groups, but it would be enhanced if greater emphasis was placed on the efforts actually made to find new members. Once the benefit package is determined, it must still be brought to the attention of those who might be most attracted to it.

MARKETING INTEREST GROUPS: DIRECT MAIL

For some interest group leaders, then, it may not be the mix of benefits they offer, but how aggressively they market their organizations, which makes the critical difference in their ultimate success. If they operate in a competitive environment, but offer goods similar to those of other groups, the question is how they reach people and persuade them to join. The segment of the interest group community in which competition is probably fiercest is among citizen groups. For almost every conceivable constituency, there are overlapping groups. Conservatives, for example, have a vast array of citizen groups to choose from, including the American Conservative Union, the American Security Council, Citizens for the Republic, Committee for the Survival of a Free Congress, the Congressional Club, the Conservative Caucus, the Eagle Forum, the Moral Majority, the National Conservative Political Action Committee, the National Right to Life Committee, the National Tax Limitation Committee, the U.S. Justice Foundation, and the Young Americans for Freedom. Some differences in coverage of issues can be found between these groups, but they still compete for many of the same donors.

When a national citizen group is in a highly competitive field, it will frequently depend on direct mail to solicit members or donations. Direct mail campaigns involve mailings of tens or hundreds of thousands of individual letters. They are popular with interest groups because they are a means of communicating individually with prospective members, bringing to their attention the good work of the organization. Contrary to the stereotype of direct mail letters being junk mail that is tossed into the wastebasket, they are frequently opened and examined.[20]

[20] Susan Rouder, "Mobilization by Mail," *Citizen Participation* 2 (September/October 1980, pp. 3 ff); and Dom Bonafede, "Part Science, Part Art, Part Hokum, Direct Mail Now a Key Campaign Tool," *National Journal*, July 31, 1982, p. 1336.

A lobby wanting to engage in a direct mail campaign begins by hiring consultants and renting mailing lists.[21] Consultants are hired because direct mail involves a number of steps requiring expertise as well as expensive computer and printing equipment that few groups have reason to own. One important aspect of their job is to help groups select a mailing list or sets of lists. The larger consulting firms have their own lists of donors to various causes that they can rent to clients. Other consultants will rent them from brokers. They can look in the direct mail magazine *ZIP* and see that Butcher-Forde, a California firm, is offering 145,000 "Known Anti-Busing Activists" at $40 per thousand.[22] Picking a list is critical, because if the mailing turns out poorly, the lobby will end up losing money, hardly a desirable outcome. For that reason, a group using lists for the first time will usually pretest them, sending out small batches to names on each list to see if any are clear winners or losers. The best lists are then used in full. The usual types of lists give names of people who are members of other interest groups, donors to political campaigns, and subscribers to magazines with a distinctly liberal or conservative point of view.

Two national consulting firms stand out because of the breadth of their direct mail operations. The Richard A. Viguerie Company, named for its founder and director, services conservative political candidates and interest groups. Viguerie was one of the pioneers in the field in the late 1960s, adapting marketing principles from advertising and public relations to the political world. Direct mail was hardly new, but it had not been used extensively in politics until Viguerie and others proved that it could work.[23] High-speed computers made direct mail increasingly feasible, allowing firms to keep an electronic file cabinet of millions of names. These names can be retrieved instantaneously and quickly printed on labels and even on the first page of letters to make them "personalized." [24]

Craver, Mathews, Smith, and Company is a liberal counterpart to the Viguerie operation. Roger Craver, the company's president,

[21] Larry J. Sabato, *The Rise of Political Consultants* (New York: Basic Books, 1981).
[22] "P.S.: Please Send Money," *California Journal*, June 1980, pp. 3–5.
[23] Richard A. Viguerie, *The New Right: We're Ready to Lead* (Falls Church, Va.: Viguerie Company, 1981).
[24] New advances in technology are described in Bill Keller, "Computers and Laser Printers Have Recast the Injunction: 'Write Your Congressman,'" *Congressional Quarterly Weekly Report*, September 11, 1982, pp. 2245–2247.

successfully launched Common Cause's initial direct mail efforts early in the 1970s. Craver, Mathews, and Smith has lists with 4 million names and addresses, just slightly fewer than Viguerie's 4.5 million.[25] People like Richard Viguerie and Roger Craver do not see themselves as simply businessmen offering a service to anyone who might want to use it. They are ideologues who started doing political work because they care deeply about political issues.[26]

Most direct mail letters have three important parts. The first is the envelope. A rose by any other name may still be a rose, but direct mail envelopes seem endlessly diverse. What's on the outside is significant because it may determine whether or not the individual will open it and read what's inside. Direct mail designers try to think of ways to spark the reader's curiosity. One way is to place a bold or scary tease on the outside. The Southern Poverty Law Center, a civil rights group, uses envelopes with a picture of six-gun-wielding Ku Klux Klansmen, camped out in the woods by a fire and a Confederate flag. The legend reads, "KKK Guerillas Training for the 'Race War.'" Handgun Control has an envelope that reads, "ENCLOSED: Your first real chance to tell the National Rifle Association to go to hell!...." Other groups will try to get recipients to open and read the letter by printing the word "Emergency" in red on the envelope. Declaring that a poll is inside is also a favorite tactic. Some groups use reverse psychology, printing nothing on the envelope but an unidentified return address in Washington or New York, forcing the recipient to open the letter to find out what it contains and who sent it.

Inside is the most important ingredient, the appeal letter. Letters that have been found to work best contain a good amount of detail along with passages that will provoke the reader's emotions. Typically, the letters are four single-spaced pages with significant passages underlined or indented to break up the long blocks of text. The key to direct mail is to make the reader angry or scared. To do so, says Roger Craver, "You've got to have a devil. If you don't have a devil, you're in trouble." [27] The "devil" in these letters is some person or group that is visibly and actively working against the soliciting group's

[25] E. J. Dionne, "The Mail-Order Campaigners," *The New York Times*, September 7, 1980.
[26] Not all consultants place a high premium on working for a party or point of view. See Sabato, *The Rise of Political Consultants*, pp. 24–34.
[27] Dionne, "The Mail-Order Campaigners."

interests. The American Civil Liberties Union uses Jerry Falwell and the Moral Majority as its foil. In a direct mail appeal to potential members, this text was used:

> Dear Friend,
> If the Moral Majority has its way, you'd better start praying.
> The Moral Majority — and other groups like them — think that children should pray in school. Not just their children. Your children. . . .
> They want their religious doctrines enacted into law and imposed on everyone.
> If they believe that birth control is a sin, then you should not be allowed to use contraceptives. . . .

As you would expect, Reverend Falwell makes similarly emotional pleas in his direct mail. He has his own set of villains though, as illustrated in the following fund-raising letter:

> I have become the victim of a vicious, orchestrated attack by the liberal politicians, bureaucrats, and amoralists. . . .
> The liberals and amoral secular humanists have tried to destroy my character and my integrity.
> And sadly enough, some of my friends who once supported the Old-Time Gospel Hour have believed some of these false reports and charges made in the Press. . . .
> I have burned the bridge behind me. You will never read it in the newspaper that Jerry Falwell quit. You may read that someone killed me — but that is the only way I can be stopped. . . .[28]

Another part of the formula is that letters ask — indeed, demand — specific action of the reader. The action, of course, is giving money. Often the request is worded so that money is being requested for a specific project or lobbying campaign, making the donor feel a direct link between the contribution and political action. The Wilderness Society used this approach in a letter featuring former Interior Secretary James Watt as its devil. Donations were asked for a "Wilderness Watch" fund to monitor the policies of Watt, whose pro-development attitude infuriated environmentalists.

A common third part of the direct mail package is one or more other pieces of literature not written in letter format. Often included

[28] Frances FitzGerald, "A Disciplined, Charging Army," *New Yorker*, May 18, 1981, p. 136.

is a reprint of a newspaper article or two offering persuasive evidence that the crisis outlined in the letter is as real as the organization says it is. The National Organization for Women (NOW) has used a reproduction of the one-sentence human-life amendment advocated by antiabortionists: "The paramount right to life is vested in each human being from the moment of fertilization without regard to age, health or condition of dependency." A "handwritten" message from NOW's president on the same sheet points out that such an amendment would outlaw some forms of birth control. A return envelope and a contributor's card round out the typical package.

Direct mail is particularly successful when it is tied to highly salient current events. During a fourteen-week period of the Watergate scandal, Common Cause used direct mail to enlist more than 100,000 new members.[29] Conservative groups did well by playing on the Panama Canal issue prior to the vote in Congress to give control of the Canal to the Panamanians. The Reagan administration opened up the wallets of liberals across the country as direct mail appeals by left-leaning groups became much more successful within a month of his election.

For all the success many groups have had with direct mail, it is still a risky enterprise because of its substantial costs. A "good" return on a new list can be 2 percent of recipients sending money. If a group can break even when it is searching for new members, it is likely to come out ahead later on when the recent recruits can be asked to donate again. Such a "house list" generally gets a response from 8 to 15 percent of those solicited.[30] Not all campaigns eventually wind up in the black, though. If the initial return drops below 1.5 percent, a group probably will end up losing money.[31] Yet the success so many groups have had with direct mail encourages others to take the risk and invest "seed" money, hoping to uncover a good harvest of donors.

MAINTAINING THE ORGANIZATION

Direct mail is but one tool by which interest groups market their "product" and retain their members once they enlist them. What-

---

[29] Rouder, "Mobilization by Mail," p. 3.
[30] Bonafede, "Part Science, Part Art," p. 1336.
[31] Tina Rosenberg, "Diminishing Returns," *Washington Monthly*, June 1983, p. 35.

ever the means, though, all organizations must *maintain* themselves by raising money on an ongoing basis so that they may continue to operate.[32] It is not simply a matter of raise money or die: Although organizations can go under if fundraising drops dramatically, the more common problem is keeping funding up to avert project or staff cutbacks. Ideally, of course, interest groups expand their base of support so that they can take on more projects. Fundraising is difficult and competitive, though, and most groups will usually do well to keep up with the annual rate of inflation.

Still, I have said throughout that the number of interest groups has grown significantly and that many interest groups that have been in business for many years have expanded their operations. Their using direct mail indicates a larger trend: Interest groups have been able to better market themselves. There are two parts to this advance. First, entrepreneurs have successfully identified new or undersubscribed markets where members could be found for their organizations. Second, interest group leaders have been able to expand their funding beyond membership dues.

The basis for the first part of this argument is detailed in Chapter 2: Success demonstrated by salient interest groups, decline of trust in government, multiplication of regulatory agencies and government programs, acceptance of pluralism as a goal, and demystification of interest group behavior. All contributed to expanding the numbers of interest groups and to the growth of many existing organizations. Interest group entrepreneurs were able to approach constituencies that were learning of the potential in interest group advocacy.

The appeal of lobbying organizations to new constituencies explains only part of their growth. Equally important has been the ability of groups to tap additional sources of money that allow them to grow beyond the limits of their rank-and-file membership dues. Competitiveness among like-minded organizations for the same group of people willing to donate money, and the increasing number of groups that have entered that competition have forced lobbies to be more aggressive to maintain themselves.

To begin with, where does interest money come from? Jack Walker's survey of interest groups provides interesting data. Various kinds of groups differ substantially in their dependence on dues.

---

[32] See, generally, Wilson, *Political Organizations*.

Groups in the "profit-sector" category (mostly trade associations) draw three-quarters (76.8 percent) of their funds from membership dues. The other types of organizations in his sample (citizen groups, nonprofits, and profit and nonprofit mixed memberships) receive only about one-third to one-half of their funds from membership dues.[33] Where does the rest of the money come from? The following sources of money supplement dues as interest group income.

FOUNDATIONS. Citizen groups, which receive the smallest part of their money from members, are the biggest beneficiaries of foundation money among all types of lobbies. Liberal public interest lobbies received extraordinary support from foundations during the 1970s. Between 1970 and 1980, the Ford Foundation contributed roughly $21 million to liberal groups under its public interest law program.[34] Likewise, foundation support for conservative public interest law firms has been instrumental to their success. The conservative National Legal Center for the Public Interest received roughly $1.8 million from Scaife Family foundations during the last decade.[35]

FEES AND PUBLICATIONS. A common source of interest group income is the money they derive from publications, conferences, and training institutes. One way in which some groups make money is by selling advertising in their magazines. *Modern Maturity*, a publication of the NRTA/AARP, appeals to advertisers who have products to sell to older consumers, such as health insurance, wheat germ, and nonprescription pain relievers.

For the majority of groups that just have newsletters, selling advertising is not feasible because they are not a particularly attractive medium. Staffers' expertise can be put to use for profit in other ways, though. With their unusually good command of their issues, interest group activists and researchers are able to produce handbooks, booklets, and even full-size books that can be marketed to the general public. Staffers for the Health Research Group produced

---

[33] Jack L. Walker, "The Origins and Maintenance of Interest Groups in America," *American Political Science Review* 77 (June 1983), p. 400.

[34] *The Public Interest Law Firm* (New York: Ford Foundation, 1973; *Public Interest Law: Five Years Later* (New York: Ford Foundation, 1976); and "Ford Ends Public Interest Law Program," *Citizen Participation* 1 (January/February 1980), p. 9.

[35] James W. Singer, "Liberal Public Interest Law Firms Face Budgetary, Ideological Challenges," *National Journal*, December 8, 1979, pp. 2052–2056; and "Where the Money Goes," *Common Cause*, August 1981, p. 15.

a bestseller, *Pills That Don't Work*, which brought roughly $1 million to the organization. Sales of that magnitude are uncommon, but it is not at all unusual for a group to count on publications for a modest segment of its income.[36] Interest groups can also use specialists on their staffs to attract individuals for training institutes. The American Bankers Association runs many institutes to help bank personnel develop skills, including a four-day institute on regulatory compliance. Those who attend are promised a program that "will give students an advanced level of regulatory knowledge and skills to develop and manage systems, policies, and procedures to cope with complex regulations." Cost of tuition, room, board, and materials is $950 for ABA members and $1,100 for nonmembers.[37]

SUGAR DADDIES. Leaders of organizations know that they can substantially increase the group's activities if they can add large individual donations to the sum they raise through regular membership fees. Furthermore, for groups with little or no membership support, large donations from sugar daddies may be their lifeblood. This was the source for the National Welfare Rights Organization during the few years that it flourished. Its dynamic leader, George Wiley, was effective in face-to-face meetings with wealthy liberals. Some of these, like Anne Farnsworth Peretz (heiress to the Singer Sewing Machine fortune) and Audrey Stern Hess (granddaughter of the founder of Sears, Roebuck), contributed large sums to keep the militant civil rights organization going for a while.[38]

A group representing people on welfare certainly needs large donations, yet many other kinds of interest groups rely in part on such gifts. The National Association of Manufacturers receives a disproportionate share of its funds from a few very large firms that are members. These large gifts in the form of "dues" give the lobby tremendous financial resources while allowing it to keep dues reasonable for smaller manufacturers and thereby hold them in the organization.[39]

[36] Michael deCourcy Hinds, "Advocacy Units Seek New Funds," *The New York Times*, January 9, 1982.
[37] "ABA Newsletter," *Banking Journal*, April 1982, p. 24b.
[38] Nick Kotz and Mary Lynn Kotz, *A Passion for Equality* (New York: Norton, 1977), pp. 241–242.
[39] Moe, *The Organization of Interests*, pp. 193–194.

GOVERNMENT GRANTS. A main factor in interest groups' growth since the 1960s is the parallel growth in domestic spending by the federal government. The categorical grant programs of the 1960s and 1970s made funds available to citizen groups, nonprofit professional organizations, and trade associations. These interest groups aggressively seek federal grant money for training, planning, economic development, and other activities and projects.

The Council of State Community Affairs Agencies (COSCAA) is an example. It started in 1974 with a budget for the year of $25,000. Its two staff members were supported by dues from nine states. Within six years it had grown to a nine-person staff and an annual budget of more than one-half million dollars. All fifty states had become members, but most of the budget's growth came from grants by the Economic Development Administration, the Farmers' Home Administration, the Office of Personnel Management, and the National Science Foundation.[40]

The cuts in domestic spending by the Reagan administration reduced the grant money available to interest groups. Even so, prospects for groups that receive a good part of their budget from the federal government are not necessarily dim. Interest groups have flourished precisely because they have found diverse sources of income.[41] Groups that lose federal money will explore other possible sources of funding, and if the past twenty years are any indication, many will be successful. When additional sources of income outside the membership are not available, a group may find that it needs to intensify its efforts to find new members. Sometimes consultants are hired to suggest new membership strategies, or more of the existing resources are devoted to membership recruitment. Larger organizations with some financial reserves may invest in some new service designed to make membership more attractive. When membership of the National Association of Realtors dropped during the severe 1982 recession, the organization allocated $500,000 for a telecommunications network for member realtors across the country who could use it to list and search for properties.[42] Whatever the attractiveness

[40] *COSCAA: Six Years and Beyond* (Washington, D.C.: COSCAA, 1980), p. 4.

[41] Walker, "The Origins and Maintenance of Interest Groups." The rise of the public interest movement in particular would not have been possible without a strong base of nonmembership funds. See Jeffrey M. Berry, *Lobbying for the People* (Princeton: Princeton University Press, 1977), pp. 71–76.

[42] Timothy D. Schellhardt, "Layoffs, Cutbacks Spread to Trade Groups in Autos, Housing, Other Hard-Hit Fields," *Wall Street Journal*, March 3, 1982.

of a group's issue coverage and benefits package, it must work hard to seek out new funds from potential members or outside donors. Otherwise, it risks organizational decline.

CONCLUSION

During the last two decades people became increasingly aware of the potential for interest group advocacy. The civil rights and Vietnam War movements catalyzed formation of countless citizen groups. Business reacted aggressively to new challenges by the consumer and environmental movements by redoubling its efforts in Washington. Growth in government gave more and more constituencies a direct stake in policy decisions being made at the federal level. The development of new interest groups and expansion of old ones has drawn support from the groups' improving ability to market themselves. By heavy investment in fundraising and by developing new sources of funding, Washington lobbies have been able to attract greater financial resources.

The rapid expansion of interest group advocacy in recent years highlights shortcomings in prevailing theories of interest group origins and maintenance. None of the three theorists we have discussed — David Truman, Robert Salisbury, or Mancur Olson — offers a completely satisfactory framework for understanding the development of interest groups. Still, parts of each work provide insight into the ways in which interest groups form and attract money from constituents. Technological changes and disturbances do create a climate in which interest groups can form. Benefits do attract members to lobbies, and members' satisfaction with those benefits is related to their decisions on renewal. Further research is needed, however, to improve our understanding of the relationship between membership incentives and the origins and maintenance of interest groups.

In short, interest groups have prospered because of broad political changes that have made people aware of the advantages of interest group advocacy, and because individual entrepreneurs have grown skilled in organizing and maintaining interest groups. This, in turn, has brought greater representation to more and more constituencies.

CHAPTER FIVE

Interest Groups as Organizations

Membership dues and other funds raised by interest groups must be "converted" into actions representing the donors' interests. This work is critical to any lobby's overall effectiveness. Interest groups are *organizations*, and the way in which each organization makes decisions about its resources directly affects how well members' interests are represented before government.

Three aspects of organizational life deserve attention. First, what are the groups' governing structures? How much do the professional staff and rank-and-file members influence an organization's decision making? Second, how does a lobbying group allocate its resources, including both staff responsibilities and issue priorities? Third, how do lobbying organizations change?

WHO GOVERNS?

Like any other type of organization, interest groups must have a means for governing themselves. Even the smallest group with no more than a handful of staff members creates roles giving some workers more authority than others. The authority structure of an interest group generally provides a framework for decision making on allocating resources, selection of issues, personnel, change in leadership, lobbying tactics, bylaws, and accountability of staff.

Authority

Despite the tremendous diversity among interest groups, they approach self-governance with the same impulse to create democratic organizational structures.[1] The founding bylaws of an interest group almost always prescribe a procedure whereby some body representing the membership, such as a board of directors or an annual convention, has final authority over all major decisions. Even if, like some public interest groups, a group has no real membership, it is still likely to have an independent governing board with formal (if rarely exercised) authority over staff operations.[2]

Just as it is true that interest groups almost always appear on the outside to be democratic, it also seems that they are almost always oligarchic on the inside.[3] This contradiction will not surprise anyone who has belonged to a voluntary organization of some kind. A small cadre of workers invariably seem to dominate such organizations. Relatively few of the rank and file feel they have much time to devote to the organizations they belong to. The full-time staff, with their greater command over information and organizational resources, easily gain preeminent influence within the organization. This natural tendency, which sociologist Robert Michels described as the "iron law of oligarchy," is pervasive among interest groups.[4]

Although interest groups are generally oligarchic, groups differ in the amount of influence the rank and file or the board of directors have within the organization. In some lobbies, members do actually exert some significant and direct influence on organizational decisions, yet these differences do not seem easily explained by the way lobbying organizations are designed. Compare the American Hospital Association (AHA) and the U.S. Conference of Mayors. Both have conventions twice yearly at which the memberships have an opportunity to formulate policy. Both also have boards that meet periodically during the year to make timely decisions about questions of policy.

The similarity in the formal governing structures of these organizations tells little about the way they are actually run. Mayors have a much larger part in their organization than hospital administrators do in theirs. An AHA spokesman said that issues are not brought

[1] David B. Truman, *The Governmental Process* (New York: Knopf, 1951), pp. 129–139.
[2] Jeffrey M. Berry, *Lobbying for the People* (Princeton: Princeton University Press, 1977), pp. 195–199.
[3] Truman, *The Governmental Process*, pp. 139–155.
[4] Robert Michels, *Political Parties* (New York: Free Press, 1958). Originally published in 1915.

"raw" to House of Delegates' conferences. Rather, the staff "massages the issues through the system," so that by the time they hit the agenda of the House of Delegates, the positions are fairly clear. A spokesman for the Conference of Mayors paints a different picture. The large conventions and board meetings give the mayors an opportunity to set priorities. "Lobbying is completely determined by the policies passed by the mayors," said one staffer.

Why the differences between the organizations? To the AHA lobbyist, the marginal role played by rank-and-file members makes perfect sense. "Statutory and regulatory problems are the business of AHA. The hospital administrators are too busy running their hospitals." Mayors, on the other hand, see statutory and regulatory problems as very much their business. As elected officials, they feel more comfortable and confident dealing in the political world. They are much more aware of the direct influence of Washington policy on their jobs. Finally, the partisan differences between Republican and Democratic mayors places an unusual constraint on the organization. Mayors of the party controlling the White House do not want the staff of the organization working against the president's domestic policies unless they give them specific permission to do so.

Some organizations make a concerted effort to elicit the membership's views before setting policies.[5] Common Cause polls its members, then its board uses the responses in setting priorities. Yet the vast majority of interest groups use a governing structure like that of the AHA and the Conference of Mayors, whose board and possibly national conference are the means by which members theoretically "control" the staff. In most of these groups, the staff runs the organization with modest guidance and little direct interference.

In sum, then, we have two conclusions. First, the governing structures of lobbies, as laid out in their written charters, usually do little to stop the iron law of oligarchy from taking hold. Only if a group takes exceptional steps to build in polling or some other device for direct control by the membership does the formal structure of a lobbying organization make much difference in the way the group is governed. Second, if rank-and-file members of an organization are going to have anything more than a passive role in making decisions, they have to prove to the lobbying staff that they will be highly

5 Rarely are there regular, competitive elections within a group. See Seymour Martin Lipset, Martin Trow, and James Coleman, *Union Democracy* (Garden City, N.Y.: Anchor Books, 1956).

active and will not acquiesce to faits accomplis. Few organizations have this type of membership.

Anticipation

Dominance by staff in most interest groups may seem to be a rather undemocratic and disconcerting part of interest group politics. Still, though members generally have very little direct influence over the staff of their organization, they do have a great deal of indirect influence. Remember that most interest groups are voluntary organizations. Members can "vote with their feet" by leaving the group if they don't like what the organization is doing.[6]

That membership is generally voluntary is fundamental to the relationship between leaders and followers in these organizations. Members join groups because they agree strongly with its goals. As we saw in Chapter 4, even if some material benefit or service is an attractive inducement to join, political goals can remain an instrumental part of the decision. Consequently, rank-and-file members usually do not worry about how important organizational decisions are made because they observe the lobbying group pursuing the issues they feel strongly about. One trade association lobbyist said of his membership: "They care about the results, not how we get them."

Despite the trust members have in their staffs, continued support of those members is not ensured. The initial issues that bring people into a group may lose importance and be replaced by others. The staff must anticipate reactions by members to these new issues as they rise to the fore.[7] As the organization leaders consider how to approach an issue, they ask themselves what their members want. It is not usually difficult for them to anticipate the membership's preferences, however, because limited resources largely restrict groups to their most important issues. Environmental groups do not have to stop to think about whether their members are in favor of strengthening the Clean Air Act when it comes before Congress.

At times, however, those governing an interest group cannot take the membership's stance on an issue for granted. A difficult problem

[6] Albert O. Hirschman, *Exit, Voice, and Loyalty* (Cambridge: Harvard University Press, 1970).

[7] Norman R. Luttbeg and Harmon Zeigler, "Attitude Consensus and Conflict in an Interest Group," *American Political Science Review* 60 (September 1966), pp. 655–666.

arises when an issue affects some members of a group differently from others. This divergence can be particularly troublesome to large peak associations such as the Chamber of Commerce, whose membership includes almost all kinds of businesses.[8] Even a trade association representing one industry can be constrained by the differential effects of an issue. The American Petroleum Institute (API) is an example. Many proposals pertaining to the oil industry affect companies quite differently because they vary in size, ranging from behemoths like Exxon and Mobil to the small independent wildcatter. Smaller companies often want to be treated separately by Congress when it is writing tax laws for the industry, knowing that there is more sympathy for the "little guy" than for the giant corporations. As a result, says one API lobbyist, consensus on many issues is a "long time coming." On broad issues cutting across the membership, API's stand is sometimes "no stand" due to lack of consensus.

When the leaders of a group perceive a strong view in some segment of the membership that is contrary to the organization's general policy, they will usually prefer to shy away from fighting the issue out. The American Farm Bureau Federation has long espoused a free market for agricultural products. When the free-market Reagan administration proposed changes in price supports for peanuts in 1981, the Farm Bureau decided discretion was the better part of valor. Knowing that some of its members in the Southeast would be furious if the organization agreed with weakening peanut supports, the group did not back the Reagan plan, fearing to lose those members.[9]

Sometimes, however, interest groups are subjected to outright rebellion by dissidents in the organization. Among interest groups, labor unions seem most susceptible to open conflict within the ranks. A primary reason is that labor union members cannot really vote with their feet and leave the organization if they are dissatisfied. Workers who begin employment at a plant or office where union membership is required, are not given a choice as to the union they might like to join. Their union has already been determined by collective bargaining agreements. In recent years, the Teamsters, the United Steelworkers, and the United Mine Workers have all been subjected to

---

[8] See William J. Lanouette, "Chamber's Ponderous Decision Making Leaves It Sitting on the Sidelines," *National Journal*, July 24, 1982, pp. 1298–1301.
[9] William P. Browne, "Farm Organizations and Agribusiness," in Don F. Hadwiger and Ross B. Talbot, *Food Policy and Farm Programs* (New York: Academy of Political Science, 1982), p. 211.

serious internal conflicts. A dissident movement in the United Mine Workers (UMW) was spurred on in 1981 by an unpopular contract settlement that the union negotiated with mine owners. The anger of UMW members led to defeat of incumbent union President Sam Church in 1982 at the hands of insurgent candidate Richard Trumka.[10] When dissatisfaction comes out in a voluntary organization, though, dissent is more likely to be manifested by people declining to renew their memberships. After the American Civil Liberties Union (ACLU) defended the right of the American Nazi party to march in the heavily Jewish suburb of Skokie, Illinois, they suffered a drop in membership. Many Jewish members cast a negative vote toward the ACLU leadership by leaving the organization.[11]

For every UMW or ACLU case, however, hundreds of interest groups hear nary a discouraging word from their members. Harmony continues in most groups because of congruence between members' opinions and the avowed purposes of the organization. Also, because in voluntary organizations, most internal protest consists of the relatively passive act of failing to renew one's membership. Finally, peace usually reigns within interest groups because staff members are careful not to move the organization toward policy positions that are likely to alienate a significant portion of the membership. For almost all interest group staffers, maintaining the organization is more important than ideological purity.

Corporations

Our discussion of business lobbies has been focused on trade associations, which, of course, represent a number of businesses in an industry. With the rapid increase in interest group representation in Washington, more and more individual corporations have opened a Washington office for "public affairs" or "governmental relations."[12] These lobbies have no real memberships and are accountable only to top corporate officers. Their governing structure is rather different from anything described above.

---

[10] William Serrin, "President-Elect of United Mine Workers," *The New York Times*, November 11, 1982.

[11] Tom Goldstein, "The ACLU Finds Another Issue: Itself," *The New York Times*, April 23, 1978; and Jim Mann, "Hard Times for the ACLU," *New Republic*, April 15, 1978, pp. 12–15.

[12] *Public Affairs Offices and Their Functions* (Boston: Boston University School of Management, 1981).

Although corporations differ substantially from trade associations, they must still develop an authority structure to determine *who* decides what when it comes to government relations. Who in the corporate chain of command does the head of the Washington office report to? How much authority does the Washington office have for making decisions on its own?

Usually the head of a corporation's Washington lobbying office reports to a senior vice-president of the firm. If the person running the office is a company vice-president, that officer may report directly to the chief executive officer of the company or to a higher vice-president at headquarters. The important question is not how the boxes on a company's organization chart are formally arranged, but where the decision-making authority really lies. The answer is that the corporate world has not determined any best way of structuring relationships between headquarters and Washington. Rather, companies vary considerably in the manner and degree to which they supervise their lobbying offices.[13]

The various relationships between the Washington office and the corporate headquarters can best be thought of as a continuum. At one end is a mostly independent Washington office, such as the Washington operation of LTV, a large conglomerate. One of the company's lobbyists describes his office:

> Most of the issues that we take positions on, we know our business and we know what affects it. We don't need a lot of research. My deputy and my boss and I have been here so long that we pretty well know [what to do]. There aren't too many new issues. We formulate the policies for the company. There is no formal structure.

At the other end of the continuum is a highly formal decision-making structure, in which the headquarters office carefully considers positions the Washington office should take. Bethlehem Steel operates in this fashion. Says one of its Washington lobbyists:

> We have a system here where we are the early warning. We determine which items are going to be issues and which are not. If they will have an impact on our organization, we send it back to the home office. The home office develops a position and it's sent back to us.

[13] Phyllis S. McGrath, *Redefining Corporate-Federal Relations* (New York: Conference Board, 1979).

Other companies represent intermediate points on this continuum, with varying levels of headquarters involvement in Washington operations. All companies, though, must rely heavily on their Washington people for advice because determining a company's official position on issues is only part of the job.[14] Important strategic decisions must also be made about what to compromise on, what to fight for, and what to give up on so as not waste scarce resources. Washington staffers have to take the lead in such day-to-day strategizing. Lobbyists are a company's eyes and ears in the capital. No matter who makes the final decisions, they will be based mainly on information supplied by the government relations staff.

DESIGN OF THE ORGANIZATION

The differences between a consultative operation like Bethlehem Steel and a freehand operation like LTV raises a central issue. How does the organizational design of an interest group's Washington office affect its ability to accomplish its lobbying mission?

A lobbying office can be broken down by hierarchy and roles in many ways. In the smaller offices, the structure is usually much less hierarchic and highly informal. Often, most of or all the professionals will hold a similar rank under the director's supervision. A lobbyist for the ACLU described the Washington office as one in which "There is very little hierarchy, which makes for a very pleasant working environment. All the lobbyists have to do all the same things and are paid the same. We have to testify, lobby, travel, do speaking engagements, etc." The number of lobbyists in the ACLU is five, making it practical to run an office in this manner.

An office of five professionals is in the medium-sized category for Washington. We have no precise number for the mean (average) number of professionals who work in all types of Washington lobbies, but evidence indicates that a typical office employs five or fewer.[15] (When interest group representatives are interviewed, they usually refer to employees who have responsibilities directly related to trying to influence government, the media, or constituents as "professionals." "Support staff" usually means clerical workers and

---

[14] See "Government Relations at TRW, Inc.," Harvard Business School Case 0-382-053 (1981).

[15] Berry, *Lobbying for the People*, p. 62; McGrath, *Redefining Corporate-Federal Relations*, p. 62; and *Public Affairs Offices and Their Functions*, p. 8.

researchers.) The relatively small size of most Washington lobbying operations makes the idea of a command or authority structure within the offices rather meaningless. There is the director and everyone else.

Staff Specialization

The lack of a meaningful organization chart in small and medium-sized groups does not mean that no important differences appear in the way division of labor is handled. Even if decision making is informal, staff responsibilities still must be assigned. Groups handle it differently, but the most common way of dividing the work is by either *functional specialization* or *issue specialization*. The simplest arrangement, a group that has two Washington lobbyists, could have one cover Congress and the other administrative agencies. Or it could assign the first to cover one set of issues while giving the second another set. A lobbyist would do the advocacy work on these issues whether they were before Congress or an agency.

These are pure types, and often functional assignments and issue assignments overlap. The American Association of State Highway and Transportation Officials has four professionals. One, the director, is a lobbyist who handles legislative and administrative advocacy, and three are engineers, whose technical expertise contributes to all aspects of the director's work.

As organizations grow, the division of labor becomes more complex and offices are set up with increasing diversity. The National Education Association (NEA) has twenty-eight employees in the Division of Government Relations. The president, vice-president, and executive director of the NEA are involved with this division daily, overseeing its operations and making policy decisions for the organization. Beneath them are two managers, one in charge of legislative lobbying and the other responsible for administrative lobbying. Six full-time lobbyists work in the division along with seven researchers and writers in its "Information" section. There is also a coordinator for the congressional district contact team and a staff person for each of six NEA regional offices (each responsible for one-sixth of the congressional districts and states). The clerical staff rounds out the government relations division's own employees, but this unit draws heavily on other divisions, such as legal counsel and communications, when the need arises.

As organizations grow, more specialized roles in organizational maintenance also develop. These are jobs dealing with membership services and recruiting of members. The organization chart (Figure 5.1) of the National Association of Manufacturers (NAM) is instructive. Under one of the senior vice-presidents is a Field Operations Division, which includes a Membership Development Department as well as regional coordinators. Aggressive marketing of the organization is particularly important to a group like the NAM because of its highly competitive situation. As a large peak association, it overlaps with numerous trade associations in various fields of manufacturing. It is also in an especially competitive position with the Chamber of Commerce, which serves much of the same clientele. The Chamber's membership has been growing in recent years while the NAM's has been declining.[16]

A clear division of labor between advocacy and maintenance of the organization makes obvious sense because very different skills are involved in dealing with the government and dealing with members' requests for services, organizing membership drives, designing recruitment materials, and evaluating marketing efforts. What may be less clear to interest group officials is the comparative value of assigning advocacy staffers on the basis of issue or functional specializations. As will be argued here and in Chapter 6, expertise on issues is exceptionally valuable to lobbyists in day-to-day work before Congress or administrative agencies. Nevertheless, many interest group offices are not organized to maximize the issue specialization of their lobbyists.

Effects of Size

The best explanation for interest groups' not uniformly adopting issues as a basis for organizing their lobbyists seems to be the size of Washington offices. For the small offices that predominate, the number of issues and volume of work may make division of labor by specializing on issues difficult if not impractical. For a two-person office to conduct a major lobbying effort on one issue, it may well take each of them months of nearly full-time work while a bill works its way through the congressional committees. If that office has many

16 Robert S. Greenberger, "Manufacturers' Lobby Alters Style to Combat Its Obstructionist Image," *Wall Street Journal*, May 5, 1981; and Lanouette, "Chamber's Ponderous Decision Making."

Figure 5.1
Organization of the National Association of Manufacturers

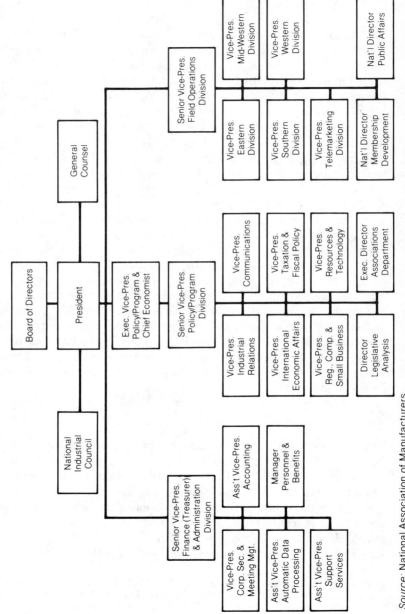

Source: National Association of Manufacturers.

such issues to follow, work assignments may readily evolve so that one person works the House and the other the Senate. Lobbyists in the office may come with different backgrounds, which may also structure their work assignments. A former agency official may easily feel more comfortable doing administrative advocacy, leaving the legislative lobbying to one or more colleagues.

For large Washington offices, specialization on issues may not be the principle of organization because of the sheer scope of their lobbying efforts and the research and support staff available to the lobbyists. A large staff such as that of the National Education Association can aim a concerted lobbying effort at just about all the members of Congress rather than focusing only on key committee members. Hence, a number of staff positions are assigned solely to coordinating grassroots campaigns so that it will complement the group's Capitol Hill lobbying.

In large interest groups and individual corporations it is only natural that separate research staffs develop to service many types of organizational tasks. They are needed as a resource for everything from publications to speeches for the director. Expertise on issues at the lobbying level may seem to duplicate expertise at other organizational levels, and therefore some interest group managers may seem to feel that *political* qualities, such as legislative or administrative experience, should guide staffing of their lobbying unit.

Lobbying is, of course, much more than just quoting facts and figures to government officials and their staffers. Building coalitions with other interest groups and catalyzing grassroots support are critical in congressional or administrative lobbying campaigns. Yet day in, day out, most of a lobbyist's job has to do with the sum and substance of issues. Profound knowledge of an issue is an advantage a lobbyist carries into battle. Other attributes can outweigh lack of superior expertise, but expertise can only help a lobbyist in his or her work.[17]

When a group has a strong support staff in Washington, the disadvantages of not organizing by issues are at least minimized. Having

---

[17] Hugh Heclo, "Issue Networks and the Executive Establishment," in Anthony King, ed., *The New American Political System* (Washington, D.C.: American Enterprise Institute, 1978), pp. 87–124; Robert W. Kweit and Mary Griesez Kweit, "Bureaucratic Decision-Making: Impediments to Citizen Participation," *Polity* 12 (Summer 1980), pp. 647–666; and Jeffrey M. Berry, "Beyond Citizen Participation: Effective Advocacy Before Administrative Agencies," *Journal of Applied Behavioral Science* 17 (October 1981), pp. 463–477.

people at their fingertips can shore up lobbyists by giving them quick responses for information they need. The problem can be exacerbated when the lobbyist or office manager has to reach further back into the organization, such as a trade association having to go to individual companies, or a corporate public affairs office having to go to line managers of the firm. The head of Gulf Oil's Washington office explains:

> One of my most difficult jobs is getting managers to provide me with detailed data on an issue. I have to first convince them that these are not useless exercises wasting thousands of dollars and their valuable time. They sometimes have the attitude of "let the boys in Washington handle this one. We're in the middle of a refinery turnaround and don't have time to gather this information." Or they say: "This is private Gulf information; if the government wants it, let them find it."[18]

To counteract this type of problem, the TRW company, a diversified manufacturer, has institutionalized the "quarterback system." When an issue develops, a quarterback at the headquarters office in Cleveland is identified to give the responsible Washington lobbyist a partner to work with. The quarterback communicates with people in the operating units and secures the information and cooperation that is necessary.[19]

Expertise is, of course, a matter of degree. Interest group lobbyists all have some familiarity with the issues; it is really a question of how much. Organizations must, therefore, decide if they want their lobbyists to develop technical mastery of a few issues by allowing them to concentrate on those issues, or if they want to sacrifice some expertise to maximize the lobbyists' coverage. No textbook gives rules for organizing a lobbying office, and so each organization follows its instincts and experience to find what will work best. Yet, as issues have become more and more complex, expertise on issues more and more determines how well lobbyists carry out their job. Indeed, a study of corporate-government relations concludes, "A growing trend seems to be for Washington offices to organize on an issues basis rather than assigning a person, or persons, to each branch of the government."[20]

[18] J. Ronald Fox, "Gulf Oil Corporation: Public Affairs and the Washington Office," Harvard Business School Case 9-380-143 (revised, 1981), p. 12.
[19] "Government Relations at TRW," pp. 11–13.
[20] McGrath, *Redefining Corporate-Federal Relations*, p. 67.

Within the constraints (or opportunities) of an interest group's resources, it makes great sense to try to create roles that maximize the lobbyist's proficiency with issues.

MAKING DECISIONS

We have dwelt on how organizations are designed to carry out their tasks, and who has the authority to decide what those tasks will be. We can now study the actual dynamics of how decisions are made. On a continuum of authority with staff dominance at one end and direct membership involvement at the other, staff-dominated organizations are more common. In organizations whose members are heavily involved, the decision-making structure becomes complex because of broader participation. Such organizations must develop a practical means of selecting issues to lobby upon. No matter how democratic an organization sincerely wants to be, it is unwieldy to involve large numbers of people in making decisions. Annual conventions can do little more than offer broad direction to the professional staff. One means of getting periodic membership input into decision making is to have an executive council of members that meets every few months. Unless the members of such a council are aggressive in staking out their role, however, they can easily come to play a minor role in the organization. Another method is the task force, on which the Business Roundtable relies to draw upon the prestige and influence of chief executive officers (CEOs) of member firms.[21] To successfully involve these CEOs and to get them to commit time to the organization, they must be given a real say in deciding its direction.

The Business Roundtable has task forces in international trade, regulatory reform, antitrust, taxation, energy, and many other areas, all chaired by a CEO of a member firm. By the staff's account, the chairmen of these task forces are quite active in developing the policy recommendations to be made. Yet in the Roundtable, as in so many other lobbies, deciding on issue positions is not the dilemma they face. Rather, says a top official of the group, the real question the CEOs find themselves asking is, "Why do *we* have to get in on this issue?"

[21] Mark Green and Andrew Buchsbaum, *The Corporate Lobbies* (Washington, D.C.: Public Citizen, 1980); and Kim McQuaid, "The Roundtable: Getting Results in Washington," *Harvard Business Review* 59 (May/June 1981), pp. 114–123.

Even this relatively wealthy organization, with its own budget in the low millions and access to the resources of member firms, is limited in the number of issues it can work on. For interest groups, the law of resources is that *on any given day, any given group will have many more relevant issues before it than it can possibly handle.* Whether a group is staff dominated or has some direct membership influence, allocating resources between issues is the most troublesome part of making decisions.

How do organizations deal with this problem of setting priorities? There are no clear-cut decision rules, but this description by a lobbyist for the National Council of Senior Citizens (NCSC) is instructive:

> We try to [make decisions] on as rational a basis as possible. We first judge the potential impact on older people. Generally speaking, we represent all elderly people, but primarily due to our own lack of resources, we concern ourselves with the low-income elderly. We are more likely, therefore, to be more involved with an issue like a reduction in the cost of living adjustment rather than the reauthorization of the FTC — although there are issues there of concern to all elderly. We try to quantify things. We make judgments based on the [interests of the] needier. We also have to make judgments on the basis of timeliness. Things change. It's an evolving sort of process here in Washington. We have to govern our flow of work on the basis of how things come up on Capitol Hill. This tends to create some confusion. Sometimes it's not easy to decide what to let go of.

A number of important points about decision making by interest groups appear in this account. First, leaders of interest groups do try to think systematically about how to budget their resources. The National Council of Senior Citizens tries to be "rational" and to "quantify things." Yet the lobbyist also acknowledges that much of their decision making comes down to "judgment." This is the contradiction that all interest group officials must live with. They do try to think rationally about resource allocations by weighing the merits of each issue in relation to the interests of their constituency. Relative merits, though, can never be calculated by a formula or strict decision rule. Rather, human judgment must be relied upon.

Second, some issues matter so deeply to the organization that without question they must receive high priority for lobbying resources. For the NCSC, the "reduction in the cost of living adjustment" issue (proposals in 1982 to cut back the otherwise automatic indexing of social security payments to rises in the cost of living) was absolutely vital to the well-being of the group's constituents. Some issues command a large commitment of an organization's resources and other decisions must be made around those issues. As the lobbyist for another group put it, "On the hot issues, we know what they are and there's little debating."

Third, the timeliness of issues makes planning extremely hard. Interest groups do not control their own destiny, because they cannot control the political agenda. The NCSC may not have adequately anticipated that adjustment in the cost of living indexing for social security would be such a central issue in 1982. Some other cost-saving "reforms" of the system that had been raised in 1981 were judged to be such a liability to the incumbent Republican administration that they were quickly dropped. Yet when reform of the social security system reemerged on the agenda in 1982, there was more support for making changes in the cost of living provision than many people expected. No matter how carefully an interest group plans allocation of its resources over the next year, it is always going to be it-all-depends planning.

Fourth, and finally, it is much easier for an interest group to take on a new issue than to drop a current one. Just because a new issue vital to the group arises, other issues do not become unimportant. Consequently, "it's not easy to decide what to let go of." Issues can become less pressing in a relative sense as the lobbyists rush to an emergency that needs their immediate attention. Nevertheless, interest group staffers do not operate on a zero-sum principle; for every new allocation of their time they do not consciously eliminate an equally time-consuming activity. In practice, of course, the zero-sum principle must hold because the day has only so many hours. Issues get "crowded out" by the demands of more urgent issues without some official articulation of a new ordering of priorities.[22]

These generalizations describe the dynamics of resource allocation. There are, of course, variations. Some years can be stable for an interest group, with few surprise issues or relevant changes in the political environment. Eventually, though, the problems outlined here plague all types of interest groups. They have trouble planning and

[22] See Charles Lindblom, "The Science of Muddling Through," *Public Administration Review* 19 (Spring 1959), pp. 79–88.

their allocation of resources evolves out of incremental decisions, many of which are "automatic" because they involve issues at the core of the group's purpose.

ORGANIZATIONAL CHANGE

Like all other types of organizations, interest groups undergo change, sometimes deliberately, sometimes accidentally, and most often by gradual evolution. "Change" in an interest group organization can be analyzed as it affects leadership, direction of policy, and financial and membership support.

Leadership

The most critical time for an interest group to change leaders is when it must go from the founding enterpreneur to the successor.[23] During its formative years, the organization is very much a personal vehicle reflecting the founder's views of how an organization should be run. The organization's success in getting off the ground also reflects the entrepreneur's ability to raise money to maintain it. When leadership is transferred to someone new, the danger is always that the new person will not be able to raise adequate funds or manage the organization under the old bureaucratic apparatus left by the predecessor.

When the founder of a group leaves, members must decide if theirs is a faith in the organization or in the person leading it. For an organization that has some type of nonideological benefit as part of the membership package, it is easier to see that benefit as stemming from the organization. When the reason for joining is primarily ideological, the struggle of good against evil can easily take on David and Goliath imagery. When David is gone, his replacement may not rekindle the sense of struggle.

Although this problem is significant for all lobbies, it is particularly acute for citizen groups. Trade associations usually have companies as members or individuals paid for by companies. Their renewals are steadier and changes in support tend to be more gradual than in citizen groups. Because labor unions' membership is mostly involuntary because of closed-shop agreements, sudden changes in membership usually reflect economic conditions that determine employment rates.

[23] Theodore J. Lowi, *The Politics of Disorder* (New York: Basic Books, 1971).

Citizen groups, with their hypercompetitive atmosphere and tremendous vulnerability to changes in issue salience can be dramatically affected by a change at the top. An example is the Southern Christian Leadership Conference (SCLC), a civil rights group founded by the late Martin Luther King, Jr. As King became the preeminent leader of the civil rights movement during the 1960s, the SCLC prospered, drawing both blacks and whites to the organization. After King was assassinated in 1968, Ralph Abernathy was selected as his successor. Five years later, the SCLC stood "on the brink of extinction" and Abernathy resigned under pressure.[24]

Was the SCLC's decline the fault of Abernathy? It seems appropriate to place a good deal of the blame on him. Abernathy did not work as well with the staff, and particularly gifted aides left the organization. After skyrocketing at King's death, financial support began to decline. The civil rights movement was changing: segregation and voting discrimination had been outlawed by legislation, and "economic rights" became a new focus. Yet Abernathy and other black leaders were unable to coalesce the supporting elements of the civil rights movement into the same type of powerful force when it came to economic issues.

It was not Abernathy's fault that the political and social environment changed around the civil rights movement. Still, he did not cope with change as well as the leaders of other black organizations.[25] It is certainly true that no one could have filled the shoes of a charismatic figure like Martin Luther King. In retrospect, however, it seems clear that someone else could have done a better job in helping the SCLC in making the hard transition from being King's group to being the SCLC in the post-King era.

Despite the difficulty in transition between first and second leaders, many organizations handle it successfully. Common Cause did so smoothly despite the group's long identification with its founder, John Gardner. Gardner left the top position voluntarily and quietly at a time when the organization was stable. He was replaced by a highly qualified lieutenant, David Cohen, who had been with Com-

---

[24] Joel Dreyfuss, "Crisis at SCLC," *Washington Post*, June 24, 1973.
[25] Another group that declined was the Student Nonviolent Coordinating Committee, whose leadership could not successfully bring the group from a protest-oriented organization to one able to enter the mainstream of interest group politics. See Clayborne Carson, *In Struggle* (Cambridge: Harvard University Press, 1981).

mon Cause from the start. The organization already had a bureau-cratized decision-making process, or as Theodore Lowi says, it had undergone a "managerial takeover."[26] If an interest group hopes to remain successful and stable it must move beyond dependence on its leader's abilities to dependence on the *organization's* capabilities.[27]

Policy Direction

When we compare an interest group's current issues with those which preoccupied it twenty years earlier, we are likely to see substantial differences. In the 1960s, the United Auto Workers' union was not dealing with Japanese imports or job security for longtime employees. These issues are absolutely vital to today's union, which cannot focus on wage and benefit improvements as much as it did in the past.

Although the focus on issues can change considerably, such changes rarely signify an abrupt change in direction for the organization. Efforts on new issues must appear to be in line with continuing issue interests. Lobbies are not like businesses that can expand into new fields just because they have the money to do so. The *Chicago Tribune* newspaper company can buy the Chicago Cubs baseball team and though the purchase may appear odd, it can be interpreted as an effort by the *Tribune* to invest its profits and grow. Interest groups simply cannot jump so far afield because they are constrained by their general policy goals. The National Cattleman's Association, for example, will find no credibility with government or support from its membership for lobbying on issues of little consequence to the cattle industry.

Changes in focus therefore are usually incremental and in line with an organization's long-term objectives. But if the direction of an organization must appear to be consistent, the *scope* of its efforts is not similarly limited. As its financial resources permit, an interest group can usually move into many new but organizationally relevant issues without alienating its membership.

Resource Cycles

When interest groups take on new issues to augment those they already cover, they have no assurance that their evolving coverage of

[26] Lowi, *The Politics of Disorder*, p. 48.
[27] Henry J. Pratt, *The Gray Lobby* (Chicago: University of Chicago Press, 1976), pp. 94–96.

issues will continue to attract the same level of financial support. Other interest groups may be more identified with such issues, resulting in more competition for members. Benefit packages may not be as attractive as they once were. The opposite can happen as well. An organization's membership can move sharply upward as an issue they are identified with becomes highly salient.[28] The National Audubon Society, founded in 1905, saw its membership go up in the late 1960s and early 1970s as Americans worried more about the environment. Lobbying groups, of course, can help raise interest in issues by their advocacy work and efforts in the media.

Some interest groups are more susceptible to swings in issue salience than others. Citizen groups probably have the greatest risk of being hurt by temporary changes in issues, but also the greatest potential for attracting large numbers of new adherents when an issue becomes hot.[29] When such changes take place, the changed resources must be managed.

Interest groups are labor-intensive organizations. What they do, they do primarily with people and not machines. Even for the side of an organization devoted to services, those services require large staffs for publications, casework, and other duties. How new dollars get allocated is a matter of hiring new staff, either for political positions or organizational maintenance. No rule of thumb tells how much one side of interest group organizations should grow in relation to the other. Managers of interest groups surely prefer political positions in the abstract, for they see the organization's primary goal as achieving public policy objectives. Yet the more professionals are hired, the more money must be brought in continually to support their salaries; the maintenance side of the organizations must do more.

Unlike a production line, whose output can be fine-tuned by a reduction in hours, a downward spiral in an interest group's income is not so easily adjusted to.[30] In a three- or four-person office, eliminating one professional staffer can be cataclysmic for the others. Salary freezes or reductions in support staffing are acts of last resort. Larger

[28] Anthony Downs, "Up and Down with Ecology — 'The Issue Attention Cycle,' " *Public Interest* 28 (Summer 1972), pp. 38–50.
[29] Jeffrey M. Berry and Bill Fisher, "Public Interest Groups as the Loyal Opposition," *Citizen Participation* 2 (July/August 1981), pp. 14–15.
[30] See Neil Maxwell, "Civil Rights Groups Face Tough Challenge in Bid to Regain Power," *Wall Street Journal*, September 19, 1980; and Robert S. Greenberger, "Recession Forces Organized Labor to Cut Staff and Some Programs," *Wall Street Journal*, December 23, 1982.

organizations may have enough reserves to ride out a downturn for a few years. For three years in a row the National Forest Products Association was able to incur a deficit of $400,000 or more because of a $1.6 million reserve. But looking to the future, the executive vice-president acknowledged, "We're walking on eggs." [31] For most interest groups, when income begins to drop, the organization must move more quickly to shrink its staff, and hence the quantity of its advocacy work.

CONCLUSION

Despite the attention that has been given to interest groups over the years, little unanimity has been reached on how lobbying organizations ought to be governed or how the division of labor ought to be structured. Lobbies also have trouble establishing firm priorities; they often find themselves reacting rather than planning. Selecting issues often means new emergencies crowding out other policy conflicts.

Yet interest groups are not organized in an irrational or even anomalous manner. They are not the only organizations that have no fixed rules to guide their division of labor. Governmental bureaucracies are constantly undergoing reorganization to find a more efficient way of delivering services. Business organizations too have trouble planning because their environment is so unpredictable. Car manufacturers place a high premium on planning, but nowhere in the American economy are mistakes in planning so conspicuous.

Clearly, the organizational problems of lobbies are not unique, yet little effort has been exerted to understand their organizational pathologies. Few political scientists have tried to systematically study interest groups to find the kinds of structures that are most productive. Little research has been done on the decision-making process in lobbying organizations. The organizer of a new interest group who wants to go by the book in setting up the organization can't — there is no book.

With more and more people contributing to interest groups and looking to lobbies as a primary means of political representation, the

[31] Timothy D. Schellhardt, "Layoffs, Cutbacks Spread to Trade Groups in Autos, Housing, Other Hard-Hit Fields," *Wall Street Journal*, March 23, 1982.

subject deserves more recognition. An interest group's ability to accomplish its goals is affected by its organizational strengths and weaknesses. Its allocation of resources, setting of priorities, leadership, and adaptation to change in the environment are all critical in determining how well it gets its political job done.

CHAPTER SIX

Lobbyists

The word "lobbyist" still conjures up a negative stereotype: a smooth-talking armtwister. The unsavory image associated with lobbyists comes from many scandals over the years involving representatives of interest groups who offered some illegal inducement to a government official. No wonder most lobbyists bridle at the title, claiming instead that they work in "public affairs" or "government relations." They resent the name not only because of its unflattering connotations but also because it doesn't adequately describe what they do.

Little of what a contemporary lobbyist does amounts to armtwisting or pressuring a government official with some sanction if the desired option is not followed. Very few lobbyists have done anything in their work that can be described as unethical. They work long hours under trying conditions to represent their constituents before government. No matter how professional they are on their job, though, theirs is not an occupation that is highly valued by the American people, nor one that is particularly well understood.

A DAY IN THE LIFE OF A LOBBYIST

To better appreciate and understand what lobbyists do, it is best to begin by simply asking how they spend their time. In interviews, a number of legislative lobbyists were asked to describe their "typical" day. Their responses, like this from a representative for a professional association, illustrate the job.

> I am one of those people who gets to work no later than 7:45. The first hour is spent reading the papers — the *Washington Post*, *Wall Street Journal*, and *New York Times*, trade

association publications, and the *Congressional Record* from the prior day. Each of these plays into my need to plan the activities for the current day. The next activity is meeting with the staff for a brief period to check the work plans for any changes. There is then one or more hearings on the Hill in the morning. After lunch, I usually meet with committee staff or use that time to lobby specific members of Congress. I'm usually back by 4:00 to meet with the support staff to check on what's happened while I was gone and if we are on top of the work planned for the day. About 5:30 I usually leave for some reception or fundraiser to represent [our group]. These settings give me an opportunity to swap stories and positions with members and other lobbyists who are concerned with the same issues we are. I usually get home for dinner about 8:00.

The head lobbyist for one of the nation's largest corporations describes his typical Monday:

I come in at 8:30. I usually get through the mail about 9:00 or so, then check the phone messages. I touch base with friends on the staff of the Senate Finance Committee, asking "What does it look like for this week?" "When are hearings?" I need to know what's scheduled for the week because I am concerned about the president's budget. I will check bases with these friends each week. I have a standing meeting at 11:00 with a public relations company. We are about one of twenty companies who have retained Gray & Co. to help us lead the fight opposing the president's alternative minimum tax. Gray & Co. has several lobbyists to reach each member of Ways and Means and Finance. This helps us determine where we have to concentrate our efforts. This meeting will go through lunch. Back to the office afterward and then at 2:00 the home office tax [specialist] will be in and he and I will go over to Walker and Associates. We're part of a group who are supporting Safe Harbor Leasing — $150 million for [us]. . . . About 4:00 I'll be back here to return phone calls, check mail, check with each of our lobbyists and on anything that may have erupted during the day. About 5:15 or so, I'll check with the secretaries for any little problems, as well as checking with the office manager. About three nights a week I'll have a reception that I'll have to go to.

Finally, the lobbyist for a tiny public interest group offers this account of his routine:

> I don't think I have a typical day. I usually work 8:00 until 6:00. The first half hour is spent reading the papers. . . . I spend a lot of time on the phone finding out what's happening on the Hill — gathering intelligence, I guess you might say. About 9:30 or 10:00, I take off to the Hill for hearings or a markup in committee. This usually lasts all morning. I grab a quick lunch and sometimes I stay on the Hill and do some lobbying by visiting congressional aides. Oftentimes the chairman [of our group] comes with me to visit the aides. I come back to the office in mid-afternoon. I return phone calls, find out what's happened while I was out of the office — to see if there have been any new events. Usually at this point I'll go through the *Congressional Record*, answer my mail, write memos, just get caught up.

Although these three legislative lobbyists work for dissimilar organizations, their work patterns have quite a bit in common. Most striking about the way they spend their days is the premium they place on collecting the latest information. Close attention is paid to relevant sources of news. There is constant checking on the phone and with office colleagues to see if anything has happened since the last time the lobbyist was in the office. A good deal of contact they initiate with government officials is of the "what's happening?" kind.

The emphasis on current information comes, in part, from the culture of Washington. One measure of status in Washington is the amount of inside information you have. Someone who is not in the know risks being thought unimportant. More fundamental to the substance of lobbying is the bearing current information has on short-term planning. To do the job well, a lobbyist must know what amendments are being drafted, if a key senator has met with those working the other side of the issue, or if the administration is flexible on some provisions of the legislation. Day-old information is as valuable to a lobbyist as day-old bread is to a bakery. It simply does no good to try to influence the situation that used to be.

Another common work trait shared by these and other lobbyists is the effort to make their presence felt. Contrary to the image of lobbyists as back-room operators, much of their time is taken up in trying to be visible. They spend valuable time at congressional hearings even though nothing of great consequence is likely to happen there. Still, it's a chance to touch base with other lobbyists and congressional staffers.[1] They'll make repeated visits to different Capitol Hill offices, even if all they're likely to accomplish is leaving a message with a secretary that they were by to see the administrative assistant. The ubiquitous after-work receptions are a chance to exchange a word or two with members of Congress or their aides to simply remind them who the lobbyist represents. The recently retired head of a citizens' lobby said:

> I used to get irritated when I'd see my colleagues in on a Tuesday, Wednesday, or Thursday afternoon [Congress' usual days in session]. I'd ask them why they weren't on the Hill. *You have to be seen.* Even if the legislators don't know who you are, if they see you often enough, they'll start to feel you belong.

Much of what a lobbyist does then is to validate the role that the group plays in policy making. They are constantly reminding legislators, staffers, and other lobbyists that they are around and that their views ought to be considered when policy decisions are being hammered out.

A related part of the Washington representative's job is to keep in touch with interest group allies and to do whatever can be done to spur them on. Coalition politics is characteristic of all sizes and types of interest groups. The constant interaction is a means for exchanging information, but it also affords an opportunity to develop strategy, offer and receive moral support, and politely push the other group to do more.

Lobbyists differ, of course, in the way they carry out their job. The Washington representative from the public interest group does not hire expensive public relations firms as his counterpart from the large corporation does. Some lobbyists will be able to rely on letters written by their constituencies to aid their efforts; others do not have large memberships to draw on. These descriptions have dealt only with legislative lobbying. Trying to influence the content of a regulation involves considerably less time prowling the corridors than Capitol Hill work does. The reasons are various. To begin with, an agency usually has fewer relevant offices to visit on forthcoming regulations. More important, though, the civil servants who do the lion's share

[1] See, for example, Elizabeth Drew's portrait of lobbyist Charls Walker, "Charlie," *New Yorker,* January 9, 1978, pp. 32–58.

of the work in drafting regulations can feel constricted in their relations with lobbyists. They may take the attitude that frequent meetings with industry representatives can compromise their neutrality. Naturally, agency bureaucrats want others to believe that the rules and regulations they write are based solely on the facts.[2] At the same time, they recognize that meetings with interest group representatives can help them to learn what all the facts are.[3]

For all lobbyists, though, the daily work is being the eyes and ears of their organizations. They must keep the members of their group abreast of policy developments. They must stand ready to provide information for the newsletter that goes to the printer tomorrow, answer phone calls from members, and keep their superiors supplied with a steady stream of information. Lobbyists are the nerve endings of an interest group, and they spend most of each day carrying messages back and forth between their environment and their organization.[4]

EFFECTIVE LOBBYING

It is all too clear that lobbying is a difficult and sometimes frustrating occupation. The hours are long and the prestige rather low in a town of senators, ambassadors, and cabinet secretaries. The pressures can be great when a critical vote in Congress or an administrative decision approaches. Regardless of how hard they work, policy outcomes will often be determined by factors mostly out of their control.

Still, the job is not without its satisfactions. It can be heady, exciting work. Like any other job, accomplishing what one sets out to do has its own inner rewards. And like any other job, lobbying has its own valued skills and professional norms. Lobbyists are convinced that effective lobbying is maximized by close adherence to the following "rules."

---

[2] Hugh Heclo, "OMB and the Presidency — The Problem of 'Neutral Competence,'" *Public Interest* 38 (Winter 1975), pp. 80–98.

[3] In some agencies, the bureaucrats cannot do their jobs without data supplied to them by industry representatives. See Paul J. Quirk, "Food and Drug Administration," in James Q. Wilson, ed., *The Politics of Regulation* (New York: Basic Books, 1980), pp. 211–218.

[4] Richly detailed descriptions of the lobbyist's job can be found in Lester W. Milbrath, *The Washington Lobbyists* (Chicago: Rand McNally, 1963); and Lewis Anthony Dexter, *How Organizations Are Represented in Washington* (Indianapolis: Bobbs-Merrill, 1969).

CREDIBILITY COMES FIRST/ In interviewing lobbyists about a variety of subjects, no theme is repeated more frequently than their need to protect their credibility. It is the fundamental dogma of their religion. "Washington is a village," said one labor lobbyist. "You are known by your good name and integrity."

Lobbyists emphasize their reputation because in a job designed to convince others of your point of view, it is easy to stretch the truth to make one's argument seem more powerful. But it is as dangerous as it is easy. Mislead a member of Congress and "you can expect a member never to listen to you seriously," commented one veteran lobbyist. If a business lobbyist told a congressman that the tax provision he is pushing for his industry would cost the Treasury only $250 million over three years, that figure has to be relatively accurate. If the senator uses that figure and later learns that the Congressional Budget Office estimates the cost at $1 billion for the same period, the senator will be alienated and is likely to disregard the group's "facts" in the future.

For the lobbyist, then, honesty is not so much a matter of virtue as it is of necessity. Lobbyists simply cannot do the job if there are any doubts about their credibility. As one corporate representative put it, "All you have is your word."

ONLY THE FACTS COUNT) Credibility is a precondition for getting your message heard, but it is not sufficient to exert influence. What does make a lobbyist's communications persuasive? The lobbyist who represents a powerful constituency may begin with the advantage of speaking for a well-identified point of view. Individual lobbyists cannot really affect the nature of their own constituency, but they can affect the design of the message they send to policy makers. Lobbyists are unequivocal about what makes for effective "messages" — the more factual the better. In memos, handouts, reports, formal comments on regulations, and in conversations, the only content that counts is the specific fact. "You have to know how to separate the wheat from the chaff, facts from rhetoric," said a trade association lobbyist.

It is of little value to a policy maker to hear platitudes about what's in the "public interest." They are already aware of the general pro and con arguments on an issue. If a lobbyist is to do anything to influence a member of Congress or administrator beyond the opinion they already hold, they must have something new to bring to their attention.[5] In its fights against the construction of new power plants, the Environmental Defense Fund relies on a computer model to analyze the financial and power needs of the utility. Making projections of the money that can be saved through alternatives to new plant construction is seen as a more effective approach than dwelling on the perils of increased pollution.[6]

Lobbyists increase their effectiveness as they increase their knowledge of their policy area. Amid the deepening complexity of public policy issues, the lobbyist must become a determined and continuing student of these issues.[7] To be optimally effective on the toxic waste issue, the environmental lobbyist should have at least a rudimentary understanding of what the scientific and technical literature says. But though the technical complexity of issues makes lobbying a more difficult challenge, therein lies the opportunity. Lobbyists who have mastered the complexities of their policy area enter a select group of experts who talk the same language.[8] Washington representatives with a high level of policy expertise are more valuable to those in government because policy makers can draw upon their knowledge in efforts to solve difficult issues.

NEVER BURN YOUR BRIDGES. Politics makes for strange bedfellows. Alliances can shift rapidly, or, as one trade association lobbyist put it, "You may be friends on one issue and enemies on the next." Lobbyists cannot afford the luxury of venting their anger toward policy makers who act contrary to their wishes. No matter how many times liberal lobbyists have lost the vote of conservative Senator Robert Dole (R-Kansas), they still have good reason to try to remain cordial with his office. Dole is a strong advocate of the food stamp program and his support is absolutely vital to the chances of relatively liberal legislation on that issue. To keep from burning bridges while pushing hard to get the group's policies adopted, a lobbyist, says one

5 William T. Gormley, Jr., "Statewide Remedies for Public Underrepresentation in Regulatory Proceedings," *Public Administration Review* 41 (July/August 1981), pp. 454–462.
6 John R. Emshwiller, "Environmental Group, in Change of Strategy, Is Stressing Economics," *Wall Street Journal*, September 28, 1981.
7 Hugh Heclo, "Issue Networks and the Executive Establishment," in Anthony King, ed., *The New American Political System* (Washington, D.C.: American Enterprise Institute, 1978), pp. 87–124.
8 Robert W. Kweit and Mary Grisez Kweit, "Bureaucratic Decision-Making: Impediments to Citizen Participation," *Polity* 12 (Summer 1980), pp. 647–666.

trade association representative, should be "responsible, firm, and nonemotional."

Some public interest lobbyists dissent from this rule. Common Cause has made it a practice to single out members of Congress for criticism when they feel they have acted in a particularly offensive way. Ralph Nader, who provides leadership for a number of groups started under his sponsorship, has a similar philosophy toward those who act in a manner he regards as egregiously out of line with the public interest. He derided the former head of the Atomic Energy Commission, Dixy Lee Ray, by publicly declaring that she had a "distorted . . . capacity for reason." [9]

When public interest lobbyists fail to follow the don't-burn-your-bridges rule, it is not always because they place an exalted premium on principle. It is true that some of them approach their work with a degree of moralism that makes it more difficult for them to tolerate those they see as sinners and backsliders. Yet it is more than a pious attitude that leads some public interest lobbyists to go out of their way to personalize issues. Frequently they see it as a tactical advantage to identify a "villain." [10] The idea is to portray the issue at hand as a fight between good and evil, and ridicule and vilification are useful for putting their opponents on the defensive. Nader and other citizen group lobbyists who use this tactic sacrifice whatever future cooperation they might get from their targets in the expectation that other policy makers will be more fearful of such denunciation, and thus be more helpful. For most lobbyists, though, this remains a high-risk strategy. For those representing corporations and trade associations, such a moralistic approach has no credibility.

SUCCESS = COMPROMISE. It is often said that "politics is the art of compromise." If so, lobbyists must be fine artists. No interest group ever achieves all it wants, and so the difference between success and failure is achieving an acceptable compromise. An integral part of the lobbyist's job is to aggressively seek out workable compromises that can satisfy all necessary parties. The task each day, says one business lobbyist, is to "Go solution searching." Lobbyists must see themselves as a catalyst for compromise, finding and promoting policy changes

[9] Jeffrey M. Berry, "Lessons from Chairman Ralph," *Citizen Participation* 1 (November/December 1979), p. 4.
[10] Berry, "Lessons from Chairman Ralph," p. 4.

that are going to get a bill or regulation through in acceptable form. Lobbyists attempt to give up that which is least valuable to their group while persuading policy makers and other interest groups to agree to the higher priorities their group is pushing for. The skill that is involved is knowing how much to give up and just when to make those concessions. For the Congress, that skill consists of determining which trade-offs or policy changes will attract votes from legislators who have strong reservations about the bill at hand. Lobbyists and their congressional allies look for sweeteners that will make the bill more attractive by adding or subtracting particular provisions. A lobbyist for the National Education Association describes how his organization worked to make the proposal for a new Cabinet-level Department of Education more acceptable to critics of "big government."

> We just brought these programs [from different agencies] together by selling the public and officials on the idea of cutting back on the bureaucracy and achieving a total cost savings. We cut back more than 500 administrative positions — that's what the conservative element wanted. We reduced the regulations by 50 percent by pulling it all together. We cut back paperwork by more than 50 percent. We accomplished what the majority of people wanted.

Compromises are not always reached so easily, and sometimes they cannot be reached at all because one or more factions must give up too much to keep the result palatable for them. But the good lobbyist keeps searching and keeps trying to find the middle ground.

CREATE A DEPENDENCY. The optimal role for a lobbyist to play is that of a trusted source of information whom policy makers can call on when they need hard-to-find data. A reputation for credibility and high-quality factual information are prerequisites for becoming the type of lobbyist government officials request help from. The final ingredient is developing the relationship gradually with the lobbyist providing the right kind of information at the right time. "Maintain constant communication," says one public interest representative. "Churn out a lot of material at their request. Create a dependency."

Political scientists have long described this type of relationship as characterizing "policy subsystems" or "issue networks." Lobbyists in particular policy areas develop working relationships with the agency officials and congressional committee members and staffers who have responsibility for relevant programs. This familiarity in time gives lobbyists the advantage of repeated opportunities to interact with policy makers and to display their expertise. The lobbyist for a group representing urban affairs specialists mentioned that their long work with certain agencies led to calls from those agencies when the Reagan administration was developing an urban enterprise zones proposal (a plan to give tax breaks to companies investing in inner-city areas). "They needed to know how many states already had enterprise zones, how they're working, what they look like, and so on. This happens all the time." The long nurturing of the relationship with agencies handling urban issues enabled this lobbyist to get in on the ground floor of the enterprise zones issue. The same lobbyist added, "that's the key to being a good lobbyist — to establish a two-way street not only with agencies, but with members of Congress, especially for technical areas. You need to have them depend on you for your area of expertise."

These unwritten "rules" of effective lobbying are, of course, general. Because they are so widely accepted and quickly grasped by any aspiring Washington representative, simply following them does not ensure success. Wide differences in the skill and perseverance of lobbyists remain as they try to become issue experts or facilitators of compromise. Furthermore, no matter how skilled lobbyists are, they are severely restricted in accomplishing their goals by the political popularity of their group's stand on issues and the strength of the group's constituency. Yet, so far as any one lobbyist can make a difference, adhering to these norms will help to maximize his influence.

LOBBYING AS A CAREER

Lobbying is an unusual profession, in that people do not aspire to become the representative of an interest group. Surely this attitude has to do with the low prestige of lobbying and the uncomplimentary image it has had over the years. There is no career path, then, that people consciously choose in order to prepare themselves for the lobbying profession.

Recruitment

If individuals do not set out to become lobbyists, how is it that they end up in such jobs? Generally, people become lobbyists because

previous jobs lead them to it. Specific skills or areas of background
are acquired, and soon opportunities present themselves, or may even
be pursued. A common route into lobbying is government work. A
corporate lobbyist describes his career ladder:

> I graduated from law school in 1965. I was then a legisla-
> tive assistant to a congressman from upstate New York. I was
> there for five years and then I went to work for the Depart-
> ment of Health, Education, and Welfare in congressional re-
> lations for eighteen months. Then to the White House Drug
> Abuse office, where I was Director of Congressional Relations.
> I went back to the Hill in 1972 as a Counsel to the Ways and
> Means Committee.

A somewhat different path was taken by another corporate lobbyist
who came up through the ranks of his firm:

> I was an accounting major [in college] and I came into a
> division at one of our plants. I was in Cost Analysis and
> Budget Forecasting-Capital Investment. I was there until
> 1969, then transferred to Public Affairs. I was brought in to
> do state lobbying [in New York and then West Virginia].
> Then later in 1973, I went to California as District Manager
> of Public Affairs — congressional relations, grassroots politics,
> and the news media. In 1979, I was transferred to Washing-
> ton as the Director of Operations, the number two position in
> this office.

These two rather divergent career paths led both men to very similar positions for their corporations. The common denominators are
experience and *expertise*. The first lobbyist had spent many years in
government, and with his experience as an administration lobbyist
and as a staffer on the tax-writing Ways and Means Committee, he
could not have been more attractive to the large conglomerate that
eventually hired him. The second lobbyist learned his industry by
working in middle-management positions before moving over to public affairs. He finally graduated to the vital Washington office by toil-
ing many years in the corporate vineyards. Each found himself with
job offers that were extremely attractive at the time they came. The
position the first lobbyist took offered him the chance to run his own
office and to make considerably more money than he could working
for Congress. For the second, the decision to accept a transfer to the
Washington office was a major promotion within his huge corpora-

tion. He had come a long way from his earlier positions to such a crucial government-relations job.

Some do aggressively seek out lobbying positions instead of being recruited or falling into them.[11] Most commonly, those who search for and avidly pursue such jobs are citizen activists. They are looking not so much for a job as a lobbyist as for a job that will allow them to work for a cause. Take the Washington representative for a women's group:

> I was a faculty wife for eleven years, having children and moving all over the country. I ended up in Montana in 1972. After sons one, two, and three, I became interested in political organizing. I got involved with the women's movement with the National Women's Political Caucus [NWPC]. I was a volunteer helping to get women elected and, as a by-product, doing some legislative work. Based on both my education and my skills as a teacher, I found that I was very good. I helped organize Montana's NWPC — several chapters. When we moved to Boulder, Colorado, I got a Master's in Public Administration. . . . In 1979 I went to work for Senator Gary Hart as a staff assistant. This was my first paid job in eleven years. Four months later I moved to Washington and assumed a position. . . .

This woman's career reflects dedication to the women's movement and her eventual job in Washington continued her pursuit of work on behalf of her cause.[12] The satisfaction derived by pursuing ideological goals makes jobs with citizen groups highly attractive. For the private sector lobbyist, the issues they will be lobbying on may not be the main attraction to a lobbying job.[13] It's not necessary to have a "moral commitment to that which you are lobbying for," said one oil lobbyist.

Although divergent career paths lead into lobbying positions, the jobs themselves usually are filled in the same manner: by word of mouth. Although some jobs may be advertised, organizations looking for an outside candidate will rely heavily on personal recommendations from those they consult. In any issue network, most of the par-

---

[11] Jeffrey M. Berry, *Lobbying for the People* (Princeton: Princeton University Press, 1977), p. 87; and Harmon Zeigler and Michael Baer, *Lobbying* (Belmont, Calif.: Wadsworth, 1969), p. 48.
[12] See, generally, Sara Evans, *Personal Politics* (New York: Knopf, 1979).
[13] Milbrath, *The Washington Lobbyists*, pp. 109–114.

ticipants are already well known to other actors. If a farm group loses one of its lobbyists, the director of the organization will naturally consider respected staffers on the agriculture committees in Congress and officials in the Department of Agriculture, whether those people are looking for new jobs or not. Intermediaries may put the director in touch with others who might fill the group's needs. One lobbyist described his recruitment as "one of those typical Washington stories. You know, where you know someone who knows someone."

In sum, most Washington representatives work their way up through their organization or are sought out. Someone with strong qualifications (such as having spent many years as a congressional committee staffer) will receive frequent "feelers." There are some who vigorously pursue a lobbying position, but entry into the profession tends to be unplanned.

Background

Although no precise route opens into the lobbying profession, three spawning grounds nurture most Washington representatives: law, government, and business. Because expertise and experience are the most important qualities in a lobbyist, it is easy to understand why these three backgrounds predominate. Experience in government not only gives prospective lobbyists experience in the workings of Congress and agencies, it also gives expertise on policy and "contacts" that may help to open doors. Lawyers easily metamorphose into lobbyists because their education and experience make them familiar with the way statutes and regulations are written. A few years of work as an associate in a Washington law firm or in an agency's legal counsel office gives them added preparation. Business is also a common background because the majority of lobbyists represent either trade associations or individual corporations. The technical complexity of most public policy issues makes experience in one's industry a helpful credential.

One of the most serious ethical dilemmas involving interest group politics is circulation of people out of government and into lobbying.[14] The issue is this: you are working for the government at the taxpayer's expense, developing expertise and experience that make

[14] Paul J. Quirk, *Industry Influence in Federal Regulatory Agencies* (Princeton: Princeton University Press, 1981).

you attractive to the private sector. When you leave government and parlay that background into a lobbying job, it is usually at a much higher salary, and for a position designed to exploit your contacts with those you know in government. Take William Rountree, who worked for a congressional committee and then as a general counsel for legislation in the Commerce Department for the Nixon and Ford administrations. He was subsequently recruited by Standard Oil of Ohio (Sohio) to head their Washington lobbying office.[15] The oil industry draws heavily on government employees to fill its top lobbying jobs — positions that pay as much as $100,000 or more.[16] This pattern is by no means unique to the oil industry. Between 1945 and 1970, 21 of 33 commissioners leaving the Federal Communications Commission became affiliated with the communications industry.[17]

It is difficult to legislate against government workers going directly to work for industries they formerly oversaw in a regulatory or legislative capacity without restricting their personal freedom to work and associate with whomever they choose.[18] Yet this circulation of actors within an issue network is one of the reasons "subsystem politics" has been so much criticized by political scientists and others.[19] A subsystem can become a cooperative arrangement where, for example, oil lobbyists, oil industry regulators, and relevant congressional committee members and staffers work easily together toward shared interests at the expense of the public interest. With the growth in the number of interest groups, subsystems have broadened, and changes in the Congress have produced much overlap among them.[20] Little changed,

[15] Rachelle Patterson, "The Oil Lobby," *Boston Globe*, August 26, 1979.
[16] Richard Halloran, "Capital's Diverse Oil Lobbyists: Much Criticized, Often Effective," *The New York Times*, August 9, 1979; and Patterson, "The Oil Lobby."
[17] Roger Noll, Merton Peck, and John McGowan, *Economic Aspects of Television Regulation* (Washington, D.C.: Brookings Institution, 1973), p. 123. As cited in Edward S. Herman, *Corporate Control, Corporate Power* (New York: Cambridge University Press, 1981), p. 179. The revolving-door pattern in defense contracting is documented by Gordon Adams, *The Iron Triangle* (New York: Council on Economic Priorities, 1981), pp. 77–93.
[18] William J. Lanouette, "The Revolving Door — It's Tricky to Try to Stop It," *National Journal*, November 19, 1977, pp. 1796–1803.
[19] See Roger H. Davidson, "Breaking up Those 'Cozy Triangles': An Impossible Dream?" in Susan Welch and John G. Peters, *Legislative Reform and Public Policy* (New York: Praeger, 1977), pp. 30–53; Lawrence C. Dodd and Richard L. Schott, *Congress and the Administrative State* (New York: John Wiley, 1979); and Heclo, "Issue Networks and the Executive Establishment."
[20] Dodd and Schott, *Congress and the Administrative State*, pp. 58–154.

though, is the movement of lobbyists back and forth between government and interest groups, blurring the separation between the public
and private sectors.[21]

Lobbyists are impressive in their educational backgrounds, commonly holding advanced degrees beyond the bachelor's. The most
popular advanced degree is in law, but assorted masters' in fields
such as economics, business, and political science are often found
too.[22] The relatively high level of education that characterizes the
lobbying profession has to do with the requirements of the jobs that
frequently precede work as an interest group representative. But beyond the earlier need to advance in business, law, government, or
other fields, lobbyists still find their advanced educations useful, if not
essential, to their interest group work. Again, the technical nature of
many public policy areas and the need to understand administrative
law and other arcane legal matters make academic credentials highly
valuable to a lobbyist.[23]

Lobbying is mostly a "man's world." A survey of the heads of corporate government relations offices and trade associations in Washington revealed that 94 percent of the respondents were men.[24] Public interest groups are more likely to hire women lobbyists; an earlier
survey showed 24 percent to be females.[25] It may be that beyond the
more general problems facing all women entering professions long
dominated by males, lobbying presents its own special problems. "It's
tough for a woman on the Hill," said one female trade association
representative. The people in government who make decisions are
likely to be men, and the quiet off-the-record negotiations that are
part of policy making can easily turn a woman into an outsider. Yet

---

[21] On in-and-outers from citizen groups, see Juan Cameron, "Nader's Invaders
Are Inside the Gates," *Fortune*, October 1977, p. 252 ff; Linda E. Demkovich,
"From Public Interest Advocates to Administration Defenders," *National Jour-
nal*, November 25, 1978, pp. 1892–1898; James W. Singer, "That Old Public
Interest Movement Gang Moves into New — and Private — Fields," *National
Journal*, February 14, 1981, pp. 269–273; and Robert Pear, "Influence of Sub-
Cabinet Conservatives is Mixed," *The New York Times*, July 6, 1983.

[22] "The Washington Executive," Boyden Associates, Washington, D.C., 1980,
p. 2; Berry, *Lobbying for the People*, pp. 88–90; and Milbrath, *The Washington Lobbyists*, p. 68.

[23] The ability and credentials of contemporary lobbyists contrasts to the opposite
pattern found in one major study of the 1950s. See Raymond A. Bauer, Ithiel
de Sola Pool, and Lewis Anthony Dexter, *American Business and Public Policy*
(New York: Atherton, 1963), p. 345.

[24] "The Washington Executive," p. 2.

[25] Berry, *Lobbying for the People*, p. 85.

the progress women have made in public interest lobbying, where more liberal attitudes prevail, suggests that the general disparity between male and female lobbyists can some day be overcome. Major improvement is not likely to come, however, until women make more advances into the top echelons of both business and government.

No general surveys of what lobbyists make are available, but it is certain they are not an underprivileged lot. The survey of Washington executives of trade associations and corporations showed that around 60 percent had salaries of $50,000 or higher.[26] These people are at the top end of the scale, because they are the heads of their respective offices. Also, salaries on the corporate side are higher than in nonprofit and public interest groups.

Although the entrance qualifications are high and the financial rewards from private sector groups can be lucrative, the lobbying profession does not command much loyalty. Research shows that the typical lobbyist has been in the job for five years or less.[27] This record suggests rapid movement in and out of lobbying jobs. "Washington," said one lobbyist, "is a tremendously transitional place." The rapid "transition" out of lobbying for many people has to do with a variety of factors. Long hours, high pressure, and low prestige can contribute to the desire to leave. In the parlance of Washington, individuals burn out as their energy is drained by the constant demands of their jobs. Then too, highly qualified and competent Washington representatives are going to find other job opportunities coming their way. Some even go into government in the area of their expertise. Representatives of trade associations may move on to an individual corporation, and Washington corporate executives may move to the corporate headquarters. In lobbying, as in any other profession, there are the "lifers" who stay committed to the same job. For the most part, though, lobbying is a job at a stage in one's life and not a career.

LOBBYISTS FOR HIRE

To the lobbyists who are employed full time by interest groups, we can add many lobbyists for temporary hire. Lobbyists hire out on a retainer or fee for services for two reasons. First, many companies and

26 "The Washington Executive," p. 3.
27 *Public Affairs Offices and Their Functions* (Boston: Boston University School of Management, 1981), p. 5; Berry, *Lobbying for the People*, p. 87; and "The Washington Executive," p. 2.

associations do not have an office in Washington. Most such organizations need a lobbyist infrequently and it is less expensive to hire one as need be. Second, most interest group offices are small and may not have the resources for a major lobbying campaign that the parent organization wants (and is willing to pay for). Again, it is more economical to hire outsiders to do tasks that are highly specialized or require an extensive staff for a limited time than it is to carry such people on the payroll all year. In Washington, the pool of labor for lobbying work is deep. Most lobbyists for hire come from the many public relations and law firms that eagerly court government relations work.

Law Firms

The "Washington law firm" is no ordinary law firm. These firms are in the business of representing clients before government.[28] "Lawyer-lobbyists" in Washington can earn lucrative salaries by developing expertise in an area of regulatory policy. Law school graduates starting at the top firms can begin at $35,000 a year or more. Senior partners in successful firms can easily make $200,000 to $300,000 annually.[29]

The practice of law in Washington has mushroomed along with the regulatory state. Between 1970 and 1980, the number of pages in the *Federal Register* (where all agency regulations are published) went from 20,000 almost to 80,000. Not coincidentally, the number of lawyers in Washington tripled during this period. Prestigious firms like Covington & Burling (201 partners and associates), Hogan & Hartson (152), and Arnold & Porter (145) grew rapidly to take advantage of new opportunities for business.[30]

Corporations are by far the largest group of customers for Washington law firms. The complex administrative process is intimidating to corporate executives who have little Washington experience. Even the Washington representatives of a corporation can find themselves unable to adequately understand the technical jargon and legalese of administrative regulations. The stakes can also be very high, with companies willing to pay large fees to a top-notch lawyer with the

---

[28] Mark J. Green, *The Other Government* (New York: Grossman, 1975).
[29] Bryce Nelson, "A Gold Rush for Lawyers in Legal Hills of Washington," *Boston Globe*, December 8, 1980.
[30] Donald F. Pike, "Rise of the Power Brokers," *U.S. News and World Report*, March 10, 1980, pp. 52–56.

necessary specialization. When the Levi Strauss Company was negotiating to license the Soviet government to make blue jeans, it hired Surrey, Karasik & Morse, a large firm with expertise in obtaining export and licensing approvals. The company wanted to make sure that it had the best possible representation in this complex area of international trade.[31]

The individuals who join Washington law firms are aware that they are entering a special type of law practice. They know that a good part of their time will be spent pleading some corporation's cause before government. They will choose Washington law over, say, Wall Street law, arranging stock offerings and mergers, because they find it more challenging or find the politics of lawmaking and rulemaking more intriguing. Frequently Washington lawyers will enter private practice after gaining valuable experience working for a congressional committee or an administrative agency. When they move to a private firm, they can command handsome fees from the many corporations that have a problem with the federal government.[32]

Public Relations Firms

Organizations or industries in need of Washington representation will find public relations firms of particular use when they feel they need to change public opinion, or when they have an image problem. After the accident at the Three Mile Island nuclear power plant in Pennsylvania, when the reactor core came close to a meltdown, the highly regulated nuclear industry faced a massive public relations problem. The operator of the plant, Metropolitan Edison, hired Hill and Knowlton, a well-known public relations firm. Other companies and trade associations involved in the nuclear industry also used public relations firms to counter the growing perception that nuclear power plants were dangerous. The firms advised their clients on media relations, advertising, and interaction with public officials.[33]

The two largest public relations firms in the United States are Hill and Knowlton and Burson-Marsteller, each with more than $25 mil-

[31] Rich Jaroslovsky, "A Washington Lawyer Thrives by Negotiating the Bureaucratic Maze," *Wall Street Journal*, August 14, 1978.
[32] James W. Singer, "Practicing Law in Washington — An American Growth Industry," *National Journal*, February 4, 1978, pp. 172–179.
[33] Michael R. Gordon, "The Image Makers in Washington — PR Firms Have Found a Natural Home," *National Journal*, May 5, 1980, pp. 884–890.

lion a year in billings. Hill and Knowlton has a larger presence in Washington, with an office of around ninety compared to twenty-five for Burson-Marsteller. Both, however, have rapidly expanded their Washington operations to tap the growing market for their skills. There are many smaller public relations firms in Washington as well, some with a staff no bigger than a lone professional.[34] The advantage public relations firms have over law firms is that they offer more services to clients. A large public relations firm will have specialists in lobbying, advertising, and media work.[35] Some firms will even teach a corporate executive how to be effective in a television interview. Lawyer-lobbyists still receive considerably more business among those who wish to influence public policy than public relations specialists do. Yet the public relations firms are gaining popularity among those who need lobbying as well as help with their image.

Superstars

Like any other vocation, lobbying has its stars who have reached the top of the profession in both reputation and income.[36] Among Washington's galaxy of lobbying stars are:

THOMAS H. BOGGS, JR. Tommy Boggs was born with connections. His father, Hale Boggs (D-Louisiana), was majority leader in the House until his death in a plane crash. His mother, Lindy Boggs, (D-Louisiana) holds the same seat in Congress. As a young lawyer, Tommy Boggs went to work for the firm now known as Patton, Boggs & Blow, or more informally as the "Boggs firm." He helped build the firm to its present size of about eighty, and to give it a reputation as a good Capitol Hill firm. Boggs is considered a consummate legislative lobbyist for his hard work, political savvy, and assiduous efforts to raise and channel political contributions to members of Congress. He had a major role in getting the Chrysler

34 Gordon, "The Image Makers in Washington," p. 884.
35 See Bill Keller, "Do White House Ties Count?" *Congressional Quarterly Weekly Report*, March 20, 1982, pp. 603–608; William J. Lanouette, "The Influence Peddlers — Connections Still Count, But They're Not Enough," *National Journal*, February 28, 1981, pp. 355–357; and Gordon, "The Image Makers."
36 See Joseph Goulden, *Superlawyers* (New York: Dell, 1973); and Green, *The Other Government.*

bailout bill through Congress, which established guaranteed government loans for the company and saved it from likely bankruptcy. Boggs bills his own time at $250 an hour and is reported to earn $500,000 a year.[37]

ROBERT K. GRAY. Robert Gray has been part of the Washington scene since he served as secretary to the Eisenhower Cabinet. He prospered as director of the Washington office of Hill and Knowlton, but when Ronald Reagan, a friend, became president, Gray knew it was time to capitalize on his connections by starting his own public relations and lobbying firm. Within its first year of operation, Gray & Company grew from twenty-one employees to ninety, testifying to Gray's ability and his political connections.[38] Gray is considered a premier door opener, getting clients in to see important and hard-to-reach officials. His highly competent staff carries out the nuts-and-bolts lobbying. Among those clients are Warner Communications, the American Iron and Steel Institute, and the American Maritime Association. The fifty-eight-year-old white-haired bachelor is considered to be something of a man about town, and he is often seen escorting the wives of senators and presidential aides to prominent social functions. But Gray is no lightweight. At $350 an hour, there is no shortage of clients who think he's worth every penny of what he charges.[39]

CHARLS E. WALKER. If there is one man who symbolizes the clout of big business around Washington, it's Charls Walker. His "economic consulting firm," Charls E. Walker Associates, is quite simply a lobbying firm. The balding, bespectacled Walker was Deputy Secretary of the Treasury during the Nixon administration and served as Ronald Reagan's adviser on tax policy during the 1980 campaign. A Ph.D. economist by training, Walker has an incisive understanding of both the political process and the tax code. He attracts large corporations, like Eastern Airlines, Ford Motor, Procter and Gamble,

---

37 Albert R. Hunt, "Thomas Boggs Offers Full-Service Lobbying for a Diverse Clientele," *Wall Street Journal*, March 23, 1982.

38 See Keller, "Do White House Ties Count?" on other friends of Reagan who have used their connections to attract lobbying clients.

39 James M. Perry, "A PR Man Uses Access to Influential People to Lure, Help Clients," *Wall Street Journal*, March 25, 1982; and Lynn Rosellini, "Bob Gray: Public Relations Man to the Powerful," *The New York Times*, February 26, 1982.

and Union Carbide, who can gain or lose millions of dollars by one change in the tax law. Walker played a key role in coordinating big business efforts to influence the 1981 Reagan administration tax bill. The law that was passed contained numerous provisions that effectively reduced the corporate tax. Walker says his firm has "grown steadily every year since 1973." [40]

Is there an explanation for these men being so successful as lobbyists? If an identifiable formula had been derived for this type of success, everyone would be following it. Some common qualities do stand out, however. Each of these three is as highly motivated as he is intelligent. Each has been in the lobbying profession many years, gaining clients as he gained experience. All head organizations that have many other talented people to support them in what they do. Each man has "connections," but those connections would be of modest importance if it wasn't for the lobbyist's talent. Indeed, even though Boggs is strongly identified with the Democrats, and Gray and Walker with the Republicans, all three have done well regardless of which administration has been in power. [41]

The success of these men is also magnified by their specialization in lobbying for big business, where the money is greatest. Equally successful stars are working for the nonprofit and public interest groups. No matter whom they might lobby for, Boggs, Gray, and Walker would stand out for their shrewd understanding of politics and their dogged determination to be the best at what they do.

CONCLUSION

As American politics has changed since the 1960s, and interest groups have proliferated in Washington, the job of the lobbyist has changed as well. Charls Walker describes the difference in his job now compared to the 1950s:

> In those days, I would have a fifty-minute meeting with
> [Speaker of the House] Sam Rayburn. For forty-eight minutes
> we would talk about Texas, family, and friends. In the re-

[40] Lanouette, "The Influence Peddlers," p. 355; Keller, "Do White House Ties Count?"; and Drew, "Charlie."

[41] On partisanship and lobbying firms, see Barbara Gamarekian, "A Lobbying Firm Specializing in Bipartisanship," *The New York Times*, April 12, 1982; and Robert M. Kaus, "There's No Shame Anymore," *Harper's*, August 1982, p. 15.

maining two, we would settle what I had come to talk about.
He always knew what I was there for, and would say, "It's
taken care of, Charlie," or "I just can't do that for you."
Now that kind of thing just doesn't happen any more. With
the decline of parties, the decline of leadership in the Congress, business lobbying groups have to cover the field. Many
more bodies and much more time are needed to accomplish
what we did then.[42]

Walker surely exaggerates the ease with which most lobbyists could
solve their problems in the 1950s. Yet the job of a lobbyist was
simpler then. The business lobbyist had less competition from public
interest adversaries. It was also the heyday of the so-called iron
triangles, in which policy making was carried out in a consensual
manner by industry lobbyists, agency administrators, and congressional committee chairmen.[43] Industries were also less regulated, and
a lobbyist had fewer agencies to deal with and fewer sets of complex
regulations to monitor.

It seems fair to say that the job of lobbyists today is more de-
manding. Not only do they have more groups to compete with, but
the policies that lobbyists deal with are increasingly complex. The
norms or rules of lobbying have probably not changed much, but
how much expertise on issues a Washington representative brings
to the job seems increasingly important. Yet despite the proliferation
of Washington representatives, lobbying remains a profession with
imprecise entry qualifications and unplanned career paths.

Individual lobbyists may rarely make the critical difference between
a bill's passing or failing, or a favorable regulation's being imple-
mented or scuttled. But the effective lobbyist can wield influence,
even if only at the margins of public policy. Whatever effect an
interest group can have, within the limitations of its constituency,
the popularity and salience of its issue, and the political makeup
of the government, its influence is affected by the quality of its
lobbying.

[42] Anne Colamosca, "The Trade Association Hustle," *New Republic*, November
3, 1979, p. 16.
[43] See Douglass Cater, *Power in Washington* (New York: Random House, 1964);
and J. Leiper Freeman, *The Political Process*, 2nd ed. (New York: Random
House, 1965).

CHAPTER SEVEN

The Constituency Connection

The art of influencing government can take many forms. The tactics that interest groups use range from a private meeting between a lobbyist and a legislator to elaborate street demonstrations aimed at influencing the entire public. In this chapter and the two that follow, we will analyze in detail the various tactics of influence commonly used by interest groups. We will first concentrate on approaches that emphasize influencing government through the "constituency connection." These tactics are directed at changing public opinion or mobilizing supporters of interest groups. Chapter 8 examines the activities of political action committees. The focus in Chapter 9 is on the tactics involving direct contact between lobbyists and policy makers. At the end of that chapter, the question of how interest groups choose their lobbying tactics will also be addressed.

Interest groups use the "constituency connection" by appealing to different audiences. For the broadest target, lobbying organizations can try to reach the mass public. Although it may seem mere common sense for all interest groups to want to reach as many people as possible, it is frequently impractical for lobbies to try to influence mass public opinion. They can narrow their efforts, directing them instead at an "attentive public"— groups concentrating on particular issues who follow their development in Washington.[1] An organization may also confine its efforts to its own members or activists.

Ultimately, all lobbying efforts are intended to prove to those in

[1] Francis E. Rourke, *Bureaucracy, Politics, and Public Policy*, 2nd ed. (Boston: Little, Brown, 1976), pp. 42–80.

government that a constituency has an intense policy preference. Protests, campaign contributions, and letter writing are tactics that rely on citizens' taking some concrete steps to try to influence government. Another constituency approach is to first attempt to influence mass public opinion or an attentive public's opinion. This is done to create a supportive environment for subsequent lobbying of government officials.

LOBBYING FOR VALUES

Many interest groups care about the general direction of American life and culture. Political decisions of all kinds are affected by societal values, those deep-seated collective attitudes of Americans on such matters as family life, economic principles, and the purpose of government. Sometimes the lobbying to change or reinforce values is connected to a policy decision. At other times, advocacy campaigns do not involve an immediate conflict over policy, but are aimed only at general attitudes. Either way, lobbies assume that by influencing the basic values of society, they can lay the groundwork for pursuing other policies compatible with their interests.

The Struggle for America's Soul

The 1970s and early 1980s witnessed a sharp and continuing struggle to define "the American way." Interest groups fought bitterly over their competing visions of what basic American values are. Most of this struggle has been about the American family: the role of women; the primacy of parental values over those introduced by the schools or television; and the perceived moral decay of America that undermines religion and the traditional nuclear family.[2]

The conflict over the defeated Equal Rights Amendment to the Constitution illustrates the debate. For both sides, the fight over the ERA was important for its symbolic value as well as for its substantive policy implications. Those against the ERA cited many

[2] See David W. Brady and Kent L. Tedin, "Ladies in Pink: Religion and Political Ideology in the Anti-ERA Movement," *Social Science Quarterly* 56 (March 1976), pp. 565–575; Ann L. Page and Donald A. Clelland, "The Kanawha County Textbook Controversy: A Study in the Politics of Life Style Concern," *Social Forces* 57 (September 1978), pp. 265–281; and Burton Yale Pines, *Back to Basics* (New York: Morrow, 1982).

serious issues such as women and the draft and divorce laws. But underlying these policy arguments was antagonism toward the women's movement. For the homemakers who fueled the opposition to the ERA, the women's movement represented a different conception of what an American woman's life was supposed to be.[3] Many similar efforts to reclaim the traditional family model for contemporary America have come from conservative Christian fundamentalists.[4] These fundamentalists see weakening in the moral fiber of this country, which they attribute directly to the declining importance of religious values. The rising divorce rate, abortion on demand, rampant crime, and use of drugs by young people, are all viewed as the result of weakening religious influence. Few would deny that such a link between changing moral values and the trends they decry is real. The conflict comes from efforts to prescribe remedies that would inhibit these changes.

In the broadest sense, the struggle is over something fundamentalists call "secular humanism." In their eyes, this philosophy rejects biblical truths in favor of more modern views of man and morality. Groups like Jerry Falwell's Moral Majority and Phyllis Schlafly's Eagle Forum try to rid this country of secular humanism by making efforts such as trying to ban allegedly immoral books from libraries and working to eliminate sex education in the public schools.[5] Much of what they do is concentrated on reforming the public schools, because the schools are seen as places where parents lose control over values that are transmitted to their children. Likewise, television is seen as subversive to American culture, and it too is a target. One group, the Coalition for Better Television, has threatened to boycott companies advertising products on the major networks because their programs contain "excessive sex, violence, and profanity," as well as a general "anti-Christian bigotry."[6] The networks label such threats as attempts at censorship. Nevertheless, after the advo-

[3] Alan Crawford, *Thunder on the Right* (New York: Pantheon, 1980), pp. 144–164.

[4] Michael Lienesch, "Right Wing Religion: Christian Conservatism as a Political Movement," *Political Science Quarterly* 97 (Fall 1982), pp. 403–425; Crawford, *Thunder on the Right*; and Frances FitzGerald, "A Disciplined, Charging Army," *New Yorker*, May 18, 1981, pp. 53–141.

[5] Dena Kleiman, "Parents Groups Purging Schools of 'Humanist' Books and Classes," *The New York Times*, May 17, 1981.

[6] Tony Schwartz, "A Boycott of TV Advertisers Is Again Threatened," *The New York Times*, January 28, 1982.

cacy campaign began, a modest decline in the amounts of violence and sexual material on television shows led many to believe that network officials were influenced by the criticism. Those at the other end of the political spectrum have responded to the conservative attempt to save America's moral standards by raising the issue of individual rights. Typical are the arguments used by People for the American Way, a group started by television producer Norman Lear ("All in the Family," "The Jeffersons"). In full-page newspaper ads and direct mail letters, People for the American Way claimed that the fundamentalist activists would deny people the right to be different. "Cherishing religious beliefs is an American tradition. Forcing them on other Americans is not," reads their copy.[7] People for the American Way and other liberal groups are trying to convince the public that the truest American value is the right to individual liberty, where other people's religious beliefs do not interfere with one's own freedom.

Both sides in this fight have merit. Individual liberties and a strong sense of morality are both important to the well-being of any democracy. But for each side, the problem is the same: Who is to say what "liberty" and "morality" really mean? This war is played out in numerous conflicts, from local book-banning controversies to proposed constitutional amendments affecting school prayer and abortion. The broader struggle is for public opinion. Both Jerry Falwell's syndicated television sermons and Norman Lear's newspaper ads are meant to convince the man and woman on the street that their image of America is the correct one. They are lobbying for values — values they believe embody the American spirit. Once the preeminence of those values is recognized, the "right" decisions on public policy will follow.

Promoting Capitalism

Promoting American values also extends to the economic sphere. A small number of corporations have spent millions on advertisements devoted primarily to extolling the virtues of capitalism. Although the ads may generate some name recognition for the sponsoring firms, they do not directly promote their products or services. Instead, they

---

[7] Advertisement, "The Gospel According to Four Religious Leaders," *The New York Times*, May 10, 1982.

offer moderately detailed analysis of public policy questions or basic arguments in favor of the free enterprise system. These "advocacy ads" run in leading newspapers and magazines and are designed to influence both opinion leaders (politicians, business executives, journalists) and the public at large.[8]

The best-known advocacy advertising campaign is that of Mobil Oil. Mobil's ads, which appear regularly in *The New York Times,* the *Washington Post,* the *Chicago Tribune,* and six other leading newspapers across the country, cover a variety of subjects. A continuing theme, however, is the need for free market solutions to questions of public policy. Big business will best serve the nation's interests if government will restrict its regulatory activities. This view is reflected in a typical Mobil advertisement entitled "Progress *and* the Environment":

> ... we feel it's important to know that modern technology, economic activity, and a sound environment are not incompatible. In fact, they can be mutually enriching. We feel the need to express, from time to time, our belief that those who object to economic development on ecological grounds may often be expressing mere rhetoric and couching their real elitist motives in terms they see as popular and effective.[9]

Mobil's advocacy advertising consumes $5 million of the $21 million it spends on public affairs activities.[10] Smaller programs, like those run by SmithKline and Bethlehem Steel, cost about 2 to 3 million dollars annually. The high cost of purchasing advertising space in newspapers and magazines, and the need to run ads regularly to achieve some recognition for them, mean that only the very wealthy corporations can afford to undertake an advocacy advertising series.

Despite the large sums of money spent on advocacy ads in recent years, there is little solid evidence that individual campaigns do much to shift public opinion. One poll showed that only 6 percent

---

[8] See, generally, S. Prakash Sethi, "Grassroots Lobbying and the Corporation," *Business and Society Review* (November/December 1979), pp. 8–14.

[9] Advertisement, "Progress *and* the Environment," *The New York Times,* December 3, 1981.

[10] Randall Poe, "Masters of the Advertorial," *Across the Board,* September 1980, p. 21.

of those interviewed considered corporate issue ads to be "generally credible," and 53 percent found them "not credible."[11] One can speculate that the cumulative weight of repeated advertisements praising capitalism may have increased public support for free market policies in general, but this effect seems difficult to prove. Still, the businesses that have sponsored advocacy ads feel the money they have spent has been a good investment. In interviews, public affairs officials for these companies rejected the notion that their ads amounted to little more than preaching to the faithful and claimed that their campaigns were having an effect.

Spokesmen for these companies have a very clear rationale for sponsoring advocacy ads. They believe that large corporations have not been particularly successful in getting their point of view across but that other sectors of society, especially those critical of business, have been effective in capturing media attention for their opinions. "We are playing catch up," said one corporate public affairs official. Speaking of the free enterprise system, another public affairs representative said, "There are popular misconceptions which we must correct." A broad perception is that many people really don't understand the position of business on major issues, or even understand the role business plays in American society. In the words of one corporate official, "Most people have no idea what free enterprise is all about." Thus the ads carefully explain the positive benefits that will flow from the free market policies the companies endorse.

It is not only advocacy advertising that big business uses to mold opinion about the intrinsic value of capitalism. The public affairs departments of large corporations produce a great deal of educational material (pamphlets, film strips, and comic books), which they give away to school systems for use in the classroom. The purpose is to instill — critics say to propagandize — in students appreciation for business contributions to the well-being of America. Student materials produced by industry groups, like *The Atom, Electricity, and You* and *Food Additives — Who Needs Them?* naturally present glowing appraisals of the atomic power and chemical industries.[12] Corpora-

11 Sethi, "Grassroots Lobbying," p. 9; and Poe, "Masters of the Advertorial." See contra, Robert F. Dee, "The Hippos are Astir," *Public Communications Review* 1 (Fall 1981), pp. 10–13.
12 Sheila Harty, *Hucksters in the Classroom* (Washington, D.C.: Center for the Study of Responsive Law, 1979), pp. 18–62.

tions also contribute to conservative citizen groups, probusiness think tanks, and of course, through their political action committees, to candidates who share their views.

The political bottom line for business seems to be this: No matter how successful the free enterprise system has been in the past, its critics abound. Unless business aggressively promotes its fundamental philosophy, that philosophy remains in danger. One corporate public affairs official says, "In a democratic society, people vote on ideas."

Power of Ideas

The effort of a citizens' lobby trying to ban secular humanism from the classroom or a corporation distributing a booklet called *The Atom, Electricity, and You,* may seem far removed from the vital decisions that are made in Washington by Congress or agencies. Yet such activity is hardly trivial. Interest groups recognize the simple truth that ideas are powerful. If the public's collective attitudes can be altered, significant changes in policy may follow. Before there was an Environmental Protection Agency or a strong Clean Air Act, there was an underlying change in people's attitude toward the environment. Awareness grew that resources were finite, that wilderness was disappearing, and that pollution was a real hazard to both people and the environment. Gradually, the idea took hold that government must take a much more active role lest the quality of the environment and of life rapidly deteriorate. Environmentalism became a widely shared value of the 1970s, and the political ramifications were manifested in new regulatory laws.[13]

Societal values constantly evolve, surely helped along in part by interest group advocacy. It is relatively uncommon, however, for like-minded interest groups to succeed in truly replacing old beliefs with newly dominant ones. Indeed, concerted efforts by interest groups to influence the shape of values is likely to stimulate advocacy by opposing groups. Still, as feminists, environmentalists, and Christian fundamentalists have shown, the political effect of shifting values can be impressive even when strong counterpressures build to limit change.

---

[13] For a critical examination of the consequences of environmentalism, see William Tucker, *Progress and Privilege* (New York: Doubleday, 1982).

EDUCATING THE PUBLIC

At one time or another, almost all interest groups find themselves trying to educate the public about an issue. Usually the attempt takes the form of the Washington office of a lobby attempting to get attention in the media for the facts that support its side of an issue controversy. When the media ignore such an effort, wealthier interest groups will sometimes turn to paid advertising to get their point across. Finally, interest groups dealing with Congress may use voting scorecards to educate constituents about their legislators' votes. Publicizing yeas and nays cast by members of Congress is seen as a way of pressuring them to vote in line with the interest group's preferences.

Disseminating Research

Leaders of interest groups believe that part of the problem they face is that the public does not understand the issues the lobby is involved with. This is not condescension — belief that people are basically ignorant. Rather, it is a realistic assumption that most people care marginally about most political issues. Moreover, the complexity of public policy problems makes it difficult for the nonspecialist to acquire more than a superficial knowledge of issues unless they conscientiously seek information. Interest group officials believe that if they can bring their facts to people's attention, they will win them over because of the "truth" in their case.

To get their facts out to the public, interest groups frequently engage in research to uncover data on their own, or try to make people aware of largely ignored studies by academics and others. An interest group with one or more staffers who have a strong research background may go as far as to undertake a book-length study. Ralph Nader has been particularly effective in commissioning studies to document his point of view. One of the most successful Nader studies, *The Nader Report on the Federal Trade Commission*, was a thorough, highly detailed analysis of that agency's shortcomings in protecting consumers.[14] The devastating report was a major factor in reform efforts aimed at rejuvenating the FTC.

Because the demand on resources is great, and time is often of

[14] Edward F. Cox, Robert C. Fellmeth, and John E. Schulz, *The Nader Report on the Federal Trade Commission* (New York: Baron, 1969).

the essence in lobbying, major book-length studies are not usually feasible. More modest research reports are common, though, and practically every day in Washington one group or another releases a short study of some type. After the Congress made changes in the Medicaid program at the request of the Reagan administration, the Children's Defense Fund conducted an analysis of the impact of the budget cuts on the health of children. The liberal advocacy group's report estimated that 700,000 children had lost coverage under the cuts and concluded that "Reaganomics is bad for children's health." [15]

To effectively disseminate its research, a group cannot rely on its own distribution of its reports to policy makers and opinion leaders. Rather, the success of such a tactic depends mostly on the quantity and quality of press coverage. The coverage a group receives may depend partly on subjective editorial judgments as to what's "news." Still, an interest group can improve its chances of gaining news coverage by producing high-quality research — research that is original, draws upon respected sources, is thoroughly documented, and is sophisticated in its approach.

An individual lobbyist's goal is to become known for his expertise in a policy area so that those in government will solicit his or her views and data. Lobbyists want to be known and trusted by the press in the same way. To achieve this recognition, they must be able to offer information not easily available elsewhere. They must also make sure that their own bias does not so color their findings that it will damage their credibility. Given time, lobbyists who are useful sources of information may be able to develop mutually beneficial relationships with reporters. Ideally, a lobbyist wants to be able to take the group's report to a syndicated columnist like Mary McGrory, Rowland Evans, or Jack Anderson, or to a reporter from *The New York Times* or the *Washington Post*, and have that journalist feel confident enough about their source that they write a story using that information.

Public Relations

When an interest group feels that the press is not giving sufficient coverage to an issue or is unsympathetic to its point of view, it

---

[15] Robert Pear, "Decline in Health Services for the Poor Is Cited," *The New York Times*, January 17, 1983.

may decide to initiate a public relations campaign. Usually it will purchase advertising space in newspapers and magazines. By controlling its own copy, a group can bring home to the reader the terrible consequences it sees if the action they're advocating is not taken.

A public relations campaign was used by the Bi-Partisan Budget Appeal, a group formed to fight against large budget deficits. It took out two-page advertisements in some leading newspapers in an attempt to call attention to the threat posed by looming deficits. The ads declared that "The federal budget is now out of control. It is primed to generate immense deficits, year after year, for decades ahead. . . ." The group offered a highly detailed analysis of the budget problem along with its own proposal for tax and spending policy.[16]

Public relations campaigns have a number of drawbacks. First, they are enormously expensive. A campaign that puts ads in major papers across the country reaches six figures very quickly. A full-page ad in the Sunday *New York Times* alone is around $25,000.[17] Second, ads are seen as just that — ads. Advertisements by groups calling for specific policies that will benefit them are going to be interpreted by many people as self-serving political statements. Groups can only hope that the power of their argument makes their case persuasive in spite of this transparency. Third, by themselves, advertisements won't make things happen. Policy makers are not so easily moved that they will change their minds or charge into action because an ad powerfully articulates some group's proposal or grievance. Ads make most sense when they are part of a larger campaign that involves other tactics as well. Otherwise, they are likely to amount to little more than an expensive means of raising public consciousness.

Voting Records

Voting scorecards are a means by which an interest group can tell constituents in a simple manner whether their representative or senators generally support the organization's goals.[18] Probably the

---

[16] Advertisement, "To the President and the Congress," *Wall Street Journal*, January 25, 1983.

[17] *The New York Times*. Telephone interview.

[18] Linda L. Fowler, "How Interest Groups Select Issues for Rating Voting Records of Members of the U.S. Congress," *Legislative Studies Quarterly* 7 (August 1982), pp. 401–413.

best-known voting scorecards are those distributed by the Americans for Democratic Action (ADA) and the Americans for Constitutional Action (ACA). Each year, the ADA tallies how many times each member of Congress voted for the liberal position on issues the lobby regards as crucial. Likewise, the ACA counts up agreement with conservative positions on its own list of critical issues. At the end of each session, each member of Congress receives a summary score of between 0 and 100 percent. When voters back home learn that their legislator has a 70 percent ADA rating, it might cause them to feel more positive about that legislator (if they themselves are liberal) or more negative (if they are conservative).

Voting scorecards are increasingly popular with interest groups, more than seventy of which now use them, including the National Farmers Union, Common Cause, the Chamber of Commerce, the National Taxpayers Union, and the National Council of Senior Citizens.[19] Although a few groups like the ADA and ACA compose a general liberal-conservative scorecard, most rankings are constructed from a narrower range of issues that affect particular constituencies. Members of the National Farmers Union can assume that the rankings their congressmen receive from that group relate to votes on major farm issues.

Local papers sometimes carry a story of how their members of Congress scored in some group's rankings, but the scorecard is generally disseminated through an interest group's own publication. The scorecard's effect is limited here, because a relatively small percentage of voters in any one district or state belong to any one group. Some impact may come from opponents of incumbents using the rankings in their campaigning. A liberal member of Congress in a conservative district can find that a poor rating from a conservative or a business group can be cited frequently by the person running against him. All in all, though, the rankings are only a little more helpful to a congressional challenger than the votes themselves, which can be discussed in detail if the challenger so chooses. Beyond their use in campaigns, lobbies view scorecards as a source of pressure on members of Congress on votes relevant to the group. Before an important vote, the National Federation of Independent Business sends a letter to each congressman, informing him of the group's position

[19] Bill Keller, "Congressional Rating Game Is Hard to Win," *Congressional Quarterly Weekly Report*, March 21, 1981, pp. 507–512.

and indicating that the vote will likely be included in the annual scorecard.[20]

A new and important variant of the voting scorecards is the interest group's use of direct mail to inform voters of how incumbents have voted on key issues. With direct mail, an interest group can go beyond its own members and purchase a list of people that will enable them to mail to a specific district or even to selected census tracts. The typical letter will tell voters in rather negative language that their member of Congress voted the wrong way on one or more specific issues, and will ask for a donation to help defeat him. The National Conservative Political Action Committee has used this tactic, informing voters that their senator voted in favor of abortion or to give up the Panama Canal. The same group has utilized the related approach of broadcasting negative television ads that detail a liberal congressman's voting record.[21] NCPAC can do so because under current law an individual or political action committee can spend unlimited amounts of money to advocate election or defeat of a candidate, provided they work completely independent of their preferred candidate's campaign.

DEMONSTRATIONS AND HISTRIONICS

The current popularity of political demonstrations is directly rooted in the civil rights movement of the 1960s. Before blacks took to the streets to march, civil rights groups working for legislative remedies to segregation and discrimination made negligible progress. Without question these marches, many of which ended in violent confrontations with lawmen, galvanized public opinion in favor of the 1964 and 1965 civil rights acts. The first and foremost goal of all political protests is the same: to gain coverage by the media. Like a tree falling in the forest, a protest without media coverage goes unappreciated no matter how much noise it makes. As the late E. E. Schattschneider pointed out, when an interest group sees itself at some disadvantage, it is natural for it to want to expand the conflict: "the outcome of every conflict is determined by the *extent* to which the audience becomes involved in it." [22]

[20] Keller, "Congressional Rating Game Is Hard to Win," p. 509.
[21] Adam Clymer, "Conservative Political Commitee Evokes Both Fear and Adoration," *The New York Times*, May 31, 1981.
[22] E. E. Schattschneider, *The Semisovereign People* (Hinsdale, Ill.: Dryden Press, 1975), p. 2.

In short, interest groups protest because they feel no one will listen to them otherwise. They also reason that once the injustice about which they are protesting is brought to the attention of a larger audience, enough of the public will side with them to force policy makers into action. Yet attracting attention from the media for a protest is still only one step in a lobbying campaign. Few protests are convincing enough in themselves not to require other tactics as a follow-up. Usually then, they are part of a larger strategy in which the protest is designed to bolster direct lobbying efforts.[23]

The civil rights demonstrations were particularly compelling stories for the media because of the violence that some of them produced. Indeed, it seems evident from the historical record that some of the marches were undertaken with full knowledge that they would provoke outbursts of violence against blacks by antagonistic white policemen. David Garrow writes that Martin Luther King, Jr.'s Southern Christian Leadership Conference (SCLC) consciously decided to "evoke public nastiness and physical violence" from the lawmen who were to confront them at Selma, Alabama.[24] The result was a horrified nation that saw network news coverage of defenseless blacks beaten with nightsticks and chased by mounted policemen. The marches quickly became a symbol of struggle between good and evil, justice and injustice, and Americanism and racism.

Few interest groups that have relied on protest have had anywhere near the success of the SCLC and other civil rights groups. It is not only a matter of authorities learning that their violence can increase sympathy for protesters, but also that few protests are directed toward a point of view that could crumble so easily in the court of public opinion as did racial segregation. Only in the South was there any measurable public support for it, and when the marches forced the issue to the forefront of the political agenda, congressional action became inevitable.

The legacy of the civil rights movement (and less so the anti-Vietnam War movement), is that protests can work. For citizen groups the lesson seemed to be that organizations like themselves

[23] A model of a protest-oriented lobbying strategy is offered by Michael Lipsky, "Protest as a Political Resource," American Political Science Review 62 (December 1968), pp. 1144–1158. The classic community-organizing perspective on protest strategy is Saul Alinsky, Rules for Radicals (New York: Random House, 1971).

[24] David J. Garrow, Protest at Selma (New Haven: Yale University Press, 1978), p. 54.

could have an effect with such aggressive, even abrasive behavior.[25] Because citizen groups often feel that they lack the entrée to policy makers that groups in the private sector have, demonstrations are a way of forcing people to pay attention to their demands. The widespread use of protests by citizen groups has encouraged many other types of interest groups to use them. Farmers and truckers too have felt they weren't getting a hearing in Washington and have resorted to protests to attract attention to their grievance. Protests have become so popular that their frequency has made them less effective in attracting coverage by the media. Only a very large protest at the Capitol has a chance of making the network news. Because few groups can attract thousands of people to a protest, they sometimes resort to histrionics instead. To capture the attention of the media when a conventional demonstration seems unlikely to generate much publicity or when there are too few protesters available to put on a credible march, groups may decide to try some highly imaginative and unusual protest, such as driving a tractorcade into Washington or putting steers in a pen on the mall adjacent to the Capitol. (See Table 7.1.) Still, no matter how eye-catching a demonstration is, it will amount to little more than a public venting of anger unless it is coupled with other tactics in a sustained lobbying drive.

DIRECT CONSTITUENCY LOBBYING

Even though the tactics described so far are widely used, few interest groups feel they can rely on them exclusively. When a bill is being debated in Congress, or an agency is about to write a new regulation, interest groups will usually want to build on any indirect constituency lobbying they have done and proceed to activate direct constituency contact with policy makers. From this perspective, those in government must be reminded how strongly constituents feel and about the implicit risks of going against a group's constituents. Groups also feel they must match lobbying by adversary groups, who in turn will be trying to prove how strongly their members feel about the issue at hand.

[25] Jeffrey M. Berry, *Lobbying for the People* (Princeton: Princeton University Press, 1977); Frances Fox Piven and Richard Cloward, *Poor People's Movements* (New York: Pantheon, 1978); and David Vogel, *Lobbying the Corporation* (New York: Basic Books, 1978).

Table 7.1
Protest as Theater

Protesters	Gripe	Demonstration
Cattlemen	High cost of producing beef	"Beef-in": 47 steers and calves brought to Washington and put in pens on the Washington Mall
Motorcyclists	Laws requiring cyclists to wear helmets	Bike-in at the Mall
Massachusetts People's Bicentennial Commission	"Tyranny" of big business	Dumping 100-pound sugar bags (actually filled with leaves) into Boston Harbor
Alaska Anti-Abortionists	Legalized abortion	Demonstrators chained themselves to a procedure table
American Agriculture Movement	Shrinking profits	Tractorcade into Washington
Greenpeace	Proposal to open one billion acres offshore for oil and gas exploration	Dumping marbles in Interior Department's lobby because Secretary Watt "lost his marbles" in making the proposal

Organizations typically use their memberships for direct lobbying by asking them to write letters, or by asking those members seen as particularly influential to phone or see a policy maker in person. Washington lobbyists are nearly unanimous on how valuable this kind of constituency support is to their own work. In interviews, they made these kinds of comments about their members:

They're essential.
That's where the leverage is.
The strength of our organization is our grassroots.
We depend on our constituents heavily — they are the salvation of our power.

For lobbyists, the members' writing letters or telephoning is a way of legitimating their activities. One business lobbyist stated simply, "My entrée comes because I represent the people back home." When letters and phone calls are coming into the congressman's office, the role of the lobbyists is enhanced and their access is likely to be greater than normal. Lobbyists understand intuitively what political scientists have demonstrated empirically: members of Congress are more influenced by their constituents than by Washington lobbies.[26] To maximize their own influence, then, lobbyists will try to couple their efforts with those of their rank-and-file members.

Although spontaneous mail from constituents is given most weight by congressional offices, lobbyists cannot usually wait for their group's members to act on their own.[27] On most issues, too few will write on their own and the organization must try to stimulate some letter writing. When interest groups want to activate a letter-writing campaign, they will occasionally try to move the mass public by taking out full-page ads in major newspapers around the country. This is terribly expensive and is not always the most efficient way of reaching those who are most likely to write letters. Such ads urging readers to write their members of Congress or the president are most frequently sponsored by ad hoc groups without substantial membership, by relatively wealthy groups, and by groups working on issues that are highly emotional and thus more likely to stimulate readers to react. It is more common for interest groups to try to appeal to their own memberships either in their regular newsletters or in irregular "alerts." [28]

To further efforts to catalyze members into action, the Washington office of many interest groups will have its membership broken down by congressional district. A simple command to the computer storing their membership list can produce letters for all those in the organization who, for example, live in the districts of representatives on the House Education and Labor Committee.[29] In this manner, letters can be directed to the key actors prior to a crucial committee vote. Another way in which interest groups break down

---

[26] John W. Kingdon, *Congressmen's Voting Decisions*, 2nd ed. (New York: Harper and Row, 1981).

[27] See "Communications and the Congress," Burson-Marsteller and the Institute for Government Public Information Research, Washington, D.C., 1981.

[28] Berry, *Lobbying for the People*, pp. 233–237.

[29] Corporations or groups without broad memberships can hire a direct mail firm (at considerable expense) to send preprinted letters to likely prospects asking that they be sent on to the addressee's member of Congress. See Bill Keller, "Computers and Laser Printers Have Recast the Injunction: 'Write Your Congressman,'" *Congressional Quarterly Weekly Report*, September 11, 1982, pp. 2245–2247.

their memberships for lobbying is to identify a list of organizational activists. This type of list will be composed of people who hold positions with state and local affiliates, who have done lobbying work for the group in the past, or who are otherwise active in the organization. The National Restaurant Association has an "Action Network" of food-service executives who do government relations work in their own firms. Groups rely heavily on their activists for letter writing or phone calling because they feel they can make requests many times in a year and still get a high response rate. The more general membership is seen as equally valuable, and willing to write letters, but not with the same frequency or reliability.[30] Therefore, requests to the broader membership are usually done through the newsletter, and activists will get the more expensive special mailings.

The critical assumption in activating letters to members of Congress is that legislators can be moved by such efforts. This assumption seems well grounded in fact. Members of Congress do keep a close eye on how the mail is running.[31] Part of every legislator's day is spent going through correspondence, and although they can't read every letter that comes in, their staff will summarize and even tabulate the sentiments expressed. Congressmen watch the mail closely because their responsiveness to their constituencies affects their chances for reelection, and, even more simply, because it is part of their job and they take their job seriously. Letters do not usually make those with well-established positions switch sides, but they can be helpful in swaying opinion among fence sitters. Equally important, the mail can help to influence members of Congress at an early stage, before an issue has fully crystallized into legislation before a committee.

One of the most impressive letter-writing campaigns in recent years was prompted by a law that would have instituted tax withholding on interest and dividend income earned by individuals. An effort against the law was spearheaded by bank lobbies such as the American Bankers Association and the U.S. League of Savings Institutions. These groups and many banks prompted letters with ads in newspapers, posters in bank windows and lobbies, and inserts in monthly bank statements. The outpouring of mail was so great that

---

[30] James Rosenau, *Citizenship Between Elections* (New York: Free Press, 1974).
[31] See Lewis Anthony Dexter, *The Sociology and Politics of Congress* (Chicago: Rand McNally, 1969).

Congress turned around and repealed the withholding law, which they had passed only the year before.[32]

Less is known about the effectiveness of letters from interest groups on administrative behavior. When an agency goes through rulemaking, the Administrative Procedure Act generally requires that the public be given the opportunity to comment on proposed regulations. Many of those who write to agencies are representatives of interest groups, because the technical jargon in regulations generally makes them incomprehensible to anyone who is not a policy expert on the subject. Agencies do not usually change the direction of policy in response to critical letters, but overwhelming political opposition can sometimes force withdrawal or extensive revision of proposed rules. Regulations on narrow issues are more commonly modified, because comments may suggest more palatable or efficient ways of achieving the goals.

Because it is difficult to force major changes in proposed regulations, an interest group hesitates to commit resources for a letter-writing campaign aimed at an agency. If the regulatory issue is vital to a group's goals, however, it may feel that there is little choice. Planned Parenthood launched such an effort when the Department of Health and Human Services proposed a regulation that would require federally funded family planning clinics to inform parents when teenage girls request prescriptions for birth control pills, diaphragms, or IUD's. In newspaper ads, Planned Parenthood criticized the Reagan administration's policy, calling it a "squeal law" and arguing that the regulation "won't mean less teen-age sex. Just more teen-age pregnancy." [33] Health and Human Services was subsequently deluged with thousands of critical letters. The administration went ahead with the rule anyway, only to have it overturned at the federal district court level.

When the stakes are particularly high, as just prior to a close vote in Congress, lobbyists will often prevail on important people in their organization to come to Washington. As a representative for McDonnell Douglas put it, there's "no one better to talk about the F-18 fighter than the director [of the company]." Organizations that are

[32] Julie Salmon, "Fight over Withholding Splits Banks," *Wall Street Journal*, March 28, 1983; and David Shribman, "How the Bankers Lobby on Withholding Issue," *The New York Times*, April 8, 1983.

[33] Advertisement, "If Your Daughter Had Sex . . . ," *The New York Times*, April 18, 1982.

composed of elites tend to depend heavily on their membership to directly contact policy makers. A staffer for the U.S. Conference of Mayors said of the member mayors, "They are the best lobbyists on most issues because they have the impact in the districts." When the American Newspaper Publishers Association wanted Congress to keep AT&T from publishing information electronically over its telephone lines, it naturally turned to local publishers to lobby their members of Congress. They cannot help but want to be receptive to the person who is responsible for printing news about their activities in Washington. Or, as one House aide said, "You don't pick a fight with a man who buys his ink by the barrel." [34]

Bringing group members to Washington is not always practical, and not everyone is important enough to warrant a member of Congress returning a call. Still, congressmen do not limit themselves to meeting with elites, and they spend most of their time during their frequent trips home meeting with a broad range of constituents.[35] Interest groups can arrange meetings during such visits home, and local activists can buttonhole members of Congress at political events and social gatherings. The National Education Association goes as far as printing a form (in triplicate) that local members are expected to fill out after meeting with one of their members of Congress. They're specifically asked to briefly analyze the "Member's feelings about the issue discussed." The NEA's Washington representatives apparently find this useful in the lobbying that follows.

The latest variant in direct constituency lobbying is the Chamber of Commerce's "Biznet" satellite telecommunications system. The Chamber spent $5 million in setting up Biznet, which provides companies around the country with a private telecommunications channel to Washington. Subscribing companies (at $5,000 a year) can, for example, set up a two-way, televised meeting with a member of Congress to discuss an important bill. It is also designed to enable the Chamber to alert companies very quickly on matters needing urgent action.[36] If the Chamber's Biznet is perceived as successful in maxi-

[34] Margaret Garrard Warner, "Newspaper Publishers Lobby to Keep AT&T From Role They Covet," *Wall Street Journal*, July 9, 1982.
[35] Richard F. Fenno, Jr., *Home Style* (Boston: Little, Brown, 1978).
[36] "Chamber of Commerce Plans TV Net," *The New York Times*, December 5, 1981; and Timothy D. Schellhardt, "U.S. Business to Unveil TV Network Soon," *Wall Street Journal*, April 13, 1982.

mizing constituency influence in Congress, it will surely be followed by imitators from other sectors of the interest group community.[37]

CONCLUSION

The increase in interest groups has been accompanied by growing utilization of their constituents in lobbying. The explosion in numbers of groups has heightened competition among them. This spirit in turn has pushed Washington offices to search further for resources that can augment the work of their lobbyists. Moreover, as lobbying has been studied more and better understood, methods perceived to be effective are rapidly copied.

Although breakthroughs in communications have facilitated constituency lobbying, it has always been considered an important part of interest group politics.[38] Washington lobbyists know that their own efforts are aided by a strong show of support from those back home. Constituency lobbying can add to the effectiveness of a lobbying campaign by demonstrating to policy makers that people are truly concerned about an issue, and that they are waiting to see what policy actions are going to be taken.

All the various means of constituency lobbying that are being used offer opportunities for citizens to participate in politics. Clearly, many people welcome these opportunities and take advantage of them to make their voices heard in the political process. At least for those able to participate in interest group politics, activism through their lobbies is a way of trying to right the wrongs of government and to fight a personal sense of powerlessness.

[37] The Chamber's new technology is surely one of the reasons the AFL-CIO has started to rethink its own communications efforts. See David Burnham, "AFL-CIO Trying New Technologies," *The New York Times*, October 12, 1983.

[38] Kay Lehman Schlozman and John T. Tierney, "More of the Same: Washington Pressure Group Activity in a Decade of Change," *Journal of Politics* 45 (May 1983), pp. 363–364.

Political Action Committees

The lobbying done by constituents through such tactics as writing letters to and meeting with their members of Congress is considered to be a cornerstone of the democratic process. Even in this era of computers and direct mail, contacting one's legislator or any other official is still the simple exercise of the First Amendment right "to petition the Government for a redress of grievances." From grade school on, Americans are told to cherish this right and are encouraged to partake of it lest government become unresponsive to the will of the people.

Yet all rights have their limits. The right to free speech and to petition government does not mean that constituents can do whatever they wish to influence the making of policy. In practical terms, the question of limits on such freedoms is most troublesome for interest groups when they use their money to try to influence elections. There must be some restrictions on their activity because of the threat that the wealthiest groups will dominate the political system with their campaign contributions. Although there is general agreement that the activity of interest groups in the electoral process must have limits, where to place those limits is a controversial question. This issue has become more pressing because of proliferating political action committees. Their growing importance in the electoral process is forcing Americans to again confront the classic dilemma of interest groups in a democratic society: How can the freedom of people to pursue their own interests be preserved while prohibiting any faction from abuse of that freedom?

Pressure grows to readjust the limit on the electoral activities of interest groups when it seems as though some set of lobbies is gaining an unfair advantage with their campaign contributions. Subsequent legislation on campaign financing can try to reform the system by extending the right to participate in elections to groups previously held back by law, by limiting participation of one set of groups, or by limiting participation for all groups. It is difficult to choose appropriate policy not only because of the abstract question of conflicting rights, but also because it is difficult to assess the effect of campaign contributions. What exactly is the effect of interest group money on both individual races and legislative decisions? Would-be reformers must not only try to determine the answer to these questions, but must also try to assess the future consequences of their actions — consequences that are not always easy to foresee.

MOVEMENT FOR REFORM

The greatest worry today is that political action committees are donating so much money to candidates for office that other constituencies without PACs are put in an inferior position in the governmental process. Much of this attention is focused on corporate and trade association PACs. The fear of corporate wealth is familiar in American politics and as far back as 1907, corporate gifts to candidates for federal office were prohibited by law. Subsequent reform legislation tried to limit the influence of wealthy individuals by placing a ceiling on the contributions they could make to candidates. Until the reforms of the 1970s, though, the wealthy had little trouble in donating what they wanted by making small gifts to different campaign committees that supported the same candidate.

The most recent period of reform began with the sharp increase in the cost of campaigning stimulated by the use of television advertising.[1] To pay for the ever more costly campaigns, candidates had to turn more and more to the wealthy contributors who could provide large donations. The extreme was insurance magnate W. Clement Stone, who gave approximately $2.8 million to Richard Nixon's campaign for the presidency in 1968.[2]

Congress took a major step toward reforming the nation's cam-

[1] On the transformation of campaign financing, see Alexander Heard, *The Costs of Democracy* (Chapel Hill: University of North Carolina Press, 1960); Herbert E. Alexander, *Financing the 1968 Election* (Lexington, Mass.: Lexington Books, 1971); and Herbert E. Alexander, *Financing the 1972 Election* (Lexington, Mass.: Lexington Books, 1976).

[2] Herbert E. Alexander, *Financing Politics*, 2nd ed. (Washington, D.C.: Congressional Quarterly, 1980), p. 49.

paign financing system by passing the Federal Election Campaign Act of 1971. Among its major requirements was that candidates disclose an itemized accounting of all expenditures and donations of more than $100. Each contributor was to be listed by name, address, and occupation. Campaign committees were required to file periodic reports, including updates on the fifteenth and fifth day before an election.[3] A separate bill, the Revenue Act of 1971, provided a basis for public financing of presidential elections by allowing taxpayers to donate a dollar from their tax payment to a federal presidential campaign fund by checking a box on their tax return.

Just after these reforms came the Watergate scandal. Because money raised for reelecting President Nixon bankrolled the break-in at the headquarters of the Democratic National Committee and other illegal activities, pressure built for further reform in campaign financing. The result was the Federal Election Campaign Act Amendments of 1974, a major intent of which was to institute a system for public financing of presidential elections. Matching funds for small donations are made available to presidential candidates during the race for their party's nomination. Full public financing of the general election for president was set for 1976. Spending limits were also set for congressional races, although the Supreme Court subsequently struck them down.[4] In the same case, *Buckley* v. *Valeo*, the Court ruled that the 1974 amendment to the FECA that limits individual and group contributions to candidate committees was valid. The limits are $1,000 for individuals and $5,000 for groups per election. (Primaries, runoffs, and general elections all count as separate elections.) An individual is further limited to contributing $25,000 overall in any calendar year, but no limit is set on the aggregate donations made by a PAC.[5]

Another part of the 1974 FECA amendments covered the prohibition against government contractors forming political action committees. This provision had prevented most businesses from operating

---

[3] The FECA of 1971 also put ceilings on expenditures for media, but this provision was replaced by other reforms in the 1974 amendments. See Jeffrey M. Berry and Jerry Goldman, "Congress and Public Policy: A Study of the Federal Election Campaign Act of 1971," *Harvard Journal on Legislation* 10 (February 1973), pp. 331–365.
[4] *Buckley* v. *Valeo*, 424 U.S. 1 (1976). The Court permitted limits on spending by presidential candidates when those candidates accept public funding for their campaigns.
[5] See Alexander, *Financing Politics*, pp. 25–44, on the evolution of the FECA.

PACs because few major corporations do not sell some service or product to the federal government. Labor unions, which like businesses were forbidden by law to make direct contributions to campaigns, used PACs to collect voluntary membership contributions and pass them on to candidates in the name of their shadow organization. For many years, the AFL-CIO Committee on Political Education (or COPE), was the best-known PAC for its widespread contributions to supporters of labor.[6]

Concerned that litigation in the federal courts could ultimately put an end to labor PACs, the AFL-CIO sought changes in the law. Some modifications were made in 1971 at labor's request and the ban against government contractors was lifted in the 1974 act. In going to Congress, the AFL-CIO knew it was taking a risk, because the legislation would have to treat business and labor equally if it was to stand a chance of passage. Labor leaders believed, however, that businesses would not form large numbers of PACs.[7] They were wrong. Mark Green writes that after the legislation was passed, "labor PACs grew 75 percent in the next nine years, and business PACs 1,750 percent, a ratio of 1 to 23. If the labor movement has suffered a worse self-inflicted political wound, it does not come readily to mind." [8] After the FECA Amendments of 1974 were passed, the Sun Oil Company went to the Federal Election Commission, which administers the FECA, and asked for a ruling concerning the administration of its PAC. The Federal Election Commission further broadened the opportunity for active corporate participation in the electoral process by declaring that corporate PACs could solicit money from both stockholders and employees, and that general corporate funds could be used to administer and solicit donations.[9] With the amended act and the Commission's liberal interpretation, the floodgates were opened.

---

[6] See Edwin M. Epstein, "Business and Labor under the Federal Election Campaign Act of 1971," in Michael J. Malbin, ed., *Parties, Interest Groups, and Campaign Finance Laws* (Washington, D.C.: American Enterprise Institute, 1980), pp. 107–151.

[7] Epstein, "Business and Labor under the FECA," pp. 112–113.

[8] Mark Green, "Political PAC-Man," *New Republic*, December 13, 1982, p. 24.

[9] Epstein, "Business and Labor under the FECA," p. 113. Amendments to the FECA in 1976 restricted solicitations to stockholders and corporate management. Also included in the 1976 law was a nonproliferation clause. Its purpose is to prevent an organization from getting around the contribution limit by utilizing multiple committees.

PACs AND POLITICAL FINANCE

No one can understate the increasing PAC involvement in political campaigns: it has skyrocketed. In the 1981–1982 election cycle, PACs contributed $83.1 million to candidates running for the House and Senate, more than double the amount they gave in 1977–1978.[10] The relative share of PAC contributions as a percentage of all contributions has also risen sharply. Between 1972 and 1980, the PAC funds raised by congressional candidates for general election campaigns went from 13.7 percent to 25.3 percent of total contributions.[11]

When the Federal Election Commission issued its SUNPAC advisory opinion in November 1975, just 722 PACs were in business. In only two years, the number almost doubled. By the end of 1982, close to 3,400 PACs were in operation. As Figure 8.1 shows, the most significant growth came from individual corporations. The number of PACs can be a misleading indicator of strength, however, because many PACs are quite small and give only a modest amount to political candidates. One study found that 37 percent of PACs gave $10,000 or less for the 1980 election. Furthermore, 42 percent of the PAC contributions averaged $500 or less.[12]

Clearly, all PACs are not created equal. Yet the preeminence of business is also reflected in the amounts actually contributed to candidates. For the 1982 election, corporations gave $27.4 million to congressional candidates; labor unions, $20.2 million; the "nonconnected" category (which includes ideological citizen groups), $10.7 million; and trade, membership, and health organizations, $21.7 million. This latter category includes many business trade association PACs, like that belonging to the National Association of Home Builders, as well as numerous professional association PACs, like that of the American Dental Association.[13]

10 "1981–1982 PAC Giving up 51%," Federal Election Commission, April 29, 1983, p. 1. See also "FEC Releases Data on 1981–82 Congressional Spending," Federal Election Commission, May 2, 1983.
11 *Elections '82* (Washington, D.C.: Congressional Quarterly, 1982), p. 47.
12 Theodore J. Eismeier and Philip H. Pollock, "Political Action Committees: The Shaping of Strategy and Influence," paper delivered at the annual meeting of the Midwest Political Science Association, Chicago, April 1983.
13 Cooperatives gave $2.1 million and corporations without stock $1.1 million. "1981–82 PAC Giving up 51%," p. 2. The Federal Election Commission's six categories are hardly a model of clarity, and the trade, membership, and health grouping is especially troublesome. It throws together such organizations as the American Bankers Association, the National Rifle Association, and the National Association of Retired Federal Employees.

Figure 8.1
Comparative Number of PACs, 1974–1982

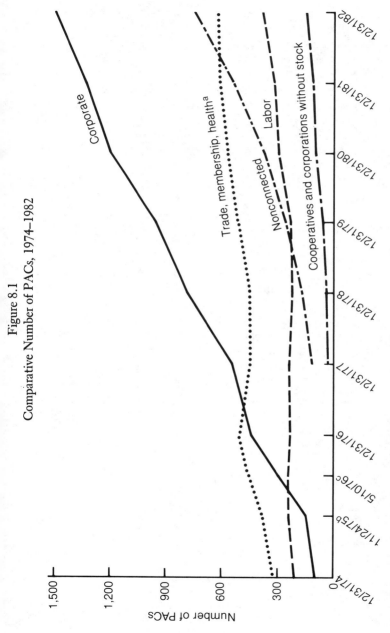

aPrior to 1977, this category includes all other PACs.
bDate of Federal Election Commission's "SunPAC" decision.
cDate FECA Amendments of 1976 were signed into law.

Source: Federal Election Commission

The explosive growth in PAC spending has come not simply because, given the opportunity, different interest groups choose to try to influence elections and public policy with their money. Groups also participate because they see themselves as competing with other interest groups. They are afraid of being at a disadvantage if they don't give. This striving to be heard extends beyond the natural antagonism between business and labor, and between ideological groups of the left and the right. Interest groups fear being lost in the shuffle among all the thousands of groups. Contributing money is seen as an important advantage in getting policy makers to pay attention to *their* problems rather than someone else's. Justin Dart, a California businessman whose Dart Industries maintains a large PAC, comments, "Talking to politicians is fine, but with a little money they hear you better." [14]

The growth of political action committees is not only a cause of increased campaign spending, but a consequence of it as well. In today's media oriented campaigns, a candidate for the Senate can easily spend more than $1 million just on television. The specific needs for television or other items, though, are almost secondary to the basic impulse of a campaign that drives candidates to spend whatever they can raise. Common Cause president Fred Wertheimer calls it the "arms-race approach" to campaigning. [15] Candidates push their fund-raising efforts to collect the greatest possible sum because they are afraid of being outspent by their opponents. They rarely see themselves as having enough. As a result, their fundraisers aggressively seek out PACs.

Because PACs are a way of gaining the gratitude of members of Congress, and presumably more access to them, we can see why so many have been formed in recent years. They seem to have been started in just about every sector of American society. It is not only PACs like the United Steelworkers of America Political Action Fund and the Realtors Political Action Committee, which represent large political constituencies, but also EggPAC, FishPAC, FurPAC, and LardPAC. The Dr. Pepper PAC is matched by the Coca-Cola PAC. The brokerage house of Merrill, Lynch, Pierce, Fenner & Smith has a PAC, as does the law firm of Dickstein, Shapiro & Morin. Inevi-

[14] Green, "Political PAC-Man," p. 20.
[15] Richard E. Cohen, "Costly Campaigns: Candidates Learn That Reaching the Voters Is Expensive," *National Journal*, April 16, 1983, p. 783.

Table 8.1
Top Ten PAC Contributors to Federal Candidates, 1981–1982

1. Realtors Political Action Committee	$2,115,135
2. American Medical Association Political Action Committee	1,737,090
3. United Auto Workers Voluntary Community Action Program	1,623,947
4. Machinists Non-Partisan Political League	1,444,959
5. National Education Association Political Action Committee	1,183,215
6. Build Political Action Committee of the National Association of Home Builders	1,005,628
7. Committee for Thorough Agricultural Political Education of Associated Milk Producers (C-TAPE)	962,450
8. American Bankers Association (BANKPAC)	947,460
9. Automobile and Truck Dealers Election Action Committee	917,295
10. AFL-CIO COPE Political Contributions Committee	906,425

Source: Federal Election Commission.

tably, beer distributors are represented by SixPAC.[16] Though not every one of these and other PACs is of great significance, it is truly important that so many constituencies feel they must contribute money if they are going to be paid attention to on Capitol Hill.

The Yield

If donating money can help to get a foot in the door, it follows that giving a lot of money can get a foot into a lot of doors. Some of the larger or wealthier constituencies have been contributing extremely large aggregate sums to congressional candidates. As Table 8.1 shows, six PACs contributed more than $1 million each to congressional candidates during 1981 and 1982. Sheer size enables these PACs to go beyond the common pattern of contributing to a modest number of candidates, most of whom are incumbents sitting on committees relevant to the group's policy interests.

It is interesting that not one of the top ten PAC *contributors* is an ideological group. Yet, counting instead money *raised* by PACs, eight of the largest ten are ideological citizen groups. Differences in the "yield" (percentage of money raised that is actually donated to candi-

---

[16] See Dom Bonafede, "Some Things Don't Change — Cost of 1982 Congressional Races Higher than Ever," *National Journal*, October 30, 1982, pp. 1832–1836.

dates) for the major categories of PACs are interesting to note. Corporate PACs contributed 62 percent of what they raised, and labor (56 percent) and trade, membership, and health (53 percent) had slightly lower yields. In contrast, groups in the nonconnected category gave as a whole only 17 percent of what they raised to candidates.[17] When we add independent expenditures for or against candidates to direct contributions, the figure rises to 23 percent of money raised that was spent on campaign expenditures or donations by nonconnected groups.[18] Most of this independent expenditure money came from the nearly $3.2 million spent by one group, NCPAC, whose abrasive, negative campaigns against liberal Democrats has generated a great deal of controversy.[19] Only a small number of other groups have used their funds for independent expenditures.

Why is it that citizen PACs don't contribute more of their money to candidates? The basic reason is overhead. Although direct mail has facilitated growth of citizen PACs, it is also the underlying problem that explains why these groups give so small a percentage of their gross to candidates (see Table 8.2). It is not only that most of the money must go for mailing lists, computer time, consultants, postage, and staff, but part of the little profit there is must be plowed back into prospecting with new lists.[20]

Compared to ideological PACs, the corporations, trade associations, and labor unions are able to utilize much more of their donors' money to pursue their political objectives. It is logical to expect that their costs for solicitation would not be as high because they are raising

---

[17] Adam Clymer, "PAC Gifts to Candidates Rose 45% in Latest Cycle," *The New York Times*, April 29, 1983.

[18] "1981–82 PAC Giving up 51%," p. 2.

[19] Not all of this money was actually spent on the independent campaigns because, according to Terry Dolan, NCPAC's chairman, Federal Election Commission requirements meant that some fundraising costs were included in the sum listed as independent expenditures. Further imprecision in the figures comes from expenditures made by the National Congressional Club, which spent money on independent campaigns not directed for or against candidates for federal office. They made a concerted effort, for example, to defeat a proposed gasoline tax in the group's home state of North Carolina. Carter Wrenn, the group's director, estimated that $1.5 million was spent on independent campaigns that were not included in Federal Election Commission figures. Wrenn says these expenditures explain why his group's yield is so far below the norm (see Table 8.2). Clymer, "PAC Gifts"; and "FEC Issues Final Report on 1981–82 Independent Spending," Federal Election Commission, October 14, 1983.

[20] The prospecting cycle is nicely illustrated in Larry J. Sabato, *The Rise of Political Consultants* (New York: Basic Books, 1981), pp. 228–229.

Table 8.2
Ideological PACs and Their Yields, 1981–1982

	Receipts	Contri-butions	Percentage of receipts donated
National Conservative Political Action Committee	$9,990,931	$263,171	2.6%
National Congressional Club	9,742,494	135,264	1.4
Fund for a Conservative Majority	2,945,874	119,595	4.1
National Committee for an Effective Congress	2,430,886	368,443	15.2
Citizens for the Republic	2,415,720	471,367	19.5
Committee for the Survival of a Free Congress	2,359,477	156,123	6.6
Fund for a Democratic Majority	2,307,605	175,959	7.6
Committee for the Future of America	2,190,264	228,562	10.4
Republican Majority Fund	1,967,119	455,547	23.2
Independent Action Inc.	1,189,059	109,840	9.2

Contribution figures do not include totals for independent expenditures for or against candidates, which totaled $3,177,210 for the NCPAC, $388,399 for the Fund for a Conservative Majority, and $132,920 for Independent Action Inc.

Source: Adam Clymer, "PAC Gifts to Candidates Rose 45% in Latest Cycle," *The New York Times*, April 29, 1983. © 1983 by The New York Times Company. Reprinted by permission.

money only from members of their organization, a fixed population who are already good prospects to contribute.[21] Such organizations do not have to purchase lists as citizen groups do. Similarly, they are not in the excessively competitive fundraising environment as the citizen PACs are. Someone whose name appears on mailing lists of known conservatives or liberals can easily receive solicitations from a dozen or more citizen groups in a month or two. (*The Washington Monthly* cited one Florida man who received 128 direct mail appeals in one month, primarily from liberal political organizations and various charities.)[22] Finally, parent organizations like corporations, trade

21 Corporations raise their money primarily from executives and most do not solicit stockholders. *An Analysis of the Impact of the Federal Election Campaign Act, 1972–78* (Cambridge, Mass.: Institute of Politics, John F. Kennedy School of Government, Harvard University, 1979, p. 5.19.
22 Tina Rosenberg, "Diminishing Returns," *Washington Monthly* (June 1983), p. 36.

associations, and labor unions can pay for the administrative and solicitation costs for running their PACs out of their general funds. Citizen PAC officials defend their groups by noting that they do not have such additional funds, that direct mail is a form of advertising, and that their PACs play a broader role than just donating money, especially in influencing the debate over issues.

Truth in Advertising?

The popularity ideological PACs have gained has a counterproductive side. The more new groups that start up, the more they plow the same ground. The Fund for a Democratic Majority (started by Senator Edward Kennedy), was one of the liberal PACs begun following the apparent success of conservative PACs in the 1980 elections. Its director, John Leslie, defended its low yield of 7.6 percent in the 1981–1982 elections as caused by its start-up costs. With an in-house mailing list of established contributors from their first time out, Leslie estimates that they will have a much improved 12 to 15 percent in the next election.[23] This optimism may or may not turn out to be justified, but the fundamental issue is that this group was sending out its direct mail letters to the same people who were being solicited by the National Committee for an Effective Congress, the Committee for the Future of America, Independent Action, Peace PAC, NOW/ERA, and other liberal PACs. As more and more groups compete for the same liberal or conservative dollar, the costs of overhead cannot help but stay at their already exorbitant peak. That a new group can aspire to improve its donation yield to just 12 to 15 percent is a measure of how dismal this situation has become.

Beyond the overhead that consumes most of the money given to ideological PACs is a further problem: accountability. The individuals who give money to an ideological PAC assume that a good part of it will end up in political campaigns. They are not told in the solicitation letters they receive what percentage of money donated actually reaches candidates. Nor is there any reason to suspect that donors are aware that so much of the money is spent on overhead. In one case identified by the *Baltimore Sun*, the Americans for Life raised $189,000 over three years but gave only $200 to one candidate. The money left

[23] Clymer, "PAC Gifts."

over after paying the overhead went back into direct mail. Yet the donors who responded to letters asking for money to help defeat "baby killers" at the polls were led to believe that their money would go to antiabortion candidates. Robert Timberg wrote, "But the ambitious political program laid out in the letters — including campaign contributions, political seminars for antiabortion activists and 'on-the-spot, up-to-the-minute' campaign aid for pro-life candidates — has never materialized." [24]

Ideological PACs not only have little accountability to their donors, but little constraint is exercised on the staff by the people with famous names that adorn the group's letterheads or by the boards of directors. Like most citizen groups, they are staff-run organizations. Direct mail contracts can be let to friends of the staff director without making that person accountable for the propriety of the action. The Progressive Political Action Committee (PROPAC), which was started by Victor Kamber, employs the Kamber Group to do much of its work. [25] Despite strict regulation by the FEC on some subjects (such as disclosure of contributions), the business practices of PACs go largely unregulated.

Until the public is made aware of the ideological PACs' yield, the current pattern will continue. Direct mail letters will keep striking at the emotions of readers who see donating as one of the few practical means available to them to fight for their political principles. For an individual, the seeming advantage of donating to a PAC rather than to a candidate is something like the advantage of buying into a mutual fund rather than directly purchasing stock in a company. Mutual funds pool the funds of many small investors to buy a wide range of stocks. And PACs pool large numbers of small donations into larger donations made to like-minded candidates. Unlike the nominal commissions charged by mutual funds, however, the donor to an ideological PAC is rarely charged less than 80 percent of the investment.

[24] Robert Timberg, "Anti-Abortion PAC Sticks to Fund-Raising," *Baltimore Sun*, July 15, 1982.
[25] Robert Timberg, "Liberal PROPAC Takes Unaccountability to Audacious Limit," *Baltimore Sun*, July 14, 1982. See also Robert Timberg, "NCPAC Means Business for Friends on the Right," *Baltimore Sun*, July 12, 1982; and Robert Timberg, "Insiders in NCPAC Operate Group Like a Family Business," *Baltimore Sun*, July 13, 1982.

DOES MONEY MATTER?

It is much easier to document the amounts of money being contributed than to account for its influence. We have no way of knowing for sure whether any group's contribution made a difference in an election. Likewise, interpreting the influence of money on votes in Congress is always a matter of inference.

Elections

Although the effect of any one group's contribution is difficult to measure, the influence of aggregate spending on congressional outcomes has been examined. Political scientist Gary Jacobson concludes after careful statistical analysis that campaign contributions are very important to the electoral chances of a nonincumbent. "In contests between incumbents and challengers, the critical variable is the amount spent by the challenger." [26] The amount spent by incumbents has less consequence for them because they enter elections with a decided advantage in public recognition. Increased spending by incumbents can little affect that recognition, but money is absolutely vital if the challenger is to become known to the electorate.[27]

Ironically, though money given to challengers is much more likely to affect their chance of winning an election, the largest share of PAC money goes to incumbents. For the 1982 election, PACs contributed $54.8 million to congressional incumbents, $16 million to challengers of incumbents, and $12.3 million to those seeking an open seat.[28] Most contributions by most PACs are not given primarily to influence election outcomes; rather, most is given to improve a group's access to members of Congress.[29] Consequently, a powerful congressman like House Ways and Means Chairman Dan Rostenkowski (D-Illinois) can easily collect $400,000 in contributions almost a year before his race — a race in which he would face token opposition at best. Most of the money comes from conservative business interests,

[26] Gary C. Jacobson, *Money in Congressional Elections* (New Haven: Yale University Press, 1980), p. 51.
[27] Jacobson, *Money in Congressional Elections*, pp. 33–50.
[28] "1981–82 PAC Giving up 51%," p. 2.
[29] See Edward Handler and John R. Mulkern, *Business in Politics* (Lexington, Mass.: Lexington Books, 1982); and W. P. Welch, "The Allocation of Political Monies," *Public Choice* 35 (1980), pp. 97–120.

such as oil companies and public utilities, who believe access to Rostenkowski is a much better bet than supporting a more conservative but long-shot Republican.[30]

Committee chairmen and party leaders are in an especially good position to receive campaign donations because of their crucial role in the legislative process. They can sometimes determine whether a bill or amendment will even be considered. Members on committees that have well-endowed constituencies are similarly blessed. The House Committee on Energy and Commerce, with its jurisdiction over a large number of industries, is a critical target for business PACs who need good relations with its members. The Ways and Means Subcommittee on Select Revenue Measures, where special tax provisions originate, is known around Congress as "Santa's workshop" for all the PAC contributions that are showered upon its members.[31] Yet the simple fact is that all incumbents do well with PACs — some just do a little bit better.

The access interest groups seek with their contributions is willingness of congressmen and their staffs to spend time with the organization's lobbyists. They also hope that congressmen who have received an interest group's contribution will be more inclined to act in the lobby's behalf. A sympathetic member of Congress can help a group beyond voting the right way by intervening in agency policy making, helping to organize legislative coalitions, and trying to persuade other members on key votes. Just as the value of access is indisputable, so too is the propensity of incumbents to win reelection. In the House, members choosing to run for reelection usually win at the rate of 90 percent or more. In the Senate, incumbents have won about 60 to 80 percent of the time in most recent elections.[32] PACs would be foolish to ignore this trend. Many House and Senate races are foregone conclusions, with incumbents facing only token opposition.

Beyond the inherent advantage an incumbent has, however, the behavior of PACs can make the incumbent's victory a self-fulfilling prophecy. By determining that specific candidates are likely to win and thereby withhold support from challengers, PACs further under-

---

[30] Brooks Jackson, "Lawmakers' Success with Fund Dinners Hinges on Lobbyists," *Wall Street Journal*, February 25, 1982.

[31] Elizabeth Drew, "Politics and Money — I," *New Yorker*, December 6, 1982, pp. 121–122.

[32] Barbara Hinckley, *Congressional Elections* (Washington, D.C.: Congressional Quarterly, 1981), p. 39.

mine the challengers' chances. Once deemed unlikely to win, a challenger's chances are even worse because of the critical need for contributions to make the campaign viable. This tendency is exacerbated by PACs watching other PACs' donation patterns. One representative of a business PAC said in an interview, "The majority of people watch the big ten [business PACs]. If they haven't given, none will." Even when an attractive challenger appears to stand a chance of winning, PACs sympathetic to the challenger's politics may fear the repercussions of failing to support the incumbent should the incumbent win.

Although access is the commodity that PACs value most, the amount of money donated to challengers and open-seat candidates is hardly insignificant. This money is spread over a smaller number of races than incumbent money because there are fewer competitive than safe seats. In this era of sophisticated polling and political analysis, the campaigns where the money will do most good are widely identified and monitored closely. As we will explore in detail, PACs are well versed on which candidates are running well and are guided by this knowledge in targeting donations.

Of the four major categories of PACs, only the nonconnected groups gave less than half their donations to incumbents in the 1982 election. As ideological organizations, they would be expected to emphasize principle more than the expediency of access. Another reason is that most of these nonconnected groups do no lobbying on Capitol Hill and therefore have little need for access to congressmen. Corporations and trade associations, on the other hand, are much more prone to giving to incumbents, including large numbers of Democrats whom they would ideally prefer to see replaced by Republicans. This has helped the Democrats maintain their edge in PAC donations over the Republicans. Toward the end of the 1980 campaign, Richard Lesher, president of the Chamber of Commerce, suggested that this practice be changed. "Business should quit trying to buy access and start buying a new forum for private enterprise. A lot of companies are putting their narrow, selfish interest ahead of the broader interests of the business community." [33]

Despite the Chamber's leadership among business lobbies and busi-

[33] Jerry Landauer, "Hedging Political Bets, Firms Give to Liberals in Positions of Power," *Wall Street Journal*, October 13, 1980.

ness PACs, Lesher's plea seemingly fell on deaf ears. In the 1980 elections, incumbents received roughly 57 percent of all corporate donations.[34] In the 1982 elections the figure for incumbents rose to 72 percent.[35] Surely the Republican gains in the 1980 elections and the strong Democratic tide in 1982 helped to fuel the rise in incumbency giving. Still, the basic pattern for corporations (as well as trade associations) is clearly one of strong support for incumbents.

Public Policy

The sharply increasing amount of PAC contributions is most worrisome because members of Congress rely more on those funds than they did in earlier years. This money has seemingly brought more groups more entrée into Capitol Hill offices. At the very least the interest groups believe it gets them more access to legislators and their staffs. One does not have to be a cynic to think that the money and increased access eventually influence public policy. Many Americans would agree with veteran Washington reporter Norman Miller that PAC money has made Congress "a scandal waiting to happen." [36]

The problem of interest groups and campaign finance is not new, however. There were PACs active, of course, prior to the FECA amendments. Moreover, corporations and their broader industries were represented outside the PAC system by large, individual contributions from executives in various businesses. The oil industry did not have to wait for the FECA amendments to have a say on Capitol Hill. One turning point was the 1940 elections, when a young Texas congressman, Lyndon Johnson, aggressively sought out wealthy oilmen and channeled their money into the hands of his Democratic colleagues across the country.[37]

Political action committees in recent years have broadened and furthered attempts by interest groups to influence public policy with campaign contributions. The change has still been significant. In the 1982 election, 106 members of the House received 50 percent or more

---

[34] "Costs of Campaigning Increase," Federal Election Commission, August 10, 1981, p. 2.
[35] "1981–82 PAC Giving up 51%," p. 2.
[36] Norman C. Miller, "The Pernicious Influence of PACs on Congress," *Wall Street Journal*, February 17, 1983.
[37] See Robert Caro, *The Path to Power* (New York: Random House, 1982), especially pp. 606–664.

of their contributions from PACs.[38] With the number of PACs rising each year (an increase of over 800 in the most recent two-year period of FEC filings), they are increasingly seen as instrumental to an interest group's policy goals.[39] Does this money influence public policy? The simple answer is that it can. One telling example is about money donated by the National Association of Automobile Dealers. Its PAC, fourth largest donor in the 1980 elections, gave $1,035,276 to congressional candidates of both parties. The leading issue for the auto dealers in the next Congress was the Federal Trade Commission's consumer protection regulation for used cars. The regulation required used-car dealers to list known mechanical defects and warranty information on a window sticker. A legislative veto resolution was subsequently introduced in both houses. In the House, 186 of the 216 representatives who cosponsored the resolution to overturn the regulation had received contributions from the auto dealers in the previous three years. Sixteen members became cosponsors within ten days of receiving their contributions. The average donation members received was $2,300.[40]

Does the fact that the Congress passed the veto of the used-car regulation mean that the auto dealers bought a favorable decision that they might not otherwise have gotten? No one knows for sure how Congress would have voted without the extensive campaign contributions. Yet it was Congress in 1975 that originally instructed the FTC to draft a used-car rule. The country did grow more conservative in the following years and the changing Congress mirrored this sentiment. The auto dealers, however, became increasingly active during this time as well. It is surely a reasonable inference that the contributions affected at least some votes on this issue. The donations were widespread, the issue relatively minor, and legislators had little to lose with the electorate by voting with the car dealers.

Few PACs have as much money as the car dealers and must instead concentrate their funds on a few legislators on the key committees. The National Office Machine Dealers Association, hardly

[38] Adam Clymer, "PAC Money's Role in Congress Raises Suspicions," *The New York Times*, January 19, 1983.

[39] "PACs Increase in Number," Federal Election Commission, January 14, 1983.

[40] Michael deCourcy Hinds, "Used-Car Rule: Lesson in Lobbying," *The New York Times*, May 12, 1982. See also Kirk F. Brown, "Campaign Contributions and Congressional Voting," paper delivered at the annual meeting of the American Political Science Association, Chicago, September 1983.

a major force in American politics, was led by its concerns to form a PAC to give it some clout on Capitol Hill. Their contributions during the 1982 campaign came to just $48,800, but those went mostly to a few members who could move a bill to restrict allegedly unfair business practices by suppliers of office machines. Representative James Florio (D-New Jersey), who guided the bill through his subcommittee, got $5,000 for his primary and an additional $5,000 for the general election. The group gave another $5,000 to the bill's Senate sponsor, James J. Exon (D-Nebraska), though he wouldn't be up for reelection for two more years. Legislators resent the implication that they worked for the bill only because of the contributions. Senator Exon, a former office equipment dealer himself, said "We could successfully get [the bill] passed without PACs to influence people." He added that until the office PAC's check arrived, "I didn't even know they had a PAC." [41]

Exon's point is important. Members of Congress do not market their vote for a price. They are more than willing to act on behalf of their constituents without PACs; that's part of their job. But they do not have the time to work strenuously on behalf of all constituency groups that approach them (and with whom they agree). It seems inevitable that their choice of how to spend their time will be affected by PAC contributions. It is simply more difficult to offer little or no assistance to a group that has made a sizable contribution. Representative Barney Frank (D-Massachusetts) says, "We are the only human beings in the world who are expected to take thousands of dollars from perfect strangers on important matters and not be affected by it." [42] Yet Congressman Frank leaves something out: Because legislators usually have at least some sympathy for most of the groups that contribute to them, they and their staffs are easily able to justify their efforts as having little to do with money.

In the day-to-day workings of Capitol Hill, it is the mundane activity of putting together compromises that will get a bill through committee or subcommittee that is the most common goal of interest groups. Maximizing their access to legislators and their staffs is helped along by contributions, as well as by other factors, such as the skills of their lobbyists and the character of their constituency. The aver-

[41] Brooks Jackson, "Office-Machine Dealers' PAC, Unlike Most, Uses Cash to Single-Mindedly Push One Bill," *Wall Street Journal*, April 6, 1983; and "How to Word-Process Congress," *The New York Times*, July 13, 1983.
[42] Green, "Political PAC-Man," p. 21.

age PAC like that of the Office Machine Dealers does not have enough funds to make influencing floor votes the goal of its contributing strategy. Although the larger PACs can work to influence the whole Congress with their money, the heart of lobbying remains committee work.

Although the primary focus of lobbyists is on committee work, journalists and political scientists trying to trace the effects of PAC money look more toward floor votes; the relationship between money and floor votes can at least be quantified, as in the used-car rule. Even though such efforts are not a precise measure of influence, they are more feasible to do than assessments of long-term committee lobbying, which is less visible and less quantifiable. The stumbling block is determining what the votes would have been without donations. In the end, judgment must be applied to each case to examine the pattern of donations considering all other factors in the legislative environment.

The lack of precision in estimating how influential PAC money is surely makes it easier for people to overestimate money's effect. Lobbyists for groups with PACs vigorously deny that contributions give their organizations undue influence in the legislative process. They argue that the improved access they may get from PAC donations enable them to get a better hearing for their members' views and nothing more. As is often pointed out, large donations are no assurance against adverse policy decisions. Furthermore, money can cut both ways on an issue, as in a dispute between business and labor.

But whatever the exact dimension of the relationship between money and public policy, there remains a widespread perception that money plays far too important a role in Washington politics. This perception is fueled not only by congressional decisions on particular issues, but by the breadth of some groups' giving and by postelection gifts as well. For some wealthy groups, contributions extend beyond the ideological preferences of members or even the need for access to key committees. The American Medical Association is one such lobby. More than 90 percent of House members serving for the past three terms have received at least one donation from the AMA.[43] In a recent Nevada senate race, the National Asso-

---

[43] Fred Wertheimer, "Common Cause Declares War on Political Action Committees," *Common Cause* (March/April 1983), p. 44.

ciation of Realtors gave to both incumbent Democrat Howard Cannon and his primary opponent, Representative James Santini. After Republican challenger Chic Hecht defeated Cannon in the general election, the same group then gave Hecht a $5,000 contribution.[44]

When gifts from one group become as widespread as those of the AMA, it stretches the justification for PAC donations as merely being an expression of the right to petition government. The AMA is simply using its great wealth to give to as many members of Congress as possible. After-election gifts also contribute to cynicism about the role of money in elections. When a group chooses not to support a candidate in the general election, but then contributes after his or her victory, it may be doing nothing more than using its wealth to cover placing a bet on the wrong candidate. Candidates understand the system, too, which encourages them to spend more than they have during a campaign. When they get to Washington, they can hold fundraisers and reduce their debt with PAC donations. After personally going into debt to win a seat in the House, New Mexico Democrat Bill Richardson raised $22,000 in one evening at a reception in a Capitol Hill restaurant. The money came primarily from energy concerns wanting good relations with the new member of the House Energy and Commerce Committee. The same groups were nowhere to be found during Richardson's campaign.[45]

TARGETING AND COOPERATION

For all the millions of dollars that are collectively given by the PACs, donations are still doled out in small increments, from a few hundred dollars to $5,000. For each PAC, large or small, decisions must be reached on whom to give to and how much they should receive. The decisions that groups make reflect their own needs and judgments as well as judgments of the broader political community in Washington.

The most difficult decisions involve contributions to challengers, open-seat candidates, and even incumbents locked in tight races. Though a group may have little difficulty in allocating money to safe-seat incumbents to whom access is most important, making

---

[44] Brooks Jackson and John Fialka, "New Congressmen Get Many Offers of Money to Cut Campaign Debt," *Wall Street Journal*, April 21, 1983.
[45] Jackson and Fialka, "New Congressmen Get Many Offers."

contributions in races where it will most affect the outcome is far more problematic. A group that has held back $20,000 or $30,000 for close races wants to make sure that it invests that money wisely. They are most eager to find out if particular races really are close rather than being foregone conclusions. Much of the information they get comes from other like-minded PACs. One trade association PAC official said, "The Washington, D.C.-based PACs are a close-knit community. Most people associated with the PACs know each other from other political work."

The communication between those affiliated with various interest groups and their PACs leads not only to a trading of information on which candidates are doing well, but to requests for assistance to particular candidates. One bank lobbyist said it was common for him to get calls from trade associations and PACs saying, "We have a candidate. Come meet him." The PACs and their parent organizations will actually hold a meeting or reception for a candidate and invite other PAC representatives to come by.

The PACs have more formal means for gathering political data as well. Business groups with general Republican leanings can draw on an easily accessible information network to find the races where their money will do the most good. The Republican National Committee and its House and Senate campaign committees, the Chamber of Commerce, and BIPAC work in tandem to keep business-oriented PACs abreast of congressional races across the country.

The Republican National Committee has PAC liaison officers to supply polling data and other political intelligence to sympathetic PACs. This system is part of a broader Republican party effort to utilize interest groups to aid congressional candidates and to help achieve the party's goals in Congress. In the most recent election, lobbyists Clark MacGregor and William Timmons worked in conjunction with the Republican campaign committees to hold breakfast meetings with representatives of various industry groups to encourage them to channel money to selected congressional races. They also helped to set up fundraisers for individual candidates with Vice-President Bush or a Cabinet secretary as the star attraction.[46]

The Chamber of Commerce acts as a communication link for business PACs with its publication, *Opportunity Races.* The purpose

---

[46] Drew, "Politics and Money," p. 71.

of *Opportunity Races* is to give PAC managers information on close races in which business interests have a decided stake. It comes out four times in an election year and, by the Chamber's estimate, is seen by 1,000 business and industry PACs. Each issue contains ten- to twelve-line capsule summaries of the hundred or so House and Senate races currently seen as presenting the greatest "opportunities" for business. Despite a veneer of nonpartisanship, the candidates deserving support are invariably Republicans. In the 1982 election, *Opportunity Races* told readers that in the second district of Mississippi (an open seat), the "Philosophical difference could not be more clear between liberal Democratic nominee, state Representative Robert Clark, and Republican candidate, attorney Webb Franklin." The summary of the race concluded, "*Urge business PACs support Franklin immediately.*" [47] (Franklin did edge out Clark.) Many of the races listed are reasonably close, but in some the group's ideology clouds its political judgment, as by telling PACs to support Ohio Senate challenger Paul Pfeifer because incumbent Howard "*Metzenbaum's negatives indicate race is winnable for Pfeifer.*" (Metzenbaum won in a widely expected landslide.) [48]

It is not clear just how much influence *Opportunity Races* has in channeling business money to its selected candidates. It seems the publication would be of most use to small PACs not headquartered in Washington. For these groups outside the issue networks in the capital, access to campaign intelligence may be less immediate. Still, PACs outside Washington can consult with any Washington-based lobbyists for the parent organization, and with representatives of relevant trade associations.

BIPAC also helps transmit information about congressional races to business PACs. It was formed in 1963 to help elect probusiness candidates to office. With so many other business and industry PACs starting up, its own role expanded to even greater leadership.[49] During election years it holds monthly meetings with PAC officials to go over races and candidates. Their endorsements are particularly important because they do extensive research on both races and candidates and they are looked to by the business community as a good

[47] *Opportunity Races*, October 5, 1982, p. 8E.
[48] *Opportunity Races*, October 5, 1982, p. 8I.
[49] See Bernadette A. Budde, "Business Political Action Committees," in Malbin, *Parties, Interest Groups, and Campaign Finance Laws*, pp. 9–25.

judge of a candidate's value to business. Although it supports an occasional Democrat, BIPAC is fundamentally a Republican organization. The Democrats do not have such an advanced PAC-relations operation. Said one trade association official with disdain, "The Democrats are not as geared up to deal with the PACs as the GOP is." Nevertheless, the AFL-CIO's COPE is a vital PAC for liberals and for the Democratic party. The National Committee for an Effective Congress is best known among the liberal citizen PACs because it has been around for more than thirty years. It holds meetings for people from other liberal PACs and publishes a list of close races in which money could be crucial. Yet it does not appear to have as extensive a following as the Chamber of Commerce or BIPAC. Few corporations and industry groups are interested in supporting liberal Democrats unless they're incumbents, and labor has an impressive political operation of its own. The Democratic National Committee and its congressional campaign committees have begun an effort to improve and expand its ties to PACs, and it may not be long before their operation is as sophisticated as that of the Republicans.

Decisions on endorsements and donations are usually handled by a small group of people within each PAC. Along with the director of the PAC may be individuals representing the parent organization (such as a corporation) or other organizations whose members give to the PAC. When a PAC has a Washington lobbying office, one of the top people from it will generally be part of this group. If a group goes beyond making donations to more than a handful of incumbents, it will often use some systematic framework for evaluating candidates. A beginning can be the political intelligence it receives from one of the national party committees or a leadership group like BIPAC. The decision-making committee of a PAC will also look at the voting records of incumbents, possibly concentrating on a few key votes on issues crucial to the group. The voting scorecards compiled by various interest groups provide further data; these scorecards have become so plentiful that a PAC can easily find one that is useful.

Political action committees may develop their own scorecards, going beyond just roll call votes. The TRW Good Government Fund has an evaluation form that is filled out by one of the corporation's Washington lobbyists, who grades candidates on eight criteria. They use a zero-to-five scale for such items as "influence in the Congress," "probusiness philosophy," and "chances of winning." Whether or not a TRW plant is located in the district or state is also noted.[50] Although the cumulative scores are added up, final decisions do not follow strict numerical comparisons. The degree of interest in issues of primary concern to TRW and other considerations come into play as well.[51]

A few of the larger PACs go further, requesting that candidates fill out questionnaires that quiz them about their views on various issues. The Realtors Political Action Committee assesses candidates' stands on matters relating to the economy and real estate with a seven-page questionnaire. Respondents are asked to rank the leading "contributors to the continuation of record-high interest rates." The items listed are: "record-level deficits, Federal Reserve's restrictive monetary policy, not enough time for supply-side economics to work, excessive federal spending, excessive personal federal tax cuts, and other (specify)."[52] Again, though, criteria other than the scores on the questionnaire come into play. BIPAC also sends out "PAC kits," which allow a candidate, Elizabeth Drew says, "to demonstrate why he would be a good investment."[53]

Political action committees have taken advantage of advances in polling and campaign analysis to effectively target their donations to candidates who are not sure winners. Their decisions are well informed and their aggressiveness in seeking information about new candidates is impressive. Still, many PACs allocate their funds in a simple and traditional way: giving money to incumbents who are sympathetic to the group's goals and who sit on the right committees.

CONCLUSION

The change in the campaign finance law that came with the Federal Election Campaign Act Amendments of 1974 has led to sharp growth in participation by interest groups in the electoral process. This explosion has been a mixed blessing at best. The PACs have increased

---

[50] "Government Relations at TRW, Inc.," Harvard Business School Case 0-382-053, 1981, p. 20.
[51] Letter to the author, December 23, 1981.
[52] James M. Perry, "How Realtors' PAC Rewards Office Seekers Helpful to the Industry," *Wall Street Journal*, August 2, 1982.
[53] Drew, "Politics and Money," p. 71.

participation in the political process by drawing on a broader range of donors.[54] They bring badly needed campaign funds into the electoral system. PACs also give people an important means of working on the issues they care about most, and improve the chances that their views will be heard on Capitol Hill.[55]

Unfortunately, this growth of PAC activity has also led to a greater sense that money is a necessary part of lobbying. One example is the recent formation of PACs by liberal citizen groups that have traditionally stood outside of electoral politics. Many groups began to feel they needed to "play hardball" with campaign donations if they were to accomplish their goals. The National Organization for Women created a PAC to work for election of pro-ERA state legislators and for defeat of ERA opponents. The National Abortion Rights Action League's NARAL-PAC was formed to counter the influence of LAPAC (Life Amendment Political Action Committee) and other antiabortion groups. A PAC for blacks was formed as well as one for senior citizens. But of course it is not just liberal citizen groups that have adopted this strategy. The number of PACs is growing across the board.

Although these new PACs may make funding of congressional campaigns more broadly representative, their formation is symptomatic of a disturbing and growing attitude that says, "without campaign contributions, my interests will not be heard in Congress." It seems much like the store owner who in times past has paid "protection money" to organized crime figures in the neighborhood. The ultimate result of this spiraling of group contributions to campaigns is that all types of interest groups will be donating huge sums of money to make sure their interest group opponents do not gain an advantage over them in Congress. The price of this kind of "equal representation" of PACs is that whatever policy actions Congress takes, large segments of the American people are going to believe that the "other side" bought the decision with their campaign contributions.

The Federal Election Campaign Act and its amendments were intended to reform a campaign system that had raised profound

[54] Ruth S. Jones and Warren E. Miller, "Financing Campaigns: Modes of Individual Contribution," paper delivered at the annual meeting of the Midwest Political Science Association, Chicago, April 1983.
[55] Herbert E. Alexander, "The Case for PACs," Public Affairs Council, Washington, D.C., 1983.

questions about the integrity of the political process. Undisclosed donations by fat-cat donors were seen as incompatible with the proper workings of a democracy. Strict disclosure requirements, public financing of presidential elections, increased incentives for individual giving, and an expanded role for interest groups were all part of this broad effort at reform. Expanding the role of interest groups has not, however, helped restore public confidence in the integrity of the political process. Rather, it has heightened unease about the role of interest groups in a democracy.

CHAPTER NINE

Washington Lobbying

Whether their organization makes campaign contributions or not, leaders of an interest group know that the real advocacy work on public policy issues comes between elections. Optimally, an interest group will approach a lobbying campaign with a coordinated strategy to influence public opinion, activate group members, and have their lobbyists meet with public officials continually. Such an idealized approach is not generally possible, for financial resources are limited, members can be called to action only so many times each year, and most organizations have only a few lobbyists, who must juggle a number of issues at once.

With resources of their organizations so limited, lobbyists must develop their advocacy plans with great care. Their work is complicated by the ideological differences they often find between themselves and those they wish to influence. Sometimes, neither Congress nor the executive branch seems likely to give the group what it wants, and it may turn to the courts instead. Yet going to court is expensive, and sometimes issues must be sacrificed because the organization cannot afford to add litigation to its already strained budget.

How do lobbyists and leaders of interest groups make such decisions in planning the structure of lobbying campaigns? After we examine how Washington representatives lobby the three branches of government, we will analyze how interest groups plan their advocacy and make their decisions.

CONGRESS

With most of the work done in Congress done in committees, it's no surprise that most of the work of legislative lobbyists is done there too. Usually the substantive decisions that Congress makes on questions of public policy are made either prior to formal committee deliberations or during the "markup" of a bill by committee members. When a bill reaches the floor of either house, there may be time for only a few amendments to be offered, especially in the House, where the "rule" on floor debate accompanying legislation can be quite restrictive. And because bills are not usually brought to the floor unless likelihood of passage is high, an interest group cannot afford to wait for floor action if it wants to influence legislation.

That Congress relies on its committees works to the advantage of interest groups. It enables them to concentrate their lobbyists' work on relatively few legislators and staffers. With most interest groups employing small professional staffs, communicating effectively with even half of the offices on Capitol Hill may not be possible.

In the first years of the Reagan administration, the National Clean Air Coalition made an all-out effort to keep members of the Senate Environment and Public Works Committee from amending the Clean Air Act to allow doubling of the carbon monoxide that could be emitted from automobile tailpipes. Auto manufacturers wanted the change because it would save them money and increase their cars' gasoline mileage. Lobbyists from environmental groups and the coalition worked with members of the committee and also released a report analyzing the consequences to public health of relaxing the standard. Their work was well directed toward committee members, because lobbying all 100 senators on the complex standard would have been far more difficult. When an informal head count showed that the carbon monoxide proposal would lose, the committee voted 9 to 7 to postpone action on the whole Clean Air Act, a victory for environmentalists, who felt that time was on their side with the 1982 congressional elections less than a year away.[1]

Committee-based policy making is advantageous to interest groups not just because of the committees' more manageable size, but also because it facilitates building personal relationships. One corporate lobbyist said, "Once you have established a good reputation, they will call on you." In time and with regular contact, lobbyists have the opportunity to prove that their information is reliable and that they can be of help to the committee in developing outside support for pending legislation.

Such relationships are usually begun and nurtured at the staff

[1] Philip Shabecoff, "Divided Senate Panel Puts Off Action on Clean Air Until Next Year," *The New York Times*, December 12, 1981.

level. Committee staffers are more immediately accessible and can put ideas they get from lobbyists directly into drafts of legislation or bring them to the attention of their bosses if they so choose.[2] Staff members do not act out of line with the general policy preferences of the representatives and senators they work for. Yet within this general constraint, their influence can be quite significant. Michael Malbin writes, "The staff's influence . . . pervades the legislative process."[3] In an interview, a lobbyist for a large manufacturer said bluntly: "If you have a staff member on your side, it might be a hell of a lot better than talking to the Member."

Congressional committees are not only of importance in the legislative process, but they are central to "policy subsystems."[4] The continuing interaction among agency officials, committee personnel, and lobbyists for client groups can build an easy familiarity between those with responsibility for the same policy area. The common tendency of committee staffers to move into jobs with interest groups or administrative agencies in the same policy area contributes to such close working relationships.

When interest groups turn from the committee to trying to influence a floor vote, they must develop a plan for reaching legislators they do not regularly deal with. If a number of interest groups share a point of view, they are likely to divide the task, each group taking the members of Congress it is most familiar with.[5] An interest group will also work closely with its allies in the House and Senate. When a vote loomed in the House on a new cargo plane for the military, the stakes were in the billions of dollars for the two competitors, Boeing and Lockheed. Boeing's case was spearheaded by Norman

---

[2] Staff members can be "entrepreneurs," aggressively seeking ideas and potential political support for their bosses. See David E. Price, "Professionals and 'Entrepreneurs': Staff Orientations and Policy Making on Three Senate Committees," *Journal of Politics* 33 (May 1971), pp. 316–336.

[3] Michael J. Malbin, *Unelected Representatives* (New York: Basic Books, 1980), p. 27.

[4] See Douglass Cater, *Power in Washington* (New York: Vintage, 1964); Roger H. Davidson, "Breaking up Those 'Cozy Triangles': An Impossible Dream?" in Susan Welch and John G. Peters, eds., *Legislative Reform and Public Policy* (New York: Praeger, 1977), pp. 30–53; Lawrence C. Dodd and Richard L. Schott, *Congress and the Administrative State* (New York: Wiley, 1979); J. Leiper Freeman, *The Political Process*, 2nd ed. (New York: Random House, 1965).

[5] See Walter Guzzardi, Jr., "How to Win in Washington," *Fortune*, March 27, 1978, p. 53.

Dicks, a Democratic representative from the company's home state, Washington. Georgia congressmen, led by Democrat Ed Jenkins, lobbied their colleagues, because Lockheed's entry would be built in their state if that corporation won the contract. The lobbyists for the airplane manufacturers coordinated their own work with these congressmen and their aides, but knew the congressmen would be much better "lobbyists," reaching representatives that the companies had little contact with in the past. Lockheed won the vote and congressional approval for its plane.

Congressional Hearings

The most visible part of the interest group's effort to influence pending legislation takes place at congressional hearings. Among the list of those called to testify at hearings are officials from interest groups connected with the issue at hand. Interest group leaders like to testify because it bestows status upon them and their organizations, because it shows members that their group is playing an important part in the legislative process, and because it helps to legitimize their further participation.[6] Interest groups do not testify from the naive assumption that their testimony might directly influence the members of Congress on the committee. It is clearly regarded as window dressing for the more substantive lobbying efforts made by the organization.[7]

Interest groups see more potential for influencing public policy by persuading committees to hold hearings in the first place. Even though a group's own testimony may be of little consequence, the hearings themselves can bring a great deal of publicity to an issue. In the early years of the food stamp program, representatives of the so-called hunger lobby helped to stimulate congressional hearings designed to bring public attention to the severity of hunger and malnutrition in the United States. The hearings received substantial press coverage, and testimony by doctors and nutritionists helped to create public sympathy for expanding the food stamp program.

[6] Schlozman and Tierney report that 99 percent of their sample of Washington lobbyists cite testifying at hearings as a tactic used by their organizations. Kay Lehman Schlozman and John T. Tierney, "More of the Same: Washington Pressure Group Activity in a Decade of Change," *Journal of Politics* 45 (May 1983), p. 377.
[7] Jeffrey M. Berry, *Lobbying for the People* (Princeton: Princeton University Press, 1977), pp. 223–225.

The Personal Encounter

The lobbying that is done in trying to influence public opinion in catalyzing letters, and in working with committee staff is ultimately aimed at influencing congressional votes. Yet no tactic is considered more effective by lobbyists than personally presenting their case to a member of Congress in a private meeting.[8] Other approaches can give a lobbyist entrée and create a perception of popular support for a policy, but a meeting with a legislator is an opportunity to press the case home and make him or her truly understand the virtue of the group's position.

Because lobbyists perceive meeting with a senator or representative as so important, and time they are usually allotted for their sessions is so short, professional lobbyists go into such an encounter with a clear idea of what they hope to accomplish and how they can most effectively make their case.[9] Washington representatives recognize that the session is not an end in itself, but part of a lengthier effort to establish a relationship with the legislators and their office. In working toward this goal, lobbyists are conscious of their "presentation of self": the verbal and nonverbal means of expressing themselves, which collectively create an impression of them as persons.[10] The most important part of the impression lobbyists try to convey about themselves is that they are persons of character. If the messenger is suspect, the message will be suspect. A labor lobbyist said, "The most important thing is your trust and integrity." Another lobbyist elaborated: "It's a relationship that we try to build. They know why we're there."

In trying to create favorable personal impressions, lobbyists do not neglect substance in favor of small talk designed to show what regular people (or good ol' boys) they are. There is surely some of that, but lobbyists regard information as the primary means for displaying their intelligence, political common sense, and overall character. Members of Congress don't need lobbyists as friends,

---

[8] See Lester W. Milbrath, *The Washington Lobbyists* (Chicago: Rand McNally, 1963); Harmon Zeigler and Michael Baer, *Lobbying* (Belmont, Calif.: Wadsworth, 1969); and Berry, *Lobbying for the People*.

[9] On lobbying as an interactive process, see Zeigler and Baer, *Lobbying*.

[10] Erving Goffman, *The Presentation of Self in Everyday Life* (New York: Doubleday, 1959). See also Richard F. Fenno, Jr., *Home Style* (Boston: Little, Brown, 1978).

and Washington representatives know that being seen as a good source of information is their entrée back into the office. A lobbyist who represents small business people said that in meetings, "providing information is the most effective tool. People begin to rely on you." Stressing a substantive presentation, an official of a large trade organization said his philosophy was to "Make an appointment, and then go with the issue manager."

When sugar lobbyists are meeting with members of Congress about a pending farm bill, their talk may move quickly to questions about how much the price support (a guaranteed minimum price) for sugar will ultimately cost the consumer, what different price support levels will do to farm and refiner profits, and how foreign competition is likely to affect the industry in the future. It is a rather complicated program, and lobbyists can draw upon their expertise to educate members of Congress on what they see as the facts. The "facts" about the sugar price support program are rather slippery, though, because all debate requires some assumptions about future market conditions. This is all the more reason for lobbyists to strive to show their expertise so that their case seems based more on solid evidence than on speculation.[11]

The stress on information does not stem from a belief that legislators are poorly informed about coming policy decisions. Rather, lobbyists act on the premise that legislators pay marginal attention to most issues because they are overloaded with the issues before them.[12] Even on the issues before one legislator's committees, an individual senator and representative will devote different amounts of energy in following each. When lobbyists do deal with one of the acknowledged experts on an issue, like Representative Barber Conable (R-New York) on tax policy or Senator Sam Nunn (D-Georgia) on defense policy, the sophistication in their presentation can rise accordingly.

For many years, the accepted view of a lobbyist's interaction with members of Congress was Bauer, Pool, and Dexter's conclusion from their study of foreign trade legislation in the 1950s that *"the lobbyist becomes in effect a service bureau for those congressmen*

[11] Barton Gellman, "Reagan's Deal on the Budget — A Sweetener for the Sugar Industry," *National Journal*, August 8, 1981, pp. 1417–1421.
[12] See Lewis Anthony Dexter, *The Sociology and Politics of Congress* (Chicago: Rand McNally, 1969), pp. 143–150.

already agreeing with him, rather than an agent of direct persuasion." [13] Few lobbyists today see their role as strictly one of supplying information to their strongest supporters in the House and the Senate. That is still a vital part of their job, but in interviews they clearly state that another important aspect of their job is trying to persuade undecided legislators to back their group's point of view. One public interest lobbyist said, simply, "I try to educate them and to convince them that the position we are advocating is the correct one and the one they should support."

In their encounters with legislators, lobbyists from large membership organizations have the advantage of being able to discuss the effect of the proposed bills on the members within the legislator's constituency. Some lobbyists claim that this is the type of information that members of Congress are most interested in. A Washington representative for the National Education Association describes his philosophy:

> . . . you go in there and talk to him about the specific program in his district. He isn't much interested in a national program. He needs to be able to take credit for doing something positive for the folks back home. You do it on the basis of what it does for him in his district. Your materials must be designed to reflect the district's activities.

How convincing any information is as it relates to effect on the constituency depends partly on the legislator's own reading of constituency opinion and intensity of interest. Interest groups understand this as well, which is why so many of them will spend significant resources on trying to influence and activate their members and attentive publics. If the legislator sees little constituency support for the lobbyist's argument, the latter's case may be weakened.

The effectiveness of a lobbyist's personal presentation to a legislator is difficult to determine in any instance, for members of Congress do not reveal how much they are swayed by any one source of information. Moreover, a lobbyist's presentation may reinforce an opinion instead of creating one. As for lobbyists' own belief that personal presentations are the most effective lobbying tactic, they are hardly the most objective judges of such interaction. It is all too human to believe that what each of us does has greater influence

---

[13] Raymond A. Bauer, Ithiel de Sola Pool, and Lewis Anthony Dexter, *American Business and Public Policy* (New York: Atherton, 1963), p. 353.

than it actually does. Surely, then, lobbyists exaggerate the value of this approach.

Although lobbyists may regard personal presentations to legislators as the most important part of their job, it is still the culmination of much more extensive work with congressional staffers. When lobbyists meet with staffers, their approach is much the same: providing useful information and trying to add to their own reputation as a reliable source of data. Every visit, every phone call, every research paper or issue brief they give to a staffer or legislator is part of their constant effort to build a trusting relationship. Most of all, lobbyists want that relationship to be a two-way street, where they not only have easy access to Capitol Hill offices, but also where they are called on to supply those offices with information.

THE EXECUTIVE BRANCH

Few public policies are conclusively settled by legislative action. If an interest group is to maximize its effectiveness, it must be skilled in lobbying the executive branch as well. Indeed, numerous interest groups spend far more time every day on the executive branch than on the legislative branch.[14] The National Association of Broadcasters must constantly monitor the activities of the Federal Communications Commission, which steadily issues new regulations. By comparison, Congress passes broadcast legislation infrequently.

When agencies formulate general policies, they usually do so by administrative rulemaking.[15] Rulemaking is designed to facilitate public input into the administrative process. Through the notice-and-comment procedure, draft regulations are published in the *Federal Register*, a compendium of all regulations issued each day. Interest groups take advantage of the comment period to write detailed analyses of the proposed administrative regulations. Another formal means interest groups can use in trying to influence administrative rulemaking is testifying at fact-finding hearings held by an agency to provide data on regulatory actions it is considering.

[14] Lewis Anthony Dexter, *How Organizations Are Represented in Washington* (Indianapolis: Bobbs-Merrill, 1969), pp. 1–16.
[15] See Kenneth Culp Davis, *Discretionary Justice* (Baton Rouge: Louisiana State University Press, 1969); and Kenneth Culp Davis, *Administrative Law*, 6th ed. (St. Paul, Minn.: West, 1977). An excellent brief introduction to rulemaking is offered by A. Lee Fritschler, *Smoking and Politics*, 3rd ed. (Englewood Cliffs, N.J.: Prentice-Hall, 1983).

As with their congressional lobbying, interest groups trying to influence agencies go beyond the formal opportunities available to them. As much as they can, lobbies mobilize political support to buttress their efforts. They also try to develop relationships with executive branch policy makers that allow them to express their interests through meetings and phone calls. Although most executive branch lobbying is directed at administrative agencies, some groups also try to influence the White House.

Administrative Agencies

The greatest difference lobbyists see between members of Congress and administrators is that the former are much more worried about the popularity of their actions with constituents back home. A corporate lobbyist describes the differences he sees in his work:

> A good many [in Congress] are idealists, but they have to get elected. They are concerned about their constituency and the media. He must be aware of his district. Administrative agency [administrators] are usually more specialized in their field and they're purists. They are not concerned about the press or a constituency. You bring in your technical experts and you just defend your point of view.

Agency personnel are probably not as callous toward constituency opinion as this lobbyist suggests, but the frustration he feels is very real. At the highest-ranking levels in federal bureaucracy are the president's appointees, individuals who are strongly interested in the next election. Beneath the top political stratum are the career civil servants, who by virtue of their nonpartisan status are somewhat more insulated from constituency pressures. Depending on their group's point of view, lobbyists may find either or both sets of officials unsympathetic to their cause. Likewise, depending on the issue, they can find considerable support among policy makers for the position they are advocating.

As in working with Congress, lobbyists deal more frequently with staffers than with the top officials. The career bureaucrats are not minor functionaries, but can hold important positions from which they can significantly affect the agency's policies. They are likely to see themselves as technocrats, determined to make up their minds from their own reading of the scientific or social scientific record.

Middle-level officials evaluating a drug for the Food and Drug Administration have scientific backgrounds and like to think that their decisions are based wholly on the scientific merits of test results and experimental usage. Yet, FDA evaluators are in regular contact with drug company representatives on whom they must rely for test data. Exactly how much this interaction affects their decisions is not known. Writing about FDA medical officers, Paul Quirk says, "having frequent contacts with industry representatives, getting to know and perhaps like them personally, and seeing their anxiousness to have drugs approved obviously will tend to create some sympathy for industry viewpoints and interests. Such contacts on a regular basis over a period of years may strongly shape the attitudes of FDA officials." [16]

Although the political independence of civil servants can be troublesome for lobbyists, the worst-case scenario for them is the appointment of high-level administrators who are hostile to their groups. John Chubb comments that agencies "actively structure relationships by cultivating the support and cooperation of some groups and ignoring or discouraging the input of others." [17] When President Reagan was elected, he appointed to the top positions in the Environmental Protection Agency people who shared his view that industry needed relief from burdensome regulations. Liberal environmental groups that support strong regulatory efforts to protect the environment were treated with open contempt by Reagan's first EPA administrator, Anne Gorsuch, and her aides. Gorsuch's deputy administrator, John Hernandez, reflected this attitude when he held meetings over three and a half months to assess the dangers of certain chemicals. Of the ninety-two people he met with, most were from the chemical industry and none were from an environmental group.[18] A representative from a liberal citizens' lobby said, "Reagan's people don't want to talk to us."

If agencies are hostile toward an interest group's general political philosophy, the lobbyists can do little to directly influence top agency

[16] Paul J. Quirk, "Food and Drug Administration," in James Q. Wilson, ed., *The Politics of Regulation* (New York: Basic Books, 1980), p. 211.
[17] John E. Chubb, "A Theory of Agency-Interest Group Relations," paper presented at the annual meeting of the American Political Science Association, Washington, D.C., September 1979, p. 57.
[18] Philip Shabecoff, "Environment Aide's Industry Talks Criticized," *The New York Times*, October 22, 1981; and "Spending Compromise Sought," *Boston Globe*, October 22, 1981.

administrators. They must instead try to work through public opinion or, more often, through members of Congress who share their point of view. A legislator on a pertinent committee can still have some clout with an agency even if he is of the "wrong" party or ideological persuasion. Agencies want to foster good relations with members of committees that formulate their budgets and oversee their operations. As a result, interest groups on the outs with an agency will prevail upon their congressional allies to intervene in agency policy making.[19]

There are strong incentives, however, for agency officials to want to cooperate with groups that share at least some of their policy objectives. As some students of bureaucracy have pointed out, administrators need to build outside support for their agencies.[20] Strong clientele support can help them win larger budgets in Congress, or protect them from would-be budget cutters at OMB. It can also help them win approval for new policy initiatives. Hugh Heclo writes,

> At best [administrators] would like to establish networks with outsiders who recognize the mutual advantages that can flow from a particular course of action or inaction. With that, bargains and understandings can be struck on the issues at hand. The influence of both participants is increased. Obviously the more enduring and less issue-specific the exchange becomes, the more confidence shades into trust.[21]

Interest group representatives approach a potentially receptive agency from much the same perspective. They want to build an enduring tie and not one that is issue specific. As in congressional advocacy, lobbyists know that their effectiveness is only as good as their credibility. In their personal presentations to administrators, many lobbyists see their approach being much the same as with legislators or their staffs. A lobbyist for a manufacturing firm said, "There's really not much difference. You are always trying to get them to see things your way." Some indicate, however, that their presentations are even more factual, with more data for administrators than for those on Capitol Hill. "Generally, we have to go into

---

[19] Jeffrey M. Berry, *Feeding Hungry People: Rulemaking in the Food Stamp Program* (New Brunswick, N.J.: Rutgers University Press, in press).

[20] Francis E. Rourke, *Bureaucracy, Politics, and Public Policy*, 2nd ed. (Boston: Little, Brown, 1976); Hugh Heclo, *A Government of Strangers* (Washington, D.C.: Brookings Institution, 1977); and Chubb, "A Theory of Agency-Interest Group Relations."

[21] Heclo, *A Government of Strangers*, p. 169.

much more detail. . . . We have to go into much more depth," said one lobbyist.

The ties between interest groups and agencies can become too close. A persistent criticism by political scientists is that agencies that regulate business are overly sympathetic to the industries they are responsible for regulating.[22] Critics charge that regulators often come from the businesses they regulate and thus naturally see things from an industry point of view.[23] Even if regulators weren't previously involved in the industry, they have been seen as eager to please powerful clientele groups rather than have them complain to the White House or to the agency's overseeing committees in Congress.

The relationship between agencies and interest groups seems to be influenced by a number of major factors. Clearly, the ideology and partisanship of the administration in power is a significant variable. Each interest group's constituency helps determine its ease of access. Citizen groups especially depend on having sympathetic administrators in power to gain meaningful access. In contrast, business groups are not frozen out of the administrative process when a liberal Democrat is in office, but they may develop much closer ties to regulatory agencies when a conservative Republican is in the White House. The climate of public opinion and the prominence in which an agency stands can also be important. Finally, norms of agencies guide civil servants in their interaction with lobbyists.

Thus each agency has its political needs and its own way of dealing with client groups. The relationships may change to the advantage or disadvantage of particular groups. Typically, though, lobbyists find that they have neither open entrée nor complete hostility to deal with. Rather, their day-to-day job is to get those in agencies to be attentive to the data brought before them, and to persuade them that those facts merit the action being proposed.

The White House

As the executive branch has grown, so too has White House involvement in cabinet and agency policy making. White House staffs

---

[22] See, for example, Marver H. Bernstein, *Regulating Business by Independent Commission* (Princeton: Princeton University Press, 1955); and Theodore J. Lowi, *The End of Liberalism*, 2nd ed. (New York: Norton, 1979).

[23] See, contra, Paul J. Quirk, *Industry Influence in Federal Regulatory Agencies* (Princeton: Princeton University Press, 1981).

have grown sharply over the years, giving the president the resources to control an expanding number of policy decisions.[24] Likewise, more and more interest groups find themselves needing access to the inner circle at the White House.

"Contacts" are probably more important for White House lobbying than for any other type of interest group advocacy. The president's aides can be selective in whom they choose to meet with. Sometimes they may find it preferable not to meet with interest group representatives so as to insulate the president from responsibility for a possibly unfavorable decision. Consequently, having someone who is close to the administration in power is vital for an interest group that wants some White House access. Reagan's friend Robert Gray's new public relations business boomed when the Reagan administration took office. Gray could call the president's chief of staff, James Baker, and have his phone call returned.[25] Many other public relations and law firms have prospered because they employ people whose past connections or reputation give them access to the White House staff.[26]

Some companies and trade associations will go out of their way to hire a person with such connections to head its Washington office. United Technologies, a large defense contractor, employs Clark Mac-Gregor, a well-liked and respected former Republican representative from Minnesota, as its chief Washington lobbyist. When a major contract is being awarded, such as a new jet engine selected by the Air Force, the stakes are in the hundreds of millions of dollars. Mac-Gregor says he is able to do his job well because "I see high-ranking people at the White House, in the Congress and at the Defense Department." [27]

Occasionally leaders from some sector of society, such as business, labor, or women's groups may be brought to the White House for

[24] Stephen Hess, *Organizing the Presidency* (Washington, D.C.: Brookings Institution, 1976).

[25] James M. Perry, "A PR Man Uses Access to Influential People to Lure, Help Clients," *Wall Street Journal*, March 25, 1982; and Lynn Rosellini, "Bob Gray: Public Relations Man to the Powerful," *The New York Times*, February 26, 1982.

[26] Bill Keller, "Do White House Ties Count?" *Congressional Quarterly Weekly Report*, March 20, 1982, pp. 603–608; and William J. Lanouette, "The Influence Peddlers — Connections Still Count, But They're Not Enough," *National Journal*, February 28, 1981, pp. 355–357.

[27] James M. Perry, "Affable Lobbyist Aids United Technologies in Jet-Engine Battle," *Wall Street Journal*, April 1, 1982.

a pep talk from the president on what his administration is doing for them. This practice can help the president politically by showing his special interest in a particular segment of American society. At times the president will even call interest group leaders into the Oval Office when he must give the impression that he is being responsive to some constituency. During the height of the civil rights movement, Lyndon Johnson met a number of times with prominent black leaders like Martin Luther King, Jr. and Roy Wilkins of the NAACP. The "photo opportunity" for these meetings brought them to the attention of people around the country in their morning newspapers.

Although it is difficult for lobbies to gain direct access to the Oval Office, presidents are not uninterested in the concerns of major groups.[28] Their decision making involves considering how attentive publics will react to options they are evaluating. Legislators of the president's party also act on behalf of major interests within their states or districts by lobbying the president for them. When President Reagan was deciding what to do about a grain pact with the Soviet Union, Representative Paul Findley (R-Illinois) and other Republicans from rural areas met with and warned Reagan of the negative consequences in the upcoming congressional elections if he didn't approve an export agreement. For their part, presidents feel constrained in their policy initiatives by the demands of competing interest groups. In explaining the shortcomings of their administrations, presidents are quick to cite the selfishness of "special interests" that kept them from accomplishing more.[29]

One means the White House uses to build support for administration policies is its Office of Public Liaison. First institutionalized in 1970, its job is to reach out to various constituencies and develop good relations with them. Typically, staffers will be responsible for a segment of the population, such as Jews, blacks, women, or businessmen, whom the White House is concerned about. The staffers serve as a point of contact for interest groups representing these constituencies. For lobbyists, the public liaison office is a channel for communicating their interests to the administration. If the administration

[28] See, generally, Nelson W. Polsby, "Interest Groups and the Presidency," in Walter Dean Burnham and Martha Wagner Weinberg, *American Politics and Public Policy* (Cambridge: Massachusetts Institute of Technology Press, 1978), pp. 41–52.
[29] Thomas E. Cronin, *The State of the Presidency*, 2nd ed. (Boston: Little, Brown, 1980), pp. 131–132.

is generally unsympathetic to the policy demands of the groups, this access to White House liaison staffers may be mostly symbolic.[30] Another aspect of interest group-White House relations is the politics of appointments. When a new president comes into office, the interest groups most clearly identified as part of his electoral coalition expect the president-elect to put the right kind of people into relevant cabinet and regulatory posts. The most important groups expect to be consulted on the top appointments in their area. No Democratic president could possibly contemplate appointing a secretary of Labor without first clearing the person with the head of the AFL-CIO. Even if direct consultations are not held, anticipating interest group reactions is a big factor in many major appointments.

THE COURTS

If an interest group is to maximize its influence in the policy-making process, it must stand ready to use litigation as one of its lobbying tactics. Yet because of the high cost of litigation, only the largest interest groups and public interest law firms have substantial legal staffs of their own. For the small Washington offices that predominate, having a skilled litigator on board is an unaffordable luxury. Furthermore, the lawyers employed full time by interest groups usually are more experienced in administrative lobbying than in litigation.

Still, though it is not common for Washington lobbies to have experienced litigators on their staff, court suits brought by interest groups are quite common. Most frequently, an outside law firm will be engaged (usually a Washington firm) to carry out a group's case. When the FCC made its landmark ruling that stations running cigarette commercials also had to run anticigarette public service announcements, the relevant trade associations moved immediately to hire top Washington law firms to fight the ruling in court. The National Association of Broadcasters retained Covington & Burling and the Tobacco Institute employed Arnold & Porter. Although the litigation was eventually unsuccessful, firms like Covington & Burling and Arnold & Porter have well-deserved reputations for success in the courtroom.[31]

[30] Joseph A. Pika, "Interest Groups and the Executive," in Allan J. Cigler and Burdett A. Loomis, *Interest Group Politics* (Washington, D.C.: Congressional Quarterly, 1983), pp. 315–320.
[31] Mark J. Green, *The Other Government* (New York: Grossman, 1975), pp. 147–162.

Even if a group has in-house counsel, the higher the stakes, the more likely it is that an outside firm will be hired. The major exception is the public interest law firm. Such organizations, like the Environmental Defense Fund and the Center for Law and Social Policy, were created so that the chronically unrepresented could be represented before the courts. Their "clients" are broad classes of people, such as environmentalists and consumers, who have an important collective interest but as individuals have too marginal an interest to warrant hiring an attorney on their own.[32] Many of these firms were started by foundations and still have no formal memberships, but others, like the Environmental Defense Fund, have developed into membership organizations.

Policy Change

The primary purpose of litigation is to seek a policy change or to stop a change from taking place. The Tobacco Institute initiated litigation on television ads because it failed to stop a regulatory agency from taking an action. When an industry's profits are liable to be significantly reduced by a government policy, it becomes worth the cost of litigation for a trade association to challenge the policy in court. Interest groups not only use the courts as an appeals process for adverse decisions by other branches, but they also litigate when they feel that their lack of popular support makes it fruitless for them to lobby the Congress or the executive branch.[33] The courts, though hardly impervious to popular opinion, do not demand the same type of constituency support to institute a policy change as Congress or an administrative agency does.[34]

Civil rights groups have long relied on the courts to fight discrim-

[32] On the evolution of public interest law, see *The Public Interest Law Firm* (New York: Ford Foundation, 1973); Simon Lazarus, *The Genteel Populists* (New York: Holt, Rinehart and Winston, 1974); *Balancing the Scales of Justice* (Washington, D.C.: Council for Public Interest Law, 1976); *Public Interest Law: Five Years Later* (New York: Ford Foundation, 1976).

[33] See Constance Ewing Cook, *Nuclear Power and Legal Advocacy* (Lexington, Mass.: Lexington Books, 1980); and Carol S. Greenwald, "The Use of Litigation by Common Cause," paper presented at the annual meeting of the American Political Science Association, San Francisco, Calif., September 1975.

[34] Robert A. Dahl, "Decision-Making in a Democracy: The Supreme Court as a National Policy-Maker," *Journal of Public Law* 6 (Fall 1957), pp. 279–295; and Richard Funston, "The Supreme Court and Critical Elections," *American Political Science Review* 69 (September 1975), pp. 795–811.

ination. It was lawyers from the NAACP who litigated against the separate-but-equal doctrine that was subsequently overturned by the Supreme Court in its 1954 decision, *Brown* v. *Board of Education.* It is absolutely inconceivable that Congress would have passed a law forbidding school desegregation during the same period.[35] There was too much opposition by white southerners and negligible support for civil rights by white northerners. Only the courts offered a reasonable target for lobbying by civil rights groups.[36]

In recent years the courts have been more and more popular with citizen groups as a focus for their lobbying. There are a number of reasons for this. First, as activists of the late 1960s and early 1970s began to look for constructive ways to work for political reform, they were able to find substantial foundation support for public interest litigation. Most notably, the Ford Foundation committed itself to funding projects intended to promote social justice in responsible and innovative ways. Second, the rules of standing were liberalized during this time, giving citizen groups broader opportunities to bring cases before the federal courts. Third, interest groups copy each other when a tactic appears to be working well. As citizen groups began to win major victories in the courts, litigation gained attractiveness for other such organizations.

The success of liberal citizen groups in using litigation has stimulated formation of conservative citizen groups oriented toward legal advocacy as well. Sponsored mainly by contributions from corporations and foundations, groups like the National Legal Center for the Public Interest and the Pacific Legal Foundation have become advocates for free enterprise and other conservative causes. Typical cases include suits to overturn a moratorium on construction of nuclear power plants in California, and protection of some North Carolina landowners from restrictions on access to their property proposed in new wildlife refuge rules.[37]

When they have no other means of changing a policy immediately, interest groups often turn to the courts to try to delay its implementation. When former Secretary of the Interior James Watt announced that the government was going to lease a billion acres of ocean land for offshore oil drilling, he was immediately taken to court by the

[35] *Brown* v. *Board of Education,* 347 U.S. 483 (1954).
[36] Richard Kluger, *Simple Justice* (New York: Knopf, 1976).
[37] James W. Singer, "Liberal Public Interest Law Firms Face Budgetary, Ideological Challenges," *National Journal,* December 18, 1979, pp. 2052–2056.

Natural Resources Defense Council and other environmental groups. Although Watt was acting within his statutory authority, environmental groups claimed he had made procedural violations in promulgating his new policy. Their real purpose, though, was to delay leasing of the land in the hope that rising public criticism would eventually force the administration to scale back the Watt plan. Using a variant of this approach, an interest group brings litigation to increase its bargaining leverage with an administrative agency. Groups pushing for rights for the disabled have frequently settled out of court with government agencies after filing suits when the government preferred direct negotiation to the uncertainty of a court decision.[38]

Standing

An important constraint on interest groups going to court is "standing." For an interest group to get a case heard before the courts, they must be an appropriate party to the suit. The courts' traditional test is that plaintiffs must show some direct injury to have standing. In the mid-1960s the federal courts began to expand the rules for standing, giving interest groups more latitude to litigate. One major case was *Office of Communication of the United Church of Christ* v. *FCC*. The church group had filed a petition before the FCC asking that the license to operate a television station in Jackson, Mississippi, be denied to the current operators because their programming and hiring policies were racist. The FCC denied the petition on the grounds that the station's viewers had not been tangibly injured. A federal court of appeals overturned the FCC denial, saying that standing could not be restricted to those with an economic interest in the case. The court declared that viewers of the station had legitimate standing.[39]

Not only was access expanded for citizen groups, but it was liberalized for corporations and trade associations as well. In another important case, *Association of Data Processing Service Organizations* v. *Camp*, the Supreme Court considered whether this trade group for

[38] Susan Olson Burke, "The Political Evolution of Interest Group Litigation," paper delivered at the annual meeting of the American Political Science Association, Washington, D.C., August 1980.
[39] *Office of Communication of the United Church of Christ* v. *FCC*, 359 F.2d 944 (D.C. Cir., 1966).

data processors could challenge the authority of the Comptroller of the Currency to allow banks to provide data processing services. The Association did not prevail in the lower courts because of legal precedent holding that a party had no standing if their injury was caused by competition. The Supreme Court overturned the decision, setting forth a new doctrine saying there was a valid "zone of interests" for regulated industries that warrants standing in cases where there was a claim of injury, even if that injury resulted from increased competition.[40]

These and other cases significantly increased the ability of interest groups to take their grievances before the courts, and expanded the range of conflicts between interest groups that the federal courts are called on to adjudicate. In recent years, though, a more conservative Supreme Court has been reluctant to ease the restrictions on standing. In a case brought by the Americans United for Separation of Church and State, the Supreme Court ruled that the group did not have standing to sue to stop the government from giving a surplus army hospital to a small Christian college. The Supreme Court ruled that the members of the group did not suffer any personal injury other than their displeasure with the action, and thus did not have the right to fight the property transfer in court.[41]

More frequently, it is the practical consideration of cost rather than limits on standing that keeps interest groups out of court. To see a case through its initial adjudication in a federal court and a subsequent appeal can easily cost an interest group tens of thousands of dollars. The Women's Equity Action League lost an important case because, when faced with an appeal, the group could not afford $40,000 for copies of the trial transcript and had to abandon the suit.[42] Yet interest groups recognize the potential costs and will hesitate to enter into litigation unless they see a reasonable chance for success and feel they will be able to carry a suit through an appeal and possibly on to the Supreme Court. Because the cost of litigation is so high, it is the wealthier lobbies like large corporations and trade

[40] *Association of Data Processing Service Organizations* v. *Camp*, 397 U.S. 150 (1970). See Karen Orren, "Standing to Sue: Interest Group Conflict in the Federal Courts," *American Political Science Review* 70 (September 1976), pp. 723–741.
[41] *Valley Forge Christian College* v. *Americans United for Separation of Church and State*, 454 U.S. 464 (1982).
[42] Karen O'Connor, *Women's Organizations' Use of the Courts* (Lexington, Mass: Lexington Books, 1980), p. 118.

associations that are the least likely to be deterred by the price of litigation.

Two other means are available to interest groups who wish to influence policy making in the courts. The first is the *amicus curiae* ("friend of the court") brief. In suits to which they are not a direct party but have a very real interest in the outcome, interest groups will often file such a document with the court. A group must, however, obtain consent from the parties to the suit or from the court before submitting the brief. *Amicus* briefs may offer an additional legal interpretation to those being used by the disputants in the case. Jewish groups have filed *amicus* briefs in affirmative action cases because quotas have been used in the past to discriminate against Jews, and because current policies aimed at recruiting other minorities are considered a form of "reverse discrimination." Such briefs have tried to convince the courts that affirmative action "goals" are a quota by another name and should not be a tool of public policy. It is not clear, however, what effect *amicus* briefs have on court decision making.[43]

Interest groups also can try to influence the direction of the courts by attempting to affect selection of federal judges. This task is difficult because the norm is that the Justice Department or administration officials do not meet with interest group representatives to discuss possible selections. The president may try to please some attentive publics with his selections, but it is not easy for any one organization to reach the president to influence a choice. Only the American Bar Association, which evaluates professional qualifications of potential and actual nominees, is consistently active in the selection process.

Occasionally, when a Supreme Court nominee is especially offensive to a group, it will make an effort to block the candidate's Senate confirmation. A few conservative groups launched an attack against Sandra Day O'Connor when she was nominated for the Supreme Court because they did not feel her views were sufficiently antiabortion. They had no apparent success, and it is quite rare for a confirmation to be blocked because of interest group opposition. Yet it can happen, as when civil rights groups led opposition to the Nixon administration's Supreme Court nominee, G. Harrold Carswell.

[43] See, generally, O'Connor, *Women's Organizations' Use of the Courts*, pp. 100–134.

Carswell's racial views and his poor record as a federal appeals court judge led to his ultimate rejection by the Senate. Generally, though, interest groups find that trying to influence selection of judges is a poor investment of their staff time. Only when the president makes an egregious choice, generating wide opposition, does it make sense for interest groups to become involved.

COALITIONS

Because the most common problem interest groups face is lack of resources, it stands to reason that lobbies will combine forces at times to pool their funds and staffs. By entering into coalitions, an organization can work to influence numerous policies that it would never take on by itself. Coalitions are ubiquitous in Washington, and kindred spirits are constantly working to form new coalitions as old ones dissolve.

Lobbyists are so emphatic in arguing that interest groups must form coalitions as a matter of necessity that it may seem puzzling so few permanent coalitions have endured. Most are ad hoc coalitions, lasting only until some resolution of an issue is reached. Some coalitions, of course, are supported by member groups on an ongoing basis. The Leadership Conference on Civil Rights, which was started over thirty years ago and has over 150 member organizations, is one of the best-known coalitions of this type. Yet one might assume that many other large, permanent coalitions would efficiently harness the resources of like-minded organizations.

The major reason similar interest groups do not go further to combine forces is that organizations have egos. The more resources an interest group devotes to coalition activities, the less it has for doing things in its own name. Interest group leaders and lobbyists have a personal stake in working to enhance their own reputation and that of their organizations. The broader and more lasting a prospective coalition is, the more difficult it becomes for the organizers to overcome this problem.

Take the Fair Budget Action Campaign, a coalition of eighty liberal groups such as the United Steelworkers and Friends of the Earth. The coalition was born out of liberals' frustration with conservative success in Congress in reducing spending for social programs.[44] Al-

44 Robert Pear, "Coalition to Protest Reagan's Policies," *The New York Times*, April 9, 1982.

though many groups were hurt by such budget cuts, relatively few joined the coalition and major commitment of resources by members seems unlikely. The Fair Budget Action Campaign has yet to become a major actor in budget politics. If the Campaign grew to great strength, would supporting groups get much credit from their own members for their cooperative lobbying? Probably not, for the press would surely highlight the name of the coalition in its reporting.

Even among a relatively small number of groups, organizational egos can get in the way of natural allies working cooperatively. The National Taxpayers Union and the National Tax Limitation Committee have both worked long and hard for a constitutional amendment to balance the budget. In spite of this parallel effort, they do not have a particularly warm relationship, each regarding the other as its rival for leadership of the antitax movement.[45]

Nevertheless, organizational rivalries are frequently overcome by leaders of interest groups who enter into ad hoc cooperative arrangements. They do so because they care deeply about achieving a specific policy goal, because they feel that cooperation is probably the only way the goal can be reached, and because they don't feel the coalition's drain on its resources threatens the organization's lasting well-being. Ad hoc coalitions are *limited* commitments, and thus the obstacles to participation are minimized.

Cooperative lobbying by big-business groups was a major factor in passage of a very generous tax cut for business during the first year of the Reagan administration. The ad hoc coalition had no fixed membership, but was led by some of the more important business organizations such as the Business Roundtable, the Chamber of Commerce, and the National Association of Manufacturers, each of which has member companies that could be called on to assist in the lobbying. Lobbyists from the groups met regularly during the fight to plot strategy, and they remain in more informal contact.[46]

Coalitions are easiest to form among groups who have the same basic political philosophy and have experience working together. They are natural outgrowths of policy networks, in which lobbyists have

[45] Edward Cowan, "Reagan's Speech Elates Lobbyists," *The New York Times*, May 1, 1982.
[46] William J. Lanouette, "Business Lobbyists Hope Their Unity on the Tax Bill Wasn't Just a Fluke," *National Journal*, October 24, 1981, pp. 1896–1898. The role interest groups play in framing legislative alternatives is analyzed by W. Douglas Costain and Anne N. Costain, "Interest Groups as Policy Aggregators in the Legislative Process," *Polity* 14 (December 1981), pp. 249–272.

come to know each other from their interaction on other related issues.[47] Anne Costain writes, "Since each issue generates a new coalition and a new opportunity for leadership of the coalition, conflicts and rivalries among groups are made less intense."[48] The business coalition that fought for the tax cuts had its roots in the "Carlton Group" that started meeting years earlier. Lobbyists from the leading business lobbies began having breakfast together periodically at the Sheraton-Carlton Hotel in downtown Washington. The general purpose was to exchange information and to let each group know what the other was up to in its lobbying so that they wouldn't work at cross-purposes or needlessly overlap each other's efforts. This led to more explicit working arrangements later on.[49]

Although coalitions are usually made up of like-minded groups, politics can join strange bedfellows. When a policy objective bridges the interests of groups that usually have little to do with each other, suspicions can sometimes be overcome by strong leadership and an ad hoc coalition can be welded. So began the Ad Hoc Committee for Airline Regulatory Reform, which pushed Congress to pass airline deregulation legislation it was considering. Included in its diverse membership was the American Conservative Union, Ralph Nader's Aviation Consumer Action Project, the National Taxpayers Union, the National Association of Manufacturers, Common Cause, Americans for Democratic Action, and Sears, Roebuck.[50] At the same time, differences between groups on some issues can turn to bitterness and keep them from working together on others. Many labor unions have taken such strong exception to antidevelopment positions of environmental groups that they have difficulty bringing themselves to work with them on issues on which they share a common concern, such as dangers of pollution at the workplace.[51]

In sum, coalitions are commonly formed in Washington, but are

[47] Hugh Heclo, "Issue Networks and the Executive Establishment," in Anthony King, ed., *The New American Political System* (Washington, D.C.: American Enterprise Institute, 1978), pp. 87–124.
[48] Anne N. Costain, "Organized Lobbying by Diffuse Interests," paper presented at the annual meeting of the American Political Science Association, Washington, D.C., September 1979, p. 17.
[49] Lanouette, "Business Lobbyists," p. 1896.
[50] Albert R. Karr, "As a Senate Panel Considers Deregulation of Airlines, Rival Lobbyists Press Efforts," *Wall Street Journal*, August 4, 1977.
[51] Alan S. Miller, "Towards an Environmental/Labor Coalition," *Environment* 22 (June 1980), pp. 32–39.

most likely to form under well-defined circumstances. The chances of success increase when:

1. The coalition is clearly intended to be of a temporary, ad hoc nature.
2. The coalition is limited to one specific issue.
3. The issue is of some immediacy with a good chance of government action.
4. The coalition is run informally and each group's contribution is to be lobbying by its own personnel rather than money given to a separate coalition staff.
5. The coalition's membership comes from an issue network in which the lobbyists have experience working with each other.
6. Participants believe there is "turn taking" in the leadership for ad hoc coalitions that grow from their issue network.
7. The coalition itself is not likely to take on so much public visibility that any successes in lobbying will be entirely credited to it rather than being shared with the separate organizations.

STRATEGIC DECISION MAKING

A variety of specific tactics have been described, each with its unique strengths and weaknesses. With limited staffs and funds, interest groups must be careful to use their lobbying resource efficiently. Considering the policy problem and organization, what tactics and longer-term strategies will yield the greatest influence at lowest cost?

Organizational Constraints

The decision-making process for selecting tactics and strategies resembles in many ways the making of decisions for selecting issues. As we pointed out in Chapter 5, many decisions for an interest group are hardly "decisions" at all because the issue that emerges so matches the group's purpose that there is no question they will become active on it. The AFL-CIO does not have to deliberate on whether they should lobby on proposed legislation to weaken the Davis-Bacon Act, a law requiring that workers be paid the prevailing local wage rates when construction projects are being funded by the federal government. Likewise, the organization doesn't have to decide whether or not it will try to personally lobby members of Congress. The group would not need a staff of Washington lobbyists unless it was going to use them on issues critical for their members. Thus, the most important factor in determining what tactics a group chooses is the issue they are considering.

A second major influence determining the tactics chosen by an interest group has to do with its "advocacy design." [52] The small size of the typical lobbying office means a limited range of specializations among its few professional staffers. If an office's lobbyists are primarily skilled in legislative lobbying, it must decide whether it is worth hiring an outside law firm to lobby an administrative agency when pertinent regulations are being formulated. Also, whether offices are oriented toward legislative lobbying, administrative lobbying, or both, they are not likely to employ litigators on their staffs. When a lawsuit seems possible, they will thoroughly analyze whether the chance of success and the potential benefits warrant the heavy cost of hiring an outside firm. In general, a Washington office will be very quick to respond with tactics appropriate to the staff it employs full time. Tactics requiring the expertise of outsiders, however, will be considered more deliberately.

How much an interest group is constrained by the design of its Washington office mostly depends on the resources of the parent organization. Many large corporations have small listening-post operations in Washington, but are ready to back up that office with whatever outside help it may need on key issues. Burlington Industries, a large textile manufacturer, has a Washington office with only a director and two staff lobbyists, but it has the resources to hire additional help as the need arises.[53] Handgun Control has few financial resources beyond those already expended on its Washington office. Unlike Burlington Industries, it cannot hire a Washington law firm or public relations firm whenever that would be helpful.

Appeals Court Lobbying

Within the framework of its organizational constraints and overall resources, each group makes its short-term decisions on how to influence a current issue. After assessing their resources, officials turn to two basic questions. First, at exactly what stage in the policy cycle

---

[52] Berry, *Lobbying for the People*, pp. 262–264.
[53] Phyllis S. McGrath, *Redefining Corporate-Federal Relations*, New York: Conference Board, 1979), pp. 26–28.

is the issue? Is a bill four months away from being marked up in committee, or is it already in a House-Senate conference? A major letter-writing campaign from a group's membership would not be well timed in either instance.

If a conference committee is working on the bill, it is likely that a membership group has already called on its constituents to write letters prior to a committee or floor vote. Here, a Washington lobby is likely to depend more on trying to find influential members of the organization who have ties to the conference committee members, and on personal lobbying of the legislators and aides it can reach. Clearly, lobbying tactics are situational, and must be timed to appropriate stages in the policy-making process. Congress, agencies, and the courts move slowly enough that Washington representatives can anticipate their next step in lobbying and plan accordingly.

The second question that a leader of an interest group addresses in determining tactical choices is how the group is likely to be treated by the relevant policy makers. It did not take long for consumer groups to recognize that so long as Reagan administration appointees headed the Federal Trade Commission and the Consumer Product Safety Commission, they would be treated with hostility by those agencies. Consumer lobbyists couldn't even get appointments to see top officials, much less exert any influence. They concentrated instead on working with their allies in Congress and on trying to influence public opinion.

In the American policy-making system, a program can be affected at different times by each of the three branches of government. When the Food and Nutrition Service tried to save money for the school lunch program by issuing standards reducing the amount of food required per serving, lobbyists from the Food Research and Action Center (FRAC) knew they would not be able to directly influence the agency and change its mind. Instead FRAC took the agency's decision back to Congress and prompted their allies there to hold a press event at which prominent senators were served the tiny portions that could meet the minimum requirement. The public ridicule forced the agency to change its regulations.

In short, if a group finds that policy formulation is going against its preferences, tactical decisions become a matter of finding an "appeals court." That is, when a group has suffered a setback in one institution, it may begin searching for a sympathetic audience in another branch of government or go to the public to appeal the decision.[54] As with litigation taken to a higher court, the appeal may also be brought within the same branch of government. When the Department of Health and Human Services was about to issue a rule requiring that aspirin bottles carry a warning that use of aspirin was linked to Reye's syndrome, the Aspirin Foundation persuaded an official on the Office of Management and Budget to block it.[55] The most effective interest groups surely are those with the capacity to lobby all three branches and public opinion. Those restricted to "consciousness raising" or congressional lobbying will eventually be at a disadvantage compared to adversaries who have broader capabilities.

For leaders of interest groups, short-term tactical choices thus tend to be relatively straightforward. At any stage in the public policymaking sequence, only a limited number of options are available. Organizational constraints, particularly available resources, narrow the choices. In the real world, where a lobbyist has typically worked on an issue for years, such "decisions" may be incremental changes in their daily schedules. For an experienced lobbyist, moving back and forth between a congressional committee and an administrative agency can simply be part of continuing work on an issue, not discrete decisions. Or, in some offices, where legislative and administrative duties are separated, changes in tactics may mean passing on responsibility for an issue to a colleague.

Long-Term Strategy

A theme I have emphasized throughout is that many Washington lobbyists are like fire fighters, reacting to what is thrust upon them and not able to adhere to plans as to how they are going to allocate their time and effort. Yet it is still true that interest groups occasionally try to plot long-term strategy. With little control over how the nation's political agenda develops, an interest group recognizes that its planning is highly problematic. Nevertheless, groups do try to implement a plan to reallocate their resources in the year (or years) to come, and they sometimes succeed.

A group will often reconsider its lobbying strategy when a long-

[54] Berry, *Feeding Hungry People*, Chapter 6.
[55] John J. Fialka, "Reaganites Find Plans for Deregulation Stall After EPA Revelations," *Wall Street Journal*, June 6, 1983.

term goal has been reached, when a major electoral swing has taken place, or when it has suffered a key defeat. Many women's groups began to reexamine their lobbying strategy as time was running out for ratification of the Equal Rights Amendment. With neither Congress nor the White House particularly sympathetic to women's rights issues, they renewed their emphasis on litigation as a lobbying strategy.[56] Or a change may come with new leadership. After many years of refusing to do anything but stand flatly opposed to government programs dealing with health, safety, and environmental issues, a new president of the National Association of Manufacturers decided that the group's "obstructionist" image was counterproductive. The NAM adopted a new strategy, trying to press the business viewpoint by more cooperative work with the government.[57]

It is not at all unusual for strategic reassessments to be done in conjunction with other like-minded groups. A trade association can act as a catalyst, with member groups also taking up the strategy adopted by the industrywide group. For citizen groups, a conference may serve the same purpose. After the Supreme Court held that an NAACP boycott of merchants in a Mississippi town was legal, a large conference of civil rights advocates voted to move toward a strategy of using the economic power of blacks as an additional means for advancing the rights of black Americans. This was not a binding decision on an individual organization, but the debate could not help but influence subsequent planning by different groups.[58]

A reassessment of strategy may also come after other groups — friends or enemies — appear to be gaining effectiveness by a change in strategy. Groups do not hesitate to imitate other organizations. When business PACs began to seem successful, other corporations and trade associations quickly followed suit. A successful lobbying strategy is a strategy that will be copied.

CONCLUSION

The diversity of tactics utilized by interest groups may give the misleading impression that a wide range of choices are open to a group

[56] David Margolick, "Women Turn to Courts to Gain Rights," *The New York Times*, June 29, 1982.
[57] Robert S. Greenberger, "Manufacturers' Lobby Alters Style to Combat Its Obstructionist Image," *Wall Street Journal*, May 5, 1981.
[58] Nathaniel Sheppard, Jr., "700 Rights Leaders Agree to Shift Focus from Politics to Economics," *The New York Times*, July 30, 1982.

when it contemplates how it is going to approach government. The issue at hand, the stage it is at in the policy-making process, and the organizational constraints of the group limit the choices. Many such decisions are automatic, and no alternatives other than the tactic eventually used are given serious consideration. Still, in time, a group will stop to evaluate whether an approach is working, or can work if adopted. This kind of evaluation frequently takes place when a group goes through one of its periodic attempts to set priorities, when an issue seemingly demands outside expenditures (such as a law or public relations firm), or when a group is deciding whether or not to take an issue up in the first place.

Evaluations of "what works" by officials of interest groups cannot help but be heavily colored by their experience. Like all other organizations, interest groups try to learn from experience so as not to repeat mistakes. Unfortunately, it is not easy to determine which tactics worked and which didn't in any one policy conflict. For their part, lobbyists evaluate their successes and failures in much the same way candidates for office do. Political scientist John Kingdon identified the "congratulation-rationalization" effect among candidates: winners congratulate themselves on running an astute campaign that surely keyed their victory; losers develop rationalizations as to why forces outside their control caused their defeat.[59] Lobbyists see victories in the same light: the organization's advocacy is always thought to be a significant factor in a successful outcome. Defeats are seen as beyond a group's control, caused by overwhelming political opposition by the administration or Congress, the large sums of money available to adversary groups, or the widespread ignorance of the American people. Tactical choices are far down the list of reasons in lobbyists' self-examination of what went wrong.

Lobbyists' evaluations of advocacy are further clouded by the incremental nature of public policy making. Unlike candidates for office, who either win or lose, lobbyists deal with shades of gray. When lobbying an agency or Congress, they are trying to affect a compromise. Even when a group sees no positive changes made in the direction it would like, it can still believe that things would have been worse had it not made the effort.

John W. Kingdon, *Candidates for Office* (New York: Random House, 1968), pp. 20–41. Kingdon relates the idea to interest groups in *Congressmen's Voting Decisions*, 2nd ed. (New York: Harper and Row, 1981), p. 174.

Political scientists have proved little better than lobbyists in developing appropriate means of evaluating effectiveness of advocacy tactics. Carrying out such analyses, they face formidable obstacles in developing scientifically valid measures of influence. A multiplicity of actors are always trying to influence the development of a policy. Groups begin lobbying efforts with unequal resources and with greatly different degrees of sympathy on the part of policy makers toward their points of view. Moreover, some policy options are never considered by government officials because they anticipate negative reaction from powerful interests, or have been socialized into accepting "truths" about the proper role of government. Considerable influence may thus be wielded by some sectors of society though that power is not directly observable in lobbying campaigns.[60] Finally, when research in Washington is carried out, it is handicapped by policy makers who are not fully forthcoming about being swayed by interest group pressure.

It is, of course, possible to look at a policy and identify very generally the sources of interest group influence. Policies benefiting farmers or labor union members are obviously the product of continuing advocacy by lobbies representing them. Going beyond such broad generalizations to construct scales and indices of lobbying influence is troublesome.[61] Measuring each group's influence in a discrete policy conflict, or more narrowly evaluating the success of one tactic used by a group, remains on the agenda of unfinished business for political scientists. For lobbyists, the evaluations they do continue to be based on experience, and such self-evaluations are inherently biased by rationalizations. Yet their evaluations of other groups, and the copying of tactics that appear successful for others, guide lobbyists toward consensus judgments on what works best in Washington politics.

[60] Peter Bachrach and Morton S. Baratz, "Two Faces of Power," *American Political Science Review* 56 (December 1962), pp. 947–952; and John Gaventa, *Power and Powerlessness* (Urbana: University of Illinois Press, 1980).

[61] See Michael T. Hayes, *Lobbyists and Legislators* (New Brunswick, N.J.: Rutgers University Press, 1981), pp. 43–54.

CHAPTER TEN

Conclusion

Lobbying is ages old and many of the tactics described here have changed little over the years in their basic approach. Yet never have so many interest groups been active and skilled in utilizing these tactics to influence government. And never have so many constituencies been so well represented in Washington. In this sense, the growth of interest group politics has furthered the democratic process by effectively articulating the views of more interests before policy makers. At the same time, this broadened representation has not come without costs to the political system.

THE MADISONIAN DILEMMA

In Chapter 1, we saw that the recent rise in interest group activity has once again challenged Americans to think about the dilemma outlined by James Madison in *Federalist* No. 10. Madison recognized that factions were sure to arise in any open political system, and just as surely would pursue their own selfish interests. That pursuit of self-interest was dangerous to the political system, for if any one faction came to dominate government it could use its power to oppress other groups in society. He argued persuasively, however, that the solution was not to prohibit the right to organize self-interested "factions," for that would restrict fundamental political freedoms. Rather, the system had to be constructed in such a way that no one faction could come to oppress others. Madison believed that the effects of faction would be controlled by the government proposed in the Constitution and by the great variety of interests that would compete before government.

The rise of interest group politics has threatened Madison's fragile

212

formula. Although the United States has always had many powerful groups having disproportionate influence with government, today's threat is disturbing beyond the "normal" inequality of group influences for two reasons. First, the recent rise of interest groups has taken place during a period of party decline. Second, political action committees have become such a large source of campaign funds that they are changing the relationship between interest groups and members of Congress.

Why did this happen?

A number of causes have contributed to the growing role of interest groups in American politics. The course of interest group politics was clearly altered by the civil rights movement and the anti-Vietnam War movement. They served as a model for thousands of other citizen groups that formed around the country. Espousing varied issues, all gave their members an appealing means of trying to advance causes they cared intensely about. The early successes of civil rights and antiwar groups were soon followed by successes of environmental, consumer, and other kinds of citizen groups. Once people became confident that these lobbies could have influence, they became an important channel of activism for those frustrated with the direction of public policy.

The pluralist vision of politics furthered the rise of interest group politics. By helping to educate and convince people that policy decisions were the outcomes of interest group bargaining with government, the subsequent acceptance that not everyone was well represented by interest groups pointed inevitably in one direction. "Balance" had to be introduced into the system so that all important interests were represented at the bargaining table. This attitude was especially important to the early rise of citizen groups, leading to major support by foundations for Washington-based public interest groups and to creation of many new citizen participation programs at the federal, state, and local levels. But the legacy of pluralism went beyond its effect on citizen advocacy. Interest group politics was given increased legitimacy. The answer to the question "Who Governs?" was that interest groups govern.

An important manifestation of this changing attitude toward interest groups was the reforms in the campaign finance law, which permitted widespread formation of corporate political action committees. This change went against the grain of government policy, which had long kept corporate contributions out of electoral politics.

Once interest groups were accepted as leading actors with a positive role in the policy-making process, and the government even began to encourage advocacy by citizens, it became less defensible to keep the hands of business tied. The explosive growth in all types of PACs, in turn, has hurt the party system by giving people an attractive means of participating in elections through their interest groups.

The growth of government itself stimulated interest group advocacy. The reach of regulatory agencies expanded, and more trade associations and corporations came to view Washington representation as essential. As interest group activity increased, so too did our understanding of how they operate. Technological change gave interest groups more tools, such as computerized direct mail. Both of these factors improved the marketing capability of interest groups.

All these reasons, described more fully in earlier chapters, led to proliferation of interest groups since the mid-1960s. The result has been heightened visibility for interest groups and heightened worry about their influence on the governmental process. Because people are generally distrustful of interest groups other than their own, the perception of great interest group activity can only contribute to the alienation and cynicism that have characterized public opinion since the 1960s. Even worse, the increased role of PACs in financing campaigns has given people added reason to believe that interest groups have undue influence in government. Although everybody believes that new groups started to represent themselves pose no threat to the political system, few believe that the overall growth of interest group politics is an entirely positive development.

REFORM?

If the system is ailing, why not fix it? One need look no further than *Federalist* No. 10 to recognize the difficulty of reforming that system. As Madison wrote, efforts to cure the "mischiefs of faction" could end up "destroying" our political freedom:

> Liberty is to faction what air is to fire, an aliment without which it instantly expires. But it could not be a less folly to abolish liberty, which is essential to political life, because it nourishes faction than it would be to wish the annihilation of air, which is essential to animal life, because it imparts to fire its destructive agency.[1]

[1] *The Federalist Papers* (New York: New American Library, 1961), p. 78.

In considering adoption of political reforms aimed at curbing interest group activity, Madison's warning should remain a guide. Preserving people's right to form factions and to lobby within our framework of political freedoms ought to be of the utmost importance. Without a compelling reason to believe that political rights or freedoms would be threatened in the absence of such reforms, those reforms cannot be justified.

That it is difficult to fashion plans for interest group reforms is illustrated by the paucity of serious proposals put before Congress in recent years. One reform idea considered by Congress is a broad change in the lobbying registration law. As passed in 1946, the Federal Regulation of Lobbying Act required paid lobbyists to register with Congress, and required lobbyists and groups to file quarterly financial reports. The vague law was subsequently given a narrow interpretation by the Supreme Court.[2] The act is restricted to individuals and groups whose principal purpose is influencing legislation, and coverage is limited to lobbying that involves direct contact with members of Congress. As recognized by everyone familiar with it, the registration act is a toothless, ineffective law. It is easy for those engaged in legislative lobbying to reason that lobbying is not their principal activity. The registration lists and expenditure reports are patently incomplete, and cannot be used as a record of lobbying expenditures on any bill because it is likely that many participants did not bother to file.

Reform bills aimed at revising the 1946 law have received careful consideration in recent years, and the Carter administration backed such legislation. One controversial aspect of the approach proposed was that it would have required all organizations spending a minimum of $2,500 on lobbying and having a representative lobby on at least 13 days in a three-month period, to file quarterly reports detailing their activities. (The amount was raised to $5,000 in a later version.) It would also have required reporting of efforts at grassroots lobbying — times when the organization tried to activate members, stockholders, or other citizens to directly lobby their members of Congress.[3]

Such legislation does not seem wise, for it places an unwarranted

2 *United States* v. *Harriss,* 347 U.S. 612 (1954).
3 Steven V. Roberts, "Business Is Crying Havoc over New Lobbying Bill," *The New York Times,* May 7, 1978; and Stephen Chapman, "One Reform Too Many," *New Republic,* June 28, 1980, pp. 14–15.

burden on small organizations. They would have to devote too much of their scarce resources to the recordkeeping necessary to file their quarterly reports. Although this proposal was pushed by Common Cause, it was actively opposed by Ralph Nader, the Sierra Club, and other citizen groups because of the costs these organizations would have to incur. Business was also vociferous in its opposition because of the recordkeeping burden and because the bills were viewed as an effort to cast a shadow over the lobbying that they do.

There is not sufficient justification for the lobbying registration envisioned in this proposal. Strict lobbying registration and reporting would effectively introduce a fee for the constitutional right to lobby, while offering few benefits to society in return.[4] Though the reports might be helpful in drawing out the bias of wealth in interest group politics, using registration to provide more detail about this bias does not outweigh the problem expenditure reporting causes for so many groups.[5]

Tighter restrictions on the revolving door — the practice of people moving from government jobs to jobs as lobbyists in the industries they formerly dealt with — would be a welcome step. There are some rules now, such as moratoriums on contact between some ex-officials and their former agencies that were passed under the 1978 Ethics in Government Act. A broad solution remains elusive, because it is difficult to fashion a reform which would not unfairly infringe upon the freedom of individuals to work for whomever they want, and which would not overly discourage people in the private sector from joining government in the first place. Restrictions on the revolving door do not, though, violate the right of interest groups to petition their government.

Some believe that the government should also "defund" groups which receive federal grants and are involved in political advocacy. Liberal citizen groups supported by various government grant programs have frequently sued the government and been active in

---

[4] See Hope Eastman, *Lobbying: A Constitutionally Protected Right* (Washington, D.C.: American Enterprise Institute, 1977).

[5] The Foreign Agents Registration Act, which requires registration by representatives of foreign countries, is justifiable. When a foreign government hires representation in this country, it should be abundantly clear that it is the foreign government that's lobbying and not Americans sympathetic to the same interest.

administrative and legislative lobbying.[6] Such restrictions are bad public policy.[7] To keep nonprofit groups receiving government funds from doing real advocacy work would leave many disadvantaged constituencies with considerably less representation in the policy-making process. The federal government must be held accountable for its actions, especially in its transgression against the poor in administering its own programs. Although the conservative *Wall Street Journal* reminds us that "no political opinion has a moral right to representation at taxpayer expense," we must also be mindful that representation of interests should not be a function of wealth, either.[8] It is an appropriate responsibility of government to fund surrogate interest groups for poor, chronically unorganized constituencies.

CAMPAIGN FINANCE

One problem of interest group politics dwarfs all others: the enormous growth of interest group funds contributed to political candidates.

The inferences we can make connecting legislators' votes with the contributions they've received from various PACs create doubt about the basic integrity of the governmental process. The issue is not bribery of members of Congress, but that contributions still sway votes without the illegality of a quid pro quo. The perception that the contributions of business, farm, labor, and professional groups influence the votes and other activities of legislators can only produce distrust of government. It also produces distrust of interest groups. Americans do not see them as organizations furthering democracy by their participation, but as agents who subvert it with their money.

There are some, however, who defend the current system. Business is especially ardent in favoring current practices. Mobil Oil,

---

6 Nonprofit groups which want donations to them to be tax-deductible for private donors (vitally important in fundraising), are already limited in the amount of legislative lobbying they can legally engage in. They can always act in an educational capacity in communicating with legislators. *The Washington Lobby*, 4th ed. (Washington, D.C.: Congressional Quarterly, 1982), p. 39.

7 The Reagan administration professed a desire to move in this direction, but has backtracked from its initial set of proposed rules, issued by the Office of Management and Budget, to restrict advocacy by groups receiving federal funds. *Federal Register*, January 24, 1983, pp. 3348–3351. Less restrictive rules may be forthcoming.

8 "Defunding the Left and Right," *Wall Street Journal*, January 26, 1983.

distrust Govt
distrust PAC's

among the most aggressive spokesmen for business, makes an important point about PACs in one of its frequent advocacy ads, arguing that "PACs are actually among the most effective ways in which the man or woman on the street — union member, company employee or whoever — can play a more active role of citizenship." [9] If reforms are adopted that reduce the role of PACs in campaigns, the opportunity for people to participate in politics through their interest groups is curtailed.

Looking back at Madison's dictum that factions must not be fought at the expense of the political liberty that gives rise to such organizations, limiting the role of PACs may seem to fly in the face of a principle that has guided this country for so long. The pursuit of self-interest by factions could be justified in Madison's eyes because the effects of faction would be controlled. But neither the solution outlined by Madison nor current campaign finance restrictions are adequate controls against the advantage that wealthy groups have when lobbies are allowed to donate money to political candidates. As Senator Robert Dole says, "there aren't any Poor PACs or Food Stamp PACs or Nutrition PACs or Medicare PACs." [10] Political action committees further institutionalize inequities between those who have great wealth and highly effective political representation and those who have neither. This is a greater threat to liberty than the diminishment in one kind of political participation that will come from PAC reform.

There are a number of ways in which the campaign finance laws can be reformed to reduce the role of PACs in financing congressional elections. Proposals include placing a ceiling on the overall amount of money a candidate could accept from PACs, providing federal matching funds for small contributions raised by candidates, raising the limit on individual contributions, and creating a separate tax credit for party contributions.[11] Whatever the combination of

---

[9] Advertisement, "PACs — The Voice of Real People," *The New York Times*, December 2, 1982. See also Herbert E. Alexander, "The Case for PACs," Public Affairs Council, Washington, D.C., 1983.

[10] Elizabeth Drew, "Politics and Money — I," *New Yorker*, December 6, 1982, p. 147.

[11] See *An Analysis of the Impact of the Federal Election Campaign Act, 1972–78* (Cambridge: Institute of Politics, John F. Kennedy School of Government, Harvard University, 1979), pp. 1.1–1.32; and Herbert E. Alexander, *Financing Politics*, 2nd ed. (Washington, D.C.: Congressional Quarterly, 1980), pp. 145–162.

reforms adopted, they should work toward decreasing the relative amounts of money that candidates receive from PACs while increasing the amounts received from individuals and party committees. Individual participation should be encouraged and the realistic financial needs of candidates to run competitive campaigns must be recognized.

RENEWING THE BALANCE

It is tempting to make interest groups the scapegoat for the ills of American society, believing that we would have politically acceptable solutions to public policy dilemmas if lobbies didn't exist.[12] But however they may be expressed, differing interests will always abound. The attitudes and potential reactions of various constituencies must be considered by policy makers when decisions are made. Yet the organization of interests into an ever-increasing number of lobbying groups adds to the power of those constituencies.

The growth of interest group politics can be applauded for the broadened representation it has brought the political system. If there are to be lobbying organizations, it is best that they be as representative as possible of all segments of American society. Yet it would be naive to assume that interest groups are ever going to fairly reflect the different interests of all Americans. Upper- and middle-class interests will always be better represented by interest groups.

Government is realistically limited in what it can do to address this imbalance. It should continue to try to ensure representation for the chronically underrepresented. Financial support for advocacy groups for the poor should be expanded, not decreased as part of the overall move to cut back government funding of welfare and social services. Such cuts actually create a greater need for this kind of surrogate representation. Citizen participation programs, which have had mixed success, ought to be continued and improved upon. They make government more accountable to the people it serves and create a potential channel of influence for those who may not be adequately represented by interest groups. There is little that the federal government ought to do aside from changing current campaign finance practices,

---

12 See Mancur Olson, *The Rise and Decline of Nations* (New Haven: Yale University Press, 1982); and Lester C. Thurow, *The Zero-Sum Society* (New York: Penguin, 1981). See also Robert H. Salisbury, "Are Interest Groups Morbific Forces?", paper presented to the Conference Group on the Political Economy of Advanced Industrial Societies, Washington, D.C., August 1980.

however, to curb the activities of interest groups. Worrisome as the spiraling growth of interest group politics may be, it is not desirable to have the government trying generally to inhibit the efforts of various constituencies to find more effective representation in the political system.

 Because government's role will always be limited, prospects for further curbing the influence of faction must come from the political parties. They are the natural counterweight to interest groups, offering citizens the basic means of pursuing the nation's collective will. Only political parties can offer citizens broad choices about the major directions of public policy. When there is little confidence that parties are capable of providing a meaningful link between the ballot box and the policies that affect one's life, suspicion grows that government is being directed by well-organized interest groups.

A stronger party system can be furthered by the one major reform that should be imposed on interest groups: changes in the campaign finance laws that would reduce candidates' dependence on PAC funds. Otherwise, party renewal must come from the parties and not from restrictions on interest groups. Weak parties are not an inevitable condition of American politics, and the vision and capacity of those active in national politics is surely equal to the task of making the two parties more attractive to the American public. The progress that Republicans have recently made in efforts to build their party offers some reason for hope. Their sophisticated fundraising apparatus, along with their efforts at recruiting and supporting attractive congressional challengers, have helped foster a stronger, more centralized national Republican party. The Democrats, in turn, are beginning to take similar steps to strengthen themselves.

Interest groups need to continue to play their traditional role of articulating this nation's multitude of interests. They offer a direct link to government on the everyday issues that interest a particular constituency but not the nation as a whole. The role they play is not ideal, but interest groups remain a fundamental expression of democratic government.

Bibliography

Aberbach, Joel, and Bert Rockman. "Bureaucrats and Clientele Groups." *American Journal of Political Science* 22 (November 1978): 818–832.

Adams, Gordon. *The Iron Triangle*. New York: Council on Economic Priorities, 1981.

Alexander, Herbert E., ed. *Political Finance*. Beverly Hills, Calif.: Sage Publications, 1979.

———. *Financing Politics*, 2nd ed. Washington, D.C.: Congressional Quarterly Press, 1980.

———. "The Case for PACs." Washington, D.C.: Public Affairs Council, 1983.

Alinsky, Saul. *Rules for Radicals*. New York: Random House, 1971.

An Analysis of the Impact of the Federal Election Campaign Act, 1972–78. Cambridge, Mass.: Institute of Politics, John F. Kennedy School of Government, Harvard University, 1979.

Arieff, Irwin B., Nadine Cohodas, and Richard Whittle. "Sen. Helms Builds a Machine of Interlinked Organizations to Shape Both Politics, Policy." *Congressional Quarterly Weekly Report* (March 6, 1982): 499–505.

Bachrach, Peter, and Morton S. Baratz. "Two Faces of Power." *American Political Science Review* 56 (December 1962): 947–952.

Bailis, Lawrence Neil. *Bread or Justice*. Lexington, Mass.: Lexington Books, 1974.

Balancing the Scales of Justice. Washington, D.C.: Council of Public Interest Law, 1976.

Bauer, Raymond A., Ithiel de Sola Pool, and Lewis Anthony Dexter. *American Business and Public Policy*. New York: Atherton, 1968.

Bayes, Jane H. *Ideologies and Interest-Group Politics*. Novato, Calif.: Chandler and Sharp, 1982.

Bentley, Arthur. *The Process of Government*. Chicago: University of Chicago Press, 1908.

Bernstein, Marver. *Regulating Business by Independent Commission*. Princeton: Princeton University Press, 1955.

Berry, Jeffrey M. *Lobbying for the People*. Princeton: Princeton University Press, 1977.

————. "On the Origins of Public Interest Groups: A Test of Two Theories." *Polity* 10 (Spring 1978): 379–397.

————. "Lessons from Chairman Ralph." *Citizen Participation* 1 (November–December 1979): 4 ff.

————. "Public Interest Vs. Party System." *Society* 17 (May–June 1980): 42–48.

————. "Beyond Citizen Participation: Effective Advocacy Before Administrative Agencies." *Journal of Applied Behavioral Science* 17 (October 1981): 463–477.

————. *Feeding Hungry People: Rulemaking in the Food Stamp Program.* New Brunswick, N.J.: Rutgers University Press, in press.

Blair, John M. *The Control of Oil.* New York: Pantheon, 1976.

Blumenthal, Sidney. "Whose Side Is Business on, Anyway?" *New York Times Magazine* (October 25, 1981): 29 ff.

Boles, Janet K. *The Politics of the Equal Rights Amendment.* New York: Longman, 1979.

Boyte, Harry C. *The Backyard Revolution.* Philadelphia: Temple University Press, 1980.

Brady, David W., and Kent I. Tedin. "Ladies in Pink: Religion and Political Ideology in the Anti-ERA Movement." *Social Science Quarterly* 56 (March 1976): 565–575.

Broder, David. *Changing of the Guard.* New York: Penguin, 1981.

Brown, Kirk F. "Campaign Contributions and Congressional Voting." Paper delivered at the annual meeting of the American Political Science Association," Chicago, September 1983.

Browne, William P. "Benefits and Membership: A Reappraisal of Interest Group Activity." *Western Political Quarterly* 29 (June 1976): 258–273.

————. "Organizational Maintenance: The Internal Operation of Interest Groups." *Public Administration Review* 37 (January–February 1977): 48–57.

————. "Farm Organizations and Agribusiness." In Don F. Hadwiger and Ross B. Talbot, eds., *Food Policy and Farm Programs.* New York: Academy of Political Science, 1982.

————. "Mobilizing and Activating Group Demands: The American Agriculture Movement." *Social Science Quarterly* 64 (March 1983): 19–34.

Budde, Bernadette A. "Business Political Action Committees." In Michael J. Malbin, ed., *Parties, Interest Groups, and Campaign Finance Laws.* Washington, D.C.: American Enterprise Institute, 1980.

Burke, Susan Olson. "The Political Evolution of Interest Group Litigation." Paper delivered at the annual meeting of the American Political Science Association, Washington, D.C., August 1980.

Cameron, Juan. "Nader's Invaders Are Inside the Gate." *Fortune* (October 1977): 252 ff.

Carson, Clayborne. *In Struggle.* Cambridge, Mass.: Harvard University Press, 1981.

Cater, Douglass. *Power in Washington.* New York: Vintage, 1964.

Checkoway, Barry. "The Politics of Public Hearings." *Journal of Applied Behavioral Science* 17 (October 1981): 566–582.

Chubb, John E. *Interest Groups and the Bureaucracy.* Stanford, Calif.: Stanford University Press, 1983.

Cigler, Allan J., and John Mark Hansen. "Group Formation Through Protest: The American Agriculture Movement." In Allan J. Cigler and Burdett A. Loomis, eds., *Interest Group Politics.* Washington, D.C.: Congressional Quarterly Press, 1983.

————, and Burdett A. Loomis, eds. *Interest Group Politics.* Washington, D.C.: Congressional Quarterly Press, 1983.

Clark, Peter B., and James Q. Wilson. "Incentive Systems: A Theory of Organizations." *Administrative Science Quarterly* 6 (September 1961): 129–166.

Cohen, David. "Future Directions for the Public Interest Movement." *Citizen Participation* (March–April 1982): 3 ff.

"Communication and the Congress." Washington, D.C.: Burson-Marsteller and the Institute for Government Public Information Research, 1981.

Cook, Constance Ewing. *Nuclear Power and Legal Advocacy.* Lexington, Mass.: Lexington Books, 1980.

————. "Membership Involvement in Public Interest Groups." Paper delivered at the annual meeting of the American Political Science Association, Chicago, September 1983.

Costain, Anne N. "Lobbying for Equal Credit." In Bernice Cummings and Victoria Schuck, eds., *Women Organizing.* Garden City, N.Y.: Adelphi University Press, 1978.

————. "Eliminating Sex Discrimination in Education: Lobbying for Implementation of Title IX." In Marian Palley and Michael Preston, eds., *Race, Sex and Policy Problems.* Lexington, Mass.: D. C. Heath, 1979.

————. "The Struggle for a National Women's Lobby." *Western Political Quarterly* 33 (December 1980): 476–491.

————. "Representing Women: The Transition from Social Movement to Interest Group." *Western Political Quarterly* 34 (March 1981): 100–113.

Costain, W. Douglas, and Anne N. Costain. "Interest Groups as Policy Aggregators in the Legislative Process." *Polity* 14 (Winter 1981): 249–272.

Coyle, Pamela. "Reagan Budget Cuts Leave Non-Profits Slashing Staff, Scrambling for Help." *National Journal* (August 8, 1983): 1630–1633.

Crawford, Alan. *Thunder on the Right.* New York: Pantheon, 1980.

Dahl, Robert A. *A Preface to Democratic Theory.* Chicago: University of Chicago Press, 1956.

————. "The Concept of Power." *Behavioral Science* 2 (July 1957): 201–215.

————. *Who Governs?* New Haven: Yale University Press, 1961.

————. "Further Reflections on 'The Elitist Theory of Democracy.'" *American Political Science Review* 60 (June 1966): 296–305.

——. *Modern Political Analysis*, 3rd ed. Englewood Cliffs, N.J.: Prentice-Hall, 1976.

——. *Dilemmas of Pluralist Democracy*. New Haven: Yale University Press, 1982.

Davidson, Roger H. "Breaking up Those 'Cozy Triangles': An Impossible Dream?" In Susan Welch and John G. Peters, eds., *Legislative Reform and Public Policy*. New York: Praeger, 1977.

Dee, Robert F. "The Hippos are Astir." *Public Communications Review* 1 (Fall 1981): 10–13.

Demkovich, Linda. "From Public Interest Advocates to Administration Defenders." *National Journal* (November 25, 1978): 1892–1898.

Dexter, Lewis Anthony. *How Organizations Are Represented in Washington*. Indianapolis: Bobbs-Merrill, 1969.

——. *The Sociology and Politics of Congress*. Chicago: Rand McNally, 1969.

Dodd, Lawrence C., and Richard L. Schott. *Congress and the Administrative State*. New York: John Wiley, 1979.

Drew, Elizabeth. "Jesse Helms." *New Yorker* (July 20, 1981): 78–95.

——. "Politics and Money—I." *New Yorker* (December 6, 1982): 54–149.

——. "Politics and Money—II." *New Yorker* (December 13, 1982): 57–111.

Eastman, Hope. *Lobbying: A Constitutionally Protected Right*. Washington, D.C.: American Enterprise Institute, 1977.

Epstein, Edwin M. "Business and Labor under the Federal Election Campaign Act of 1971." In Michael J. Malbin, ed., *Parties, Interest Groups, and Campaign Finance Laws*. Washington, D.C.: American Enterprise Institute, 1980.

Evans, Sara. *Personal Politics*. New York: Knopf, 1979.

Federalist Papers. New York: New American Library, 1961.

Ferguson, Thomas, and Joel Rogers. "The Knights of the Roundtable." *Nation* (December 15, 1979): 620–625.

FitzGerald, Frances. "A Disciplined, Charging Army." *New Yorker* (May 18, 1981): 53–141.

Fowler, Linda L. "How Interest Groups Select Issues for Voting Records of Members of the U.S. Congress." *Legislative Studies Quarterly* 7 (August 1982): 401–413.

Freeman, J. Leiper. *The Political Process*, 2nd ed. New York: Random House, 1965.

Freeman, Jo. *The Politics of Women's Liberation*. New York: David McKay, 1976.

Frieden, Bernard J. *The Environmental Protection Hustle*. Cambridge: MIT Press, 1979.

Gamson, William. *Power and Discontent*. Homewood, Ill.: Dorsey Press, 1968.

——. *The Strategy of Social Protest*. Homewood, Ill.: Dorsey Press, 1975.

Garrow, David J. *Protest at Selma.* New Haven: Yale University Press, 1978.

Garson, G. David. *Group Theories of Politics.* Beverly Hills, Calif.: Sage Publications, 1978.

Gaventa, John. *Power and Powerlessness.* Urbana: University of Illinois Press, 1980.

Gelb, Joyce, and Marian Lief Palley. *Women and Public Policies.* Princeton: Princeton University Press, 1982.

Gilbert, Michelle. "Some Law Firms Hire Non-Lawyers as Their Lobbying Arm on Capitol Hill." *National Journal* (September 17, 1983): 1899–1902.

Goodwyn, Lawrence. *The Populist Moment: A Short History of the Agrarian Revolt in America.* New York: Oxford University Press, 1978.

Gordon, Michael. "The Image Makers in Washington—PR Firms Have Found a Natural Home." *National Journal* (May 5, 1980): 884–890.

Gormley, William T., Jr., "Statewide Remedies for Public Underrepresentation in Regulatory Proceedings." *Public Administration Review* 41 (July–August 1981): 454–462.

————. *The Politics of Public Utility Regulation.* Pittsburgh: University of Pittsburgh Press, 1983.

Green, Mark J. *The Other Government.* New York: Grossman, 1975.

————, and Andrew Buchsbaum. *The Corporate Lobbies.* Washington, D.C.: Public Citizen, 1980.

Greenstone, J. David. *Labor in American Politics.* New York: Knopf, 1969.

Greenwald, Carol S. *Group Power.* New York: Praeger, 1977.

Guzzardi, Walter. "How to Win in Washington." *Fortune* (March 27, 1978): 52–58.

Hall, Donald R. *Cooperative Lobbying.* Tucson: University of Arizona Press, 1969.

Hamm, Keith E. "Patterns of Influence Among Committees, Agencies, and Interest Groups." *Legislative Studies Quarterly* 8 (August 1983): 379–426.

Handler, Edward, and John R. Mulkern. *Business in Politics.* Lexington, Mass.: Lexington Books, 1982.

Harty, Sheila. *Hucksters in the Classroom.* Washington, D.C.: Center for the Study of Responsive Law, 1979.

Hayes, Michael T. "The Semi-Sovereign Pressure Groups." *Journal of Politics* 40 (Fall 1978): 134–161.

————. *Lobbyists and Legislators.* New Brunswick, N.J.: Rutgers University Press, 1981.

Heclo, Hugh. *A Government of Strangers.* Washington, D.C.: Brookings Institution, 1977.

————. "Issue Networks and the Executive Establishment." In Anthony King, ed., *The New American Political System.* Washington, D.C.: American Enterprise Institute, 1978.

Henig, Jeffrey R. *Neighborhood Mobilization.* New Brunswick, N.J.: Rutgers University Press, 1982.

Herbers, John. "Grass-Roots Groups Go National." *New York Times Magazine* (September 4, 1983): 22 ff.

Herman, Edward S. *Corporate Control, Corporate Power.* New York: Cambridge University Press, 1981.

Hrebner, Ronald J., and Ruth K. Scott. *Interest Group Politics in America.* Englewood Cliffs, N.J.: Prentice-Hall, 1982.

Hunter, Floyd. *Community Power Structure.* Chapel Hill: University of North Carolina Press, 1953.

Huntington, Samuel P. "The Democratic Distemper." *Public Interest* 41 (Fall 1975): 9–38.

Ippolito, Dennis S., and Thomas G. Walker. *Political Parties, Interest Groups, and Public Policy.* Englewood Cliffs, N.J.: Prentice-Hall, 1980.

Jacobson, Gary C. *Money in Congressional Elections.* New Haven: Yale University Press, 1980.

Jones, Ruth S., and Warren E. Miller. "Financing Campaigns: Modes of Individual Contribution." Paper delivered at the annual meeting of the Midwest Political Science Association, Chicago, April 1983.

Journal of Applied Behavioral Science. Symposium on Citizen Participation in Public Policy. 17 (October 1981).

Kaus, Robert M. "There's No Shame Anymore." *Harper's* (August 1982): 8–15.

Keller, Bill. "Congressional Rating Game Is Hard to Win." *Congressional Quarterly Weekly Report* (March 21, 1981): 507–512.

————. "Computers and Laser Printers Have Recast the Injunction: 'Write Your Congressman.'" *Congressional Quarterly Weekly Report* (September 11, 1982): 2245–2247.

————. "Do White House Ties Count?" *Congressional Quarterly Weekly Report* (March 20, 1982): 603–608.

Key, V. O., Jr. *Politics, Parties, and Pressure Groups,* 5th ed. New York: Crowell, 1964.

Kingdon, John W., *Congressmen's Voting Decisions,* 2nd ed. New York: Harper and Row, 1981.

Knoke, David, and James W. Wood. *Organized for Action.* New Brunswick, N.J.: Rutgers University Press, 1981.

Kotz, Nick, and Mary Lynn Kotz. *A Passion for Equality.* New York: Norton, 1977.

Kweit, Robert W., and Mary Grisez Kweit. "Bureaucratic Decision-Making: Impediments to Citizen Participation." *Polity* 12 (Summer 1980): 647–666.

Ladd, Everett Carll. "How to Tame the Special Interests." *Fortune* (October 20, 1980): 66 ff.

Langton, Stuart. "Citizen Participation in America: Current Reflections on the State of the Art." In Stuart Langton, ed., *Citizen Participation in America.* Lexington, Mass.: D. C. Heath, 1978.

Lanouette, William J. "The Revolving Door—It's Tricky to Try to Stop It." *National Journal.* (November 19, 1977): 1796–1803.

————. "The Influence Peddlers—Connections Count, But They're Not Enough." *National Journal* (February 28, 1981): 355–357.

────. "Chamber's Ponderous Decision Making Leaves It Sitting on the Sidelines." *National Journal* (July 24, 1982): 1298–1301.

Lazarus, Simon. *The Genteel Populists.* New York: Holt, Rinehart and Winston, 1973.

Lienesch, Michael. "Right Wing Religion: Christian Conservatism as a Political Movement." *Political Science Quarterly* 97 (Fall 1982): 403–423.

Lindblom, Charles E. *Politics and Markets.* New York: Basic Books, 1977.

Lipset, Seymour Martin, Martin Trow, and James Coleman. *Union Democracy.* Garden City, N.Y.: Doubleday Anchor Books, 1956.

Lipsky, Michael. "Protest as a Political Resource." *American Political Science Review* 62 (December 1968): 1144–1158.

Lowi, Theodore J. *The Politics of Disorder.* New York: Basic Books, 1971.

────. *The End of Liberalism,* 2nd ed. New York: Norton, 1979.

Luttberg, Norman R., and Harmon Zeigler. "Attitude Consensus and Conflict in an Interest Group." *American Political Science Review* 60 (September 1966): 655–666.

McCarry, Charles. *Citizen Nader.* New York: Saturday Review Press, 1972.

McConnell, Grant. *Private Power and American Democracy.* New York: Alfred A. Knopf, 1966.

McFarland, Andrew S. *Public Interest Lobbies.* Washington, D.C.: American Enterprise Institute, 1976.

────. " 'Third Forces' in American Politics: The Case of Common Cause." In Jeff Fishel, ed., *Parties and Elections in an Anti-Party Age.* Bloomington: Indiana University Press, 1978.

McGrath, Phyllis S. *Redefining Corporate-Federal Relations.* New York: Conference Board, 1979.

McQuaid, Kim. "The Roundtable: Getting Results in Washington." *Harvard Business Review* 59 (May–June 1981): 114–123.

Malbin, Michael J. "Campaign Finance Reform and the 'Special Interests.' " *Public Interest* 56 (Summer 1979): 21–42.

────, ed. *Parties, Interest Groups, and Campaign Finance Laws.* Washington, D.C.: American Enterprise Institute, 1980.

────. "The Problems of PAC-Journalism." *Public Opinion* 5 (December–January 1983): 15 ff.

Margolis, Michael, and Kevin Neary. "Pressure Politics Revisited: The Anti-Abortion Campaign." *Policy Studies Journal* 8 (Spring 1980): 698–716.

Marsh, David. "On Joining Interest Groups." *British Journal of Political Science* 6 (July 1976): 257–272.

Matthiessen, Peter. *Sal Si Puedes.* New York: Random House, 1969.

Meier, August, and Elliott Rudwick. *CORE: A Study in the Civil Rights Movement.* New York: Oxford University Press, 1973.

Milbrath, Lester W. *The Washington Lobbyists.* Chicago: Rand McNally, 1963.

Miller, Alan S. "Towards an Environmental-Labor Coalition." *Environment* 22 (June 1980): 32–39.

228 Bibliography

Miller, Arthur H. "Political Issues and Trust in Government: 1964–70." *American Political Science Review* 68 (September 1974): 951–972.

Mills, C. Wright. *The Power Elite.* New York: Oxford University Press, 1956.

Mitchell, Robert Cameron. "National Environmental Lobbies and the Apparent Illogic of Collective Action." In Clifford S. Russell, ed., *Collective Decision Making.* Baltimore: Johns Hopkins University Press, 1979.

Moe, Terry M. *The Organization of Interests.* Chicago: University of Chicago Press, 1980.

———. A Calculus of Group Membership." *American Journal of Political Science* 24 (November 1980): 593–632.

———. "Toward a Broader View of Interest Groups." *Journal of Politics* 43 (May 1981): 531–543.

Moynihan, Daniel P. *Maximum Feasible Misunderstanding.* New York: Free Press, 1969.

O'Brien, David J. *Neighborhood Organization and Interest Group Processes.* Princeton: Princeton University Press, 1975.

O'Connor, Karen. *Women's Organizations' Use of the Courts.* Lexington, Mass.: Lexington Books, 1980.

———, and Lee Epstein. "The Rise of Conservative Interest Group Litigation." *Journal of Politics* 45 (May 1983): 478–489.

Olson, Mancur, Jr. *The Logic of Collective Action.* New York: Schocken, 1968.

———. *The Rise and Decline of Nations.* New Haven: Yale University Press, 1982.

Ornstein, Norman J., and Shirley Elder. *Interest Groups, Lobbying and Public Policy.* Washington, D.C.: Congressional Quarterly Press, 1978.

Orren, Karen. "Standing to Sue: Interest Group Conflict in the Federal Courts." *American Political Science Review* 70 (September 1976): 723–741.

———. "Liberalism, Money, and the Situation of Organized Labor." In J. David Greenstone, ed., *Public Values and Private Power in American Politics.* Chicago: University of Chicago Press, 1982.

Page, Ann L., and Donald A. Clelland. "The Kanawha County Textbook Controversy: A Study in the Politics of Life Style Concern." *Social Forces* 57 (September 1978): 265–281.

Perlman, Janice. "Grassrooting the System." *Social Policy* 7 (September–October 1976): 4–20.

Pika, Joseph A. "Interest Groups and the Executive: Presidential Intervention." In Allan J. Cigler and Burdett A. Loomis, eds., *Interest Group Politics.* Washington, D.C.: Congressional Quarterly Press, 1983.

Piven, Frances Fox, and Richard Cloward. *Poor People's Movements.* New York: Pantheon, 1978.

Poe, Randall. "Masters of the Advertorial." *Across the Board* (September 1980): 15–25.

Policy Studies Journal. Symposium on Interest Groups and Public Policy. 11 (June 1983).

Polsby, Nelson W. "Interest Groups and the Presidency." In Walter Dean Burnham and Martha Wagner Weinberg, eds., *American Politics and Public Policy*. Cambridge, Mass.: MIT Press, 1978.

Pratt, Henry J. *The Gray Lobby*. Chicago: University of Chicago Press, 1976.

Public Affairs Offices and Their Functions. Boston: Boston University School of Management, 1981.

Public Interest Law: Five Years Later. New York: Ford Foundation, 1976.

The Public Interest Law Firm. New York: Ford Foundation, 1973.

Quirk, Paul J. "Food and Drug Administration." In James Q. Wilson, ed., *The Politics of Regulation*. New York: Basic Books, 1980.

————. *Industry Influence in Federal Regulatory Agencies*. Princeton: Princeton University Press, 1981.

Rabin, Robert L. "Lawyers for Social Change: Perspectives on Public Interest Law." *Stanford Law Review* 28 (January 1976): 207–261.

Rosenau, James. *Citizenship Between Elections*. New York: Free Press, 1974.

Rosenbaum, Walter A. "Public Involvement as Reform and Ritual: The Development of Federal Participation Programs." In Stuart Langton, ed., *Citizen Participation in America*. Lexington, Mass.: D. C. Heath, 1978.

Rosenberg, Tina. "Diminishing Returns." *Washington Monthly* (June 1983): 32–38.

Rouder, Susan. "Mobilization by Mail." *Citizen Participation* 2 (September–October 1980): 3 ff.

Sabato, Larry J. *The Rise of Political Consultants*. New York: Basic Books, 1981.

Sale, Kirkpatrick. *SDS*. New York: Vintage, 1974.

Salisbury, Robert H. "An Exchange Theory of Interest Groups." *Midwest Journal of Political Science* 13 (February 1969): 1–32.

————. "Interest Groups." In Fred I. Greenstein and Nelson W. Polsby, eds., *Handbook of Political Science*, Vol. 4. Reading, Mass.: Addison-Wesley, 1975.

————. "Why No Corporatism in America?" In Philippe C. Schmitter and Gerhard Lehmbruch, eds., *Trends Toward Corporatist Intermediation*. Beverly Hills, Calif.: Sage Publications, 1979.

————. "Are Interest Groups Morbific Forces?" Paper delivered to the Conference Group on the Political Economy of Advanced Industrial Societies, Washington, D.C., August 1980.

Schattschneider, E. E. *The Semisovereign People*. Hinsdale, Ill.: Dryden Press, 1975.

Schlozman, Kay Lehman, and John T. Tierney. "More of the Same: Washington Pressure Group Activity in a Decade of Change." *Journal of Politics* 45 (May 1983): 351–377.

Sethi, S. Prakash. "Grassroots Lobbying and the Corporation." *Business and Society Review* (November–December 1979): 8–14.

Singer, James W. "Practicing Law in Washington—An American Growth Industry." *National Journal* (February 4, 1978): 172–179.

Sorauf, Frank J. *The Wall of Separation.* Princeton: Princeton University Press, 1976.

Stewart, Joseph, Jr., and Edward V. Heck, "The Day-to-Day Activities of Interest Group Lawyers." *Social Science Quarterly* 64 (March 1983): 173–182.

Thurow, Lester C. *The Zero-Sum Society.* New York: Basic Books, 1980.

Truman, David B. *The Governmental Process,* 2nd ed. New York: Alfred A. Knopf, 1971.

Tucker, William. *Progress and Privilege.* New York: Doubleday, 1982.

Verba, Sidney, and Norman H. Nie. *Participation in America.* New York: Harper & Row, 1972.

Viguerie, Richard A. *The New Right: We're Ready to Lead.* Falls Church, Va.: Viguerie, 1981.

Vogel, David. "How Business Responds to Opposition: Corporate Political Strategies During the 1970s." Paper delivered at the annual meeting of the American Political Science Association, Washington, D.C., September 1979.

———. "The Public-Interest Movement and the American Reform Tradition." *Political Science Quarterly* 95 (Winter 1980–81): 607–628.

———. *Lobbying the Corporation.* New York: Basic Books, 1978.

Vose, Clement. *Caucasians Only.* Berkeley: University of California Press, 1949.

Walker, Jack L. "A Critique of the Elitist Theory of Democracy." *American Political Science Review* 60 (June 1966): 285–295.

———. "The Origins and Maintenance of Interest Groups in America." *American Political Science Review* 77 (June 1983): 390–406.

———. "The Mobilization of Political Interests." Paper delivered at the annual meeting of the American Political Science Association, Chicago, September 1983.

Wasby, Stephen L. "Interest Groups and Litigation." *Policy Studies Journal* 11 (June 1983): 657–670.

"The Washington Executive." Washington, D.C.: Boyden Associates, 1980.

The Washington Lobby, 4th ed. Washington, D.C.: Congressional Quarterly Press, 1982.

Weaver, Paul. "Regulation, Social Policy, and Class Conflict." *Public Interest* 50 (Winter 1978): 45–63.

Weisbrod, Burton A., Joel F. Handler, and Neil K. Komesar, eds. *Public Interest Law.* Berkeley: University of California Press, 1978.

Welch, W. P. "The Allocation of Political Monies." *Public Choice* 35 (1980): 97–120.

Wills, Gary. *Explaining America.* New York: Penguin, 1981.

Wilson, Graham K. *Unions in American National Politics.* London: Macmillan, 1977.

———. *Interest Groups in the United States.* New York: Oxford University Press, 1981.

Wilson, James Q. *Political Organizations.* New York: Basic Books, 1973.

Wootton, Graham. *Interest Groups.* Englewood Cliffs, N.J.: Prentice-Hall, 1970.

Zeigler, Harmon, and Michael Baer. *Lobbying.* Belmont, Calif.: Wadsworth, 1969.

Zeigler, Harmon, and G. Wayne Peak, *Interest Groups in American Society,* 2nd ed. Englewood Cliffs, N.J.: Prentice-Hall, 1972.

Index

Abalone Alliance, 7
Abernathy, Ralph, 109
abortion issue, 34, 86
Abramson, Paul R., 48n
Adams, Gordon, 127n
Ad Hoc Committee for Airline
    Deregulatory Reform, 204
administrative agencies, 190–193
Administrative Procedure Act, 153
administrative rulemaking, 189
advocacy advertising, 140–141
advocacy design, 206
AFL-CIO, 60, 61, 62, 196
    Committee on Political Edu-
    cation (COPE), 159, 178
agenda building, 7–8
Airport and Airways Development
    Act, 31
Aldrich, John H., 48n
Alexander, Herbert E., 23n, 54n,
    157n, 158n, 180n, 281n
Alinsky, Saul, 148n
Allied Chemical, 22
American Agriculture Movement,
    76–77
American Association of State
    Highway and Transportation
    Officials, 100
American Bankers Association, 89,
    152
American Bar Association, 201
*American Business and Public
    Policy* (Bauer, Pool, and
    Dexter), 44, 44n

American Civil Liberties Union
    (ACLU), 85, 97, 99
American Conservative Union, 33,
    204
American Dental Association, 160n
American Farm Bureau Federation,
    5, 58, 70, 95
American Federation of Teachers,
    61
American Hospital Association
    (AHA), 93–94
American Iron and Steel Institute,
    8
American Medical Association
    (AMA), 23, 174, 175
American Newspaper Publishers
    Association, 154
American Petroleum Institute
    (API), 96
Americans for Constitutional
    Action (ACA), 146
Americans for Democratic Action
    (ADA), 146, 204
Americans for Life, 166–167
American Soybean Association, 56
Americans United for Separation
    of Church and State, 200
American Voter, The (Campbell,
    Converse, Miller, and Stokes),
    48, 48n
amicus curiae, 201
Anderson, Jack, 144
Anderson, Wendell, 17
Anheuser-Busch, 22

233

National Forest Products Association, 112
National Funeral Directors Association, 20
National Legal Center for the Public Interest, 88, 198
National Milk Producers Federation, 5
National Office Machine Dealers Association, 172–173, 174
National Organization for Women (NOW), 28, 62, 86, 180
National Resources Defense Council, 199
National Restaurant Association, 152
National Retired Teachers Association-American Association of Retired Persons (NRTA/ AARP), 75
National Science Foundation, 90n
National Tax Limitation Committee, 203
National Taxpayers Union, 146, 203, 204
National Welfare Rights Organization, 89
National Women's Political Caucus (NWPC), 125
Nelson, Bryce, 24n, 130n
New Deal, 16, 52
New Haven, Connecticut, 9, 11
New Right, 33–35
Newsweek, 16
New York Times, 16, 144, 145
Nie, Norman H., 48n, 49n
Nixon, Richard M., 27, 34, 49, 53, 54, 60, 61, 127, 133, 157, 158, 201
Noll, Roger, 127n
nonconnected PACs, 160, 164, 170
nonprofit groups, 88, 217n
normative criticism, 11
nuclear power issue, 7
Nunn, Sam, 187

occupational health and safety issue, 7–8

Occupational Safety and Health Administration (OSHA), 36, 38
O'Connor, Karen, 200n, 201n
O'Connor, Sandra Day, 201
Office of Communication of the United Church of Christ v. *the FCC*, 199
Office of Management and Budget, 208, 217n
Office of Personnel Management, 90
Office of Public Liason, 195
Olson, Mancur, 2n, 71–72, 71n, 72n, 73, 80, 91, 219n
O'Melveny & Myers, 25
Operation PUSH (People United to Serve Humanity), 62
Opportunity Races, 176–177
organization, 5
organizational maintenance, 43
Orren, Karen, 200

Pacific Legal Foundation, 198
Page, Benjamin I., 56n
Panama Canal issue, 86
Pappas, Vasil, 21n, 22n, 36n
participation, 6–7, 14, 15, 30–32, 42
social factors in, 77–78
partisan identification, 48–49
Patterson, Rachelle, 127n
Pear, Robert, 128n, 144n, 202n
People for the American Way, 139
Peretz, Anne Farnsworth, 89
Perlman, Janice, 32n
Perry, James M., 133n, 179, 194n
Peters, John G., 127n, 184n
Petrocik, John R., 48n
Pfeifer, Paul, 177
Pika, Joseph A., 196n
Pike, Donald F., 24n, 130n
Pills That Don't Work, 89
Piven, Frances Fox, 149n
Planned Parenthood, 153
pluralism, 4, 9–15, 29–30, 41–42, 45, 68–69, 213
Poe, Randall, 140n